The Image of the City

AND OTHER ESSAYS

CHARLES WILLIAMS, 1939

CHARLES WILLIAMS

The Image of the City

AND OTHER ESSAYS

Selected by

ANNE RIDLER

with a

Critical Introduction

the apocryphile press

BERKELEY, CA

www.apocryphile.org

apocryphile press
BERKELEY, CA

Apocryphile Press
1700 Shattuck Ave #81
Berkeley, CA 94709
www.apocryphile.org

First published by Oxford University Press, 1958.
First Apocryphile edition, 2007.

ISBN 9781947826366

ACKNOWLEDGEMENTS

MY chief debt is to Mrs. Charles Williams, who has given her help and encouragement to this project from its beginning, and has allowed me to quote from her husband's writings. My thanks are also due to Charles Williams's sister, Miss Edith Williams, and to Mr. George Robinson, for information about his early years. I have quoted from his letters mainly in connexion with his Arthurian poems, for which purpose I had sufficient in my own possession: he was a splendid and prolific letter-writer, and it is to be hoped that a collection will some day be made. I understand that Mrs. Williams has in preparation a selection from the many which were addressed to herself.

It has not proved possible for me to examine all the unpublished manuscripts, but I hope that nothing of importance has been left out, and that I have made no inaccurate statements for this reason.

Further acknowledgements are due to the Oxford University Press, to the proprietors of the *Dublin Review*, *Theology*, and *Time and Tide*, and to Messrs. James Clarke & Co. Ltd.

CONTENTS

INTRODUCTION

I

WHEN Charles Williams died in 1945 there remained to us of his work, besides his published books and those which he had in preparation for the press, a number of essays which had appeared in periodicals and elsewhere, many of which contain important statements of his ideas. A selection of these is printed here, and the publishers who commissioned the book wished me to preface it by a brief account of his life and a critical account of his writings, which might supplement the valuable work already published.[1] There are three parts to my introduction, and the first is mainly biographical. It is too early for his life to be seen in its true perspective, but certain facts should be set down while memories are still alive—bearing in mind that the history of a poet's life is in his work: not that he writes his biography, but that the most important part of his biography *is* his writing. I shall then attempt to describe the chief of the ideas which are to be found in all Williams's work, whether of verse or prose, and most of which have some place in this collection. Finally, I shall consider the different forms in which he expressed himself, and especially his poetry. This would not be the place in which to attempt to add anything to Professor Lewis's indispensable commentary on the *Taliessin* poems, but it may be useful to examine their relation to the poet's earlier discarded versions, and to describe the even earlier designs which Williams recorded in a notebook during the First World War.

There are indeed many possible ways of treating this many-sided writer, and predominance may be given to one or other of his chosen forms of expression, according to the taste of the critic, but every critic will come up against the same difficulty, that consideration of any one form must include a knowledge of the others.

One may consider Charles Williams as above all a great exponent of the Affirmative, the Sacramental, Way, in the canon of Christian writing; one of the few who have written of it with a full understanding of its relation to the Negative, or Mystical, Way. Or as a

[1] See especially 'Williams and the Arthuriad', by C. S. Lewis, in *Arthurian Torso*, O.U.P., also the preface to *Essays Presented to Charles Williams*, from the same publisher; and *Charles Williams*, by John Heath-Stubbs, a pamphlet published by Longmans for the British Council. This contains a bibliography where may be found details of some other critical work on Williams: my own select bibliography adds some items to the list of published works to be found there. I have tried to avoid the repetition of points already made by these two writers, though this was not always possible.

poet—the author of a quantity of poems of wholly original content expressed in traditional form, and of an unfinished cycle of poems which are original both in form and content. Or as a critic of a remarkably catholic taste, for whom literature was a passion. Or as a writer of unequalled supernatural thrillers; as a dramatist with the rare ability to give flesh and blood to symbolic figures—any one of these ways of approach would be valid, yet with each the critic would find that he needed to presuppose a knowledge of all the rest, and that even then something of value had escaped him. For the whole man (it is an opinion expressed by more than one of those who have written about him) was greater even than the sum of his works. Those who had heard Coleridge talk felt some such discrepancy between his written and his spoken criticism. One can suggest reasons, without entirely explaining it: that the energy of the man conveyed his vision more effectively than any of the words he could find to express it; that in Coleridge, the power of organization was deficient, and that in Williams, the intellectual gifts were greater than the aesthetic; also that the loving-kindness which was so strongly a part of his personality increased the powers of apprehension in his hearers. He made those who talked with him feel that the truth was a joint discovery—and indeed he believed it. His colleague Gerard Hopkins wrote of him that 'he found out the gold in others, making it shine', and many have said that in his company they felt themselves to be better people than they really were—and not only better, but more intelligent.

Yet what remains to us, of Williams as of Coleridge, is enough. The religious writings, the plays *Seed of Adam* and *Cranmer*, certain passages from the novels, some of the criticism of Shakespeare, Dante, Milton, and Wordsworth, and above all the series of *Taliessin* poems—these alone would make good a claim for him (I had written 'his claim', but he claimed nothing of the kind) as a writer of major importance. It is when we come to apply the adjective to any particular form, to speak of him as a major poet or a major critic, that the doubt arises. This is partly because the ideas he was expressing were always more important to Charles Williams than the medium of expression, and the choice of a medium (apart from poetry) was governed for him by the demands of the moment—that is, chiefly by the need to earn money, but also by his own generous readiness to respond to any request which he had it in his power to satisfy. He himself would maintain that the need to earn money is the natural mainspring of creative writing, and that the reason that our greatest writers have come from the lower middle classes is simply that poetry needs the stimulus of the abyss of poverty close at hand. So he wrote:

I saw Shakespeare
In a Tube station on the Central London:
. . . the notes for *The Merchant*
Were in his pocket
Beginning (it was the first line he thought of)
'Still quiring to the young-eyed cherubins.'

But his chief wish was to be earning more money.

At any rate, Williams's one real grievance against his lot was that no one would pay him for writing poetry—and the unfinished cycle of *Taliessin* stands as a reproach against our economic system. He was firmly against the romantic view of the poet's office, and mocked a little at Shelley and Yeats for 'making a fuss of being a poet', quoting with approval Graves's lines:

Poetry is, I said, my father's trade,
Familiar since my childhood. . . .

Williams certainly did not lack the stimulus of the abyss, though prose and not poetry had to provide his defence against it. He was born at 3 Spencer Road,[1] Holloway, on 20 September 1886, and was christened Charles Walter Stansby. He always spoke of his birthplace in a general way as having been Islington, and that district was also the place of his father's birth and marriage. Charles Williams's sister Edith tells me that their father, Walter, was 'the delicate one of twins and was taken by a grandmother, his mother having died at the time of birth'. He worked as foreign correspondence clerk in French and German to a firm of importers (no one remembers its name), and the family lived in London until Charles was eight and Edith five years old—they were the only children. Then Walter Williams's eyesight began to fail, and the specialist whom he consulted said that he could only hope to save it if he left London and went to live somewhere near to green fields and trees. It seems that Mr. Williams rated the country as low in comparison with London as his son came to do, and it must have been a serious blow to have to change his work and his home at the age of forty-six, even apart from the threat of blindness. However, the firm for which he had worked was closing down in any case, and he and his wife determined to move to St. Albans, which they had visited and liked on a holiday exploration. With the help of Mrs. Williams's family they bought a shop, 15[2] Victoria Street, near the Art School and opposite to a disused burial ground which had been laid out as a garden—thus, writes Edith, filling the need for 'somewhere green'. The shop

[1] Its name is now Caedmon Road. It is a side street near Holloway Road, just below its junction with the Caledonian Road.

[2] Later 36.

had been a greengrocer's, but they opened it as a depot for the sale of artists' materials. Mrs. Charles Williams writes of it: 'I loved that shop and residence and its garden. The shop had two chunky windows and Mrs. Williams dressed them simply and gave just the right treatment. Her house was attractive too—Victorian furniture polished and plain in design and no Victorian hotch-potch.'

At first Mrs. Walter Williams's brother Charles Wall was a partner in the business, and as he was a trained engraver and 'had studied art in Paris' he was the buyer for the firm. But the partnership was not a success: he bought extravagantly, and the business was considerably in debt when he left it, soon after the beginning. The family struggled back to solvency. Mrs. Williams took a lodger to help with the expenses, and although the greater part of the business fell on her shoulders she found time to make the children's clothes: an Eton jacket for Charles was her most ambitious attempt. Her daughter-in-law writes of her as a woman of strong vitality, who was excellent company and full of enjoyment of life, in spite of her hard struggle against poverty. She continued to run the shop after her husband's death until she was seventy-six. She died in 1948, aged ninety-two, having outlived her son by nearly three years.

Walter Williams never became totally blind, although he could not see to read for some years before his death in 1929. At the time of the move he was able to help in dealing with customers, and to attend to his daughter's lessons until she was old enough to go to school. He had read widely, and had contributed verse and short stories to various periodicals, Dickens's *Household Words* among them. A school friend of Charles recalls his guidance of their youthful reading, and Charles himself always spoke of his father as one to whose teaching he owed much, and as a wise man, greatly saddened by blindness. The two went for long walks together ('twenty miles was nothing in those days', as Edith writes), just as Charles was later to do with his wife, and Charles's city walks continued to the end of his life—he was always a peripatetic talker. He dedicated his third book of poems[1] to 'My father and my other teachers', and in a long introductory poem, which must have been written under the shadow of his father's failing health and blindness, recalls that he had 'Rebuked the use of doth and did' in his son's early verse. Fortunate poet—he never lacked such critics all through his life, and always received their objections with humility, if without any too anxious attention.

Charles began his schooling at St. Albans Abbey School, in 1894,

[1] *Divorce*, 1920.

and in 1898 he gained a County Council scholarship to St. Albans Grammar School, as it then was. (Its title is now St. Albans School, and there is another Grammar School.) Here he made his chief early friend in another scholar of the same year, named George Robinson, who for many years shared his tastes, pursuits, and literary inventions. This boy spent much time at the Williams's house, and even lodged with them for about a year, a good while later. This was the friend to whom the poem called 'Reunion' which appears in *Divorce* was addressed, on Robinson's return from France in 1918, and their friendship, although in later years their ways diverged, was a close one.

'By temperament', writes Mr. Robinson, 'we both fell into the category of "swots", anathema to the conventional boy, and this fact I suppose caused us to find in each other some mutual support and solace.' Charles had inherited his father's weakness of sight, and games were no pleasure to him, but the two boys and Edith took great delight in acting plays to the family circle. Edith recalls a performance of *As You Like It* in which she played Rosalind (and presumably a good many other parts as well, if the cast was only three), and a play which Mr. Williams wrote for himself and his two children to act. But the most ambitious attempt by the three young people was Longfellow's *The Golden Legend*, of which they had to give two performances, so that the boys could each play the part of Prince Henry and the Devil. The theme of this dramatic poem is based on a medieval tale of a prince who is a leper, and can be cured only if a virgin will give her life for his. Elsie, a farmer's daughter, offers the sacrifice, and Lucifer persuades Prince Henry to accept it. But at the last moment he repents, is cured instead by the relics of Saint Matthew, and marries Elsie. I recall the plot here, because the play must certainly have sown seed for later fruition in Charles Williams's mind, and fragments of the verse were among his familiar quotations in after years. The opening stage direction gives the tone:

The spire of Strasburg Cathedral. Night and storm. LUCIFER, *with the Powers of the Air, trying to tear down the Cross.*

The conflict between the powers of good and evil, romantically expressed, was always one of Williams's most intense literary enjoyments, but even more deeply felt was the theme of substitution in love; and most significant of all, for his future work, are the closing lines about Lucifer:[1]

> The son of mystery;
> And since God suffers him to be,

[1] After writing this, I realized that there is a paraphrase of the lines in *Descent into Hell*.

He, too, is God's minister,
And labours for some good
By us not understood!

We shall return to this later.

Charles Williams sometimes spoke of a fantasy which he had made with a friend in boyhood, a world which they entered each day when they travelled to London together from St. Albans, and which remained in being for them during some years. 'Hardly fantasy', Mr. Robinson wrote when I asked him if he remembered it: 'it was too objective for that. It concerned a Prince Rudolph (derived from Anthony Hope), a Lord de Bracey (origin unknown), and the Lady Rosalind. It brought Charles out in a new light as a comic creator. There was a sort of George Robey flavour about his Lord de Bracey which I can still taste but not describe.' Of this Gondal country nothing seems to have been recorded in writing, but the habit of fantasy-making—I retain the word, with apologies to Mr. Robinson, since it expresses just the kind of reality which these inventions had for Charles Williams—this habit remained with him, and many of his letters contain richly worded myths and rituals in which he imagined his friends taking part, and to which they too contributed according to their power. He turned the habit to good purpose in the two masques which he wrote in the twenties to be acted by the staff at Amen House; later, when he had breathed more of life into his myth—in the *Taliessin* cycle—it was still linked to that of himself and his friends.

Charles Williams and George Robinson were both awarded Intermediate Scholarships to University College, London, which were available for three years, and they began to study in Gower Street in the autumn of 1901. Mr. Robinson writes: 'The County Scholarship scheme was then in its early stages, and the education authority did not know what it was doing in pitching boys of fifteen into University College. Certainly the two boys concerned experienced some bewilderment, but things settled down, and we matriculated (January 1903) and entered on Arts Courses.' The Latin Professor at that time was A. E. Housman, and Mr. Robinson possesses a certificate signed by him, but I do not remember that Charles Williams spoke of his teaching, and I have not been able to find a record of any such comment.

Unfortunately the family could not afford to keep Charles at college for the whole of the three years, and he left 'on financial grounds' before the end of the session 1903–4. He had taken the Civil Service examination for a Second Division Clerkship in October 1903, but was not successful. This must have been a blow to him and to his parents, and in later years he would describe the doubts which he had felt about his own powers, and the dark look of a future empty of prospects, by way of encouragement to diffident and unsettled young people such as I was.

His relations looked round for a job for the boy, and an aunt saw an advertisement which led to his being employed at the Methodist 'New Connexion Publishing Office and Book Room'. According to Edith Williams, Aunt Alice Wall did not realize that she had suggested a post in a Methodist firm to her nephew, for the family was Anglican (although Walter Williams had been Nonconformist until his marriage), and Charles had been brought up in the tradition in which he remained to the end of his days. He remained—but in a different sense. It was a favourite paradox of his that in middle life you realized that everything you had learnt at your grandmother's knee was true, and that you had travelled round the world to arrive at the same place. Trying to define the mode of his belief, he wrote (in a letter soon after the outbreak of war in 1939): '. . . it seems so odd somehow to feel as if I believed absolutely everything about death and resurrection and all that and yet somehow not here, and (also) yet somehow not anywhere else. Do I look to another life? no; I think I am obstinately determined to believe that everything is justified here and now, when it obviously[1] isn't. . . .'

In those early days he and George Robinson belonged to a discussion group in St. Albans whose members called themselves the Theological Smokers, and 'over pipes, cigarettes, coffee and cakes explored the universe, regretted nonconformity, had a sneaking regard for but kept a wary eye on His Holiness—all . . . enlivened by the fondness which Charles and I both had for changing our positions half way through the discussion so that we could see what was on the other side.' He enjoyed such dialectical discussions all through his life, up to those fortunate Oxford meetings of his last years, which Professor Lewis has described. A colleague at the Methodist Book Room, Harold Eyers, introduced him to another debating society, in London, where he met a student of literature named Frederick Page. This was an introduction of much importance for the young man's future, and although he and Page came to disagree on many points, they were to be associated together and on friendly terms for the rest of their working lives. For Frederick Page was in the London office of the Oxford University Press, and had been asked to find someone to help him in the task of reading the proofs of the complete edition of Thackeray which was then—in 1908—going through the press. On his recommendation Charles Williams entered the office of the Oxford Press in the City of London, 'whence', he wrote in the thirties, 'I hope I shall

[1] His meaning is clearer if one reads *apparently*.

never go'—nor did he, until the Second World War brought Amen House to Oxford.

The premises of the Press were then at Amen Corner—since pulled down—and it was in 1924 that they moved to Amen House. The small room which Williams shared with Frederick Page in that building looked out over the Old Bailey, a view which never lost its poignancy for him. From other windows one has a fine view of St. Paul's. The remarkable institution which rises between those two domes, and also in the City of Oxford, is as difficult as the British Constitution for the outsider to understand. But for Charles Williams, as Gerard Hopkins has written, 'The City of God in which he never ceased to dwell, contained Amen House as its noblest human monument, and all who lived and worked in it were citizens to him. . . . It is no extravagance to say that by sheer force of love and enthusiasm he created about him an atmosphere that must be unique in the history of business houses.' One must add here, that he was able to do so because of the special character of Humphrey Milford (the London publisher from 1913 onward), who allowed his staff an unusual degree of freedom, and knew Williams for the Phoenix he was, though he was sometimes puzzled how to reconcile him with commercial necessities. Humphrey Milford, who became Caesar to this poet, was a man of fine literary judgement and a quick and acute intelligence: his combination of authority and benevolence helped to give life to Williams's conception of the ideal ruler. He was laconic in utterance (especially in writing—the brevity of his memoranda was proverbial, as was his eye for a misprint and his love of teasing his staff); he had an unexpected and deep humility; he had also a dislike of unpleasant scenes which caused Williams to give him the further title of *Deus Absconditus*.

The Press gave Charles Williams stability, friendship, dialectic, work that encouraged the ranging powers of his mind, 'high experiences of goodness and beauty'. But the salary which he earned there was not, as time went on, sufficient for his needs: against this, one must set the fact that he did much private work in office hours.

The abyss, then, was still in mind: without it, many of the thirty-odd books, the innumerable reviews and lectures, would not have existed. His first book, however, brought no monetary profit, and owed its existence to the generosity of a patron. Frederick Page had come to know Alice Meynell through his devotion to the work of Coventry Patmore, and before long he introduced Charles Williams to her and her husband, taking him to spend Saturday afternoons at their London flat. Sir Francis Meynell remembers Charles as being intensely shy, but he must have impressed the older Meynells with his promise as a poet: Mr. Page remembers their helping him to compose titles for the sonnets in his sequence *The Silver Stair*, and Wilfrid Meynell paid for its publication in 1912.

The Silver Stair was addressed to Florence Conway, whom Charles had met in St. Albans in the same year that he entered the Press, when they were both helping at a parochial children's Christmas party. Her own account of their meeting and of the presentation of the sonnets must be quoted:[1]

> For the first five minutes of our meeting I thought him the most silent, withdrawn young man I had ever met. [This, added to the testimony of Francis Meynell, is as interesting as it is surprising, for no one who met Williams in later life could imagine him as tongue-tied on any occasion.] For the next five minutes I thought him the nicest young man I had ever met. For the rest of the evening I thought him the most talkative young man I had ever met, and still the nicest. . . .
>
> One January night, in the kind of weather usually associated with Good King Wenceslas, I had been to a lecture. On my homeward way . . . Charles overtook me. He put a parcel into my hands, saying he had written a Sonnet Sequence called *The Silver Stair*. Its theme was Renunciation. Would I read it and tell him my opinion? And he fled. I thought 'Oh dear! Is he going to enter a monastery?' and wondered about visiting days at such places.
>
> I read *The Silver Stair* by flickering candle-light in my cold attic room. There were eighty-two sonnets and I read them all. So lovely they seemed; I read them again and yet again. Comprehension dawned and I cried aloud 'Why, I believe they are about me!' I read them again to make quite sure.
>
> Next day I wrote my first letter to Charles. It seemed to please him, and though *The Silver Stair* had Renunciation for its theme our walks continued. . . .

The renunciation of *The Silver Stair* was, in fact, 'the rash oath of virginity That is first love's first cry'. The abstract Lady of that sequence had portrait-sketches made of her in many poems that followed. 'Dusky and brilliant', he described her; 'her dark eyes sparkle', and

> These tempers and incalculable hues,
> This motion of pretended liberty,
> This haste of waves that rush the shore in glee,
> As children scramble for their promised dues,—
> Whose is this hidden law? this impulse whose,
> So bright, so dark, so mutable, so free?
> Michal, no chance provokes you to the sea,
> But kinship that creating gods infuse.

The sketch is a good one. Unpredictable in response, keenly interested in people, Florence Conway perhaps inherited from her half-Irish mother a flair for a witty summing-up of character, and an intuition which must have been the basis for many of Charles Williams's statements about the minds of women. In those early

[1] 'As I remember', an article in the American *Episcopal Churchnews*, 12 Apr. 1953.

days the touch of exaggeration which always remained in his gestures and manner of speech must sometimes have bordered on the grotesque, and his young fiancée was embarrassed by his habit of chanting verse aloud in public places, with the vowel sounds which proudly proclaimed him to have been born within the sound of Bow Bells, and which in no way detracted from the incantatory power of his recital. Because of her protests he called her Michal, after Saul's daughter who mocked at David when he danced before the Lord; and the name replaced her own.

The First World War came, the Theological Smokers were disbanded, and some of Charles's closest friends went to France—two of them, Harold Eyers and Ernest Nottingham, to die there. He himself was unfit for the army and continued in his job, with territorial exercises at week-ends. To everyone's surprise there was a boom in publishing. And in 1917 Charles and Michal were married, and went to live in a flat in Hampstead, a neighbourhood which was always to be their home henceforward. Michal had been teaching in London and continued to teach at a school in Soho until their son was eight years old: in 1920 she compiled a book on *Christian Symbolism* to which Charles contributed some passages (notably a definition of the difference between emblem and symbol), and in later years she made two anthologies of modern verse for the young.

Their marriage was a tempestuous and a true one. No one who heard Charles Williams speak of the institution of marriage could doubt that he knew it to have been the ground of his own growth, though he never spoke of it as a grace that is easily won. He sometimes quoted from a horoscope which had been made for him, which said that he might do best to remain celibate: 'Only', he commented, 'I should have done nothing.' He was not one to take a falsely romantic view of marriage—'Romantic Love is a state of facts'.[1] He smiled at the false romanticism of Hardy's lover, so disillusioned at the sudden sight of his wife as being 'but a sample Of earth's poor average kind'. Everyone from Dante downwards has felt that, he would say, and what does it prove? Simply that we are fallen creatures and cannot maintain the strength of our vision, not that the vision was untrue. As to what comes in its place, it is 'something that they call quiet affection: it isn't affection and it is not at all quiet, but the description has to serve.' Perhaps his temperament led him to predict a more universal difficulty in the married state than can be proved true, but this only serves to throw into relief his affirmation of its positive good—something that would be a good happening, whatever distress might accompany it. 'It was, perhaps, the only *certainly* wise thing I have ever done; marrying

[1] See below, p. xliii.

you. The whole effect of You on me will only be known on the Day of Judgement.' So he wrote to his wife in 1943. He would maintain that there was not the slightest irony in the reply of George II to Caroline when she lay dying and urged him to marry again: 'Non, j'aurai des maîtresses'. The marriage relationship, once held, was absolute.

More will be said of Williams's doctrine of marriage when I come to discuss his themes. His view of parentage, an office which he held with extreme diffidence, must concern us next, for in 1922 their son and only child was born. The baby was—nobly and confusingly—christened Michael.

Actually, child, I am a god
 Communing with you, a god:

he addressed the infant, and he continued to hold the view that children were distinguished strangers, with whom communication was difficult if not impossible—a view which did not prevent him from talking amply to his son. He never 'talked down', but this was not to say that he was unaware of his hearer's response. As to his view of parental detachment—he would have appreciated the joke against himself if he had read of the parent in Elizabeth Bowen's *A House in Paris*, whose conscious forbearance has in its turn become an oppression to her daughter. But there was as much of tenderness as of irony in the sonnet which he later wrote, called 'Any Father to Any Son':

lost in many a mind
lies many a quite intelligent idea
 because a parent once delivered it,
and the wise princess, heavenly-born Sophia,
 prophesies rarely by paternal wit.
Hear therefore, O my heart, hear and be warned—
it is a father's office to be scorned.

In the autumn of the year that Michael was born, Williams began to supplement the family income by giving evening lectures for the London County Council. By the time I knew him, in the thirties, he was giving a two-hour session weekly, at the City Literary Institute and at the Balham Commercial Institute. After this he would go home and settle down to literary work, and his wife has written of her nocturnal awakenings to hear its progress. 'When Charles was writing his life of Sir Francis Bacon I was aroused at one a.m. to hear the details of that great man's passing. I heard the last two chapters of *The Greater Trumps* at three a.m. . . .'[1]

[1] From the article quoted above.

Such a régime would have led to a breakdown in many men, and no one looking at Charles Williams would have thought him strong. He was slightly built, and his hands trembled so much that he always had to get a barber to shave him—this was due to neurasthenia, but he would say that it caused his aunts to suspect him of leading a debauched life. Yet in spite of his apparent frailty he was never absent from the office for any of the minor ailments that afflict tougher-looking men.

His hands were in fact wonderfully expressive—no wonder that he found the human hand in general so significant. Apart from these, his brow was his most noble physical feature: it always seemed appropriate that the name *Taliessin* should mean 'Bright Forehead'. He used his hands much more freely than most Englishmen do, and especially, when he was lecturing, in a gesture which was his alone —raising them upward in the shape of a cup, the wrists and elbows pressed together to form the stem. This was always at some high pitch of passion aroused by the poetry of which he was speaking. And passion in the fullest sense it was. Nothing could be farther from the truth about his own lectures than the bitter words which he puts into the mouth of the don Roger Ingram in *Shadows of Ecstasy*:

> I embalm poetry there—with the most popular and best-smelling unguents and so on, but I embalm it all right. I then exhibit the embalmed body to visitors at so much a head. They like it much better than the live thing, and I live by it, so I suppose it's all right. No doubt the embalmers of Pharaoh were pleasant enough creatures. They weren't called to any nonsense of following a pillar of fire between the piled waters of the Nile.

I remember Dylan Thomas saying to him after a literary party: 'Why, you come into the room and talk about Keats and Blake as if they were *alive*.' To quote poetry certainly came to him as naturally as 'the leaves to a tree', and the store of it in his mind was inexhaustible. Lost in his incantation, he was entirely unconscious of self, so that his hearers, too, became oblivious of the person of the speaker, and felt as though they were transported to the actual fount of the words. 'There is a *chaunt* in the recitation both of Coleridge and Wordsworth', wrote Hazlitt, 'which acts as a spell on the hearer and disarms the judgment.'

The movement of Charles Williams's mind was unusually quick, and his physical movements were dartingly swift to match: in lecturing he was always in movement, but it was never fidgeting—the movements seemed to match the progress of his thought. And whatever the passion engendered, that progress was always lucidly in mind: he would announce six points to be made, or distinctions to be drawn, and without the need of reference to notes, six there surely were. He seemed so full of the energy of thought that even the most lack-lustre of his listeners felt themselves, for the time being, 'mogul diamonds'.

An hour of lecture, an hour of discussion, was the rule of the L.C.C. Most readers will have experienced the stickiness of such after-the-lecture discussions, but with Charles Williams there was rarely any difficulty. He could take the most embryonic or stammeringly expressed thought as a starting-point: he would listen with serious attention, then springing to his feet would develop the argument toward some real conclusion. Argument with him was never a battle but a method of discovery, and to watch him at work on some difficult point was such a delight that his pupils felt, as Dante with Virgil, that 'to doubt is not less grateful than to know'. Moreover, in matters of religion he always gave the arguments which were opposed to his own beliefs their full reality. As he said in 1939:[1]

> My chief objection to the champions of Christianity is that the objections to Christianity do not come from them. You may really sympathize with the other fellow, but you never *sound* as if you really felt the force of his argument. . . . Why should the objections to Christianity be left to outsiders? Let us see them, see where they are, feel them, almost create them: and then we may have the energy that belongs to Christianity. . . . It is a very doubtful thing whether in fact either the Divine City itself, or that pale and feeble image of it about which we dream, can function and thrive except by in some sense including its opposite.

Earlier in the lecture just quoted, he had something to say about the people—largely from the lower middle class—of whom his audiences were composed. After fearing that 'the two words "Christian Culture" are in danger of becoming an extremely unpleasant corpse', he goes on to say:

> I have felt myself for some years, in fact ever since I became connected with them, that these are the people who are capable of re-energizing your culture. I think myself . . . that they are, much more than your more academic students, a centre of power. There is about these people a capacity and freshness for culture, for dealing with culture, which I have on the whole, with many exceptions, yet to find elsewhere. And I think the difference is largely because their culture has not already been petrified behind them. . . .

No doubt he was idealizing his students when he said this; no doubt also he would have allowed that a sense of perspective, of relative importance, is necessary and is hard for the self-educated man to acquire. But that is how he felt, and no teacher could have given himself more unsparingly to his pupils: the discussion of general or

[1] 'The Recovery of Spiritual Initiative': a lecture delivered to the Christian School of Sociology, apparently taken down verbatim, and published in *Christendom*, Dec. 1940.

of personal problems would continue into the streets of Holborn or of Tooting, long after the statutory two hours were over.

What his pupils learned from him as a general habit of mind, apart from the profit they derived from his wisdom and his knowledge in particular instances, was a vigilance in the use of words, and about commonly accepted opinions, which made them sharply sensitive to cant in all its forms. No one, taught by him, could ever again use the word *mystical* as though it merely meant *mysterious*, or the word *eternal* as though it merely meant *everlasting*, or describe some sad event as *tragic*, or use the word *love* when they merely meant *like*, without at least an inward plea to the Truth for forgiveness. Dr. Johnson's 'Clear your mind of cant' was a maxim he never let his pupils forget. 'Your Cardinals may be trying to be safe', he wrote to me in answer to some facile Protestant criticism of the Roman Church which I had made, 'but, after all, what else in the End does one want? but to be in the security of high beauty and goodness and truth . . .'. And his comment on a Roman priest's rhetorical question 'You wouldn't ask Christ for a soft job, would you?' was: 'Well, wouldn't you?'[1] '*Serviette*', he would say: 'I can't see why one *shouldn't* talk about a serviette'—and the castle of snobbery would crumble. No one was ever more consistently free from the stock response. As Professor Lewis has said, he excelled in pointing out the virtues of some passage which was commonly ridiculed, and conversely in detecting a falsity in some admired lines. Where, in the case of Chesterton, one sometimes feels that his refusal to take anything for granted has become an affectation, with Williams it was absolutely unforced. When he wrote a poem 'On arriving anywhere in time for anything', beginning

How good the Universe can be!—What now?

or protested against being prayed for:

But thou being once set firmly on thy knees
  Bringst God's will on me in how many shapes!

he was expressing his natural reaction, not straining for effect.

No one among his students was too dull to be listened to, or too grasping to be helped. His friends, to tease him, would call him promiscuous, and perhaps would wish him to be more selective, but would then recall that the saints were not selective. And in fact, however freely he seemed to give of his energies and even of his personal confidences, he had always a certain inner detachment—in the last resort, and however perfect the give and take of his human relationships, you felt that he depended on no one: he was

[1] In the lecture quoted above.

not born under *Virgo* for nothing. The work he did for his pupils brought its rewards, and perhaps provided some recompense for the lack of general recognition of his genius, by what Ezra Pound has called 'the pleasing attitudes of discipleship', but it took much time and energy—and the sacrifice was also his wife's, of her share in his leisure.

The chronicle of his years becomes largely that of books published and friends made. One relationship which was of importance to his development dates from some time earlier than the twenties, however. He much admired the writings of A. E. Waite, and Mrs. Williams tells me that it was through a letter concerning one of Waite's books that Charles made his acquaintance, and was introduced by him to the Order of the Golden Dawn. As Mrs. Williams is sure that this did not happen until after their marriage in 1917, there is a certain difficulty about the chronology, as will appear from the following account—as brief a one as the complexities of the subject will allow. 'The occult is a shifty business', as Waite himself remarks in his autobiography, and between magian secrecies and the distortions encouraged by magian vanity, it is extremely difficult to get at the truth. However, it seems certain that the hermetic Order of the Golden Dawn was founded in 1887 by three English Rosicrucians, though their accounts of the source from which its rituals were derived do not agree. Of these three, S. L. MacGregor Mathers—who had been responsible for the working out of the rituals—became the leader, and remained so until 1900, by which time the Order had some 200 members and five 'temples'. An easily accessible account of its early history is given in John Symonds's life of Aleister Crowley, *The Great Beast*.[1] He there describes the initiation ceremony, when the novice was threatened with death by a hostile current (cf. the death of Mornington in *War in Heaven*) if he broke his oath of secrecy. Charles Williams kept this oath, though he outgrew the sect, but he sometimes spoke of it in general terms to me, laughing to remember the quarrels for precedence among the children of the Second Birth.

As the result of the earlier and even more bitter quarrels in the society, there had been a rebellion against Mathers and his emissary Crowley, which ended in schism in 1900. W. B. Yeats, who had led the revolt, became head of the dissident London temple ('Isis-Urania'), and continued so, in spite of bickering, until 1904, when there was a further split. Yeats then followed Dr. Felkin, who

[1] Panther Books. The source of his information about the Golden Dawn was Mr. Gerald Yorke, who has kindly put his extensive knowledge at my disposal also.

founded the Order of the Stella Matutina,[1] and Waite took over the leadership of the Isis–Urania temple, altering the rituals to bring them closer to the tradition of Rosicrucian Christianity as he interpreted it. He also discouraged the working of 'white' magic, which had been an essential part of the original practices.[2] It was at this period that Evelyn Underhill belonged to the Order;[3] Arthur Machen, who refers to it contemptuously in his autobiography as the 'Order of the Twilight Star', had belonged to it in its original form. Then 'In 1914', to quote Waite's own account in his rather pompously written autobiography,[4]

> I put an end to the Isis–Urania or Mother Temple, owing to internecine feuds on the authenticity of documents. A few persons attempted to carry on by themselves, but it proved a failure. Of a new Rite which arose, as if from the dead ashes, there . . . is no story to tell, either by myself or another. May that most sacred centre give up no outward form.

Waite's wish has been granted, at least as far as this inquirer is concerned, but it would seem (according to the date given by Mrs. Williams) that it must have been to this later unnamed Order that Charles Williams belonged. Yet he always spoke of himself as having belonged to the Golden Dawn. Waite is nowhere explicit about his rituals: he speaks contemptuously of those of the Golden Dawn, except in that they contain 'the notion of a candidate ascending the Tree of Life'. But it is evident from Waite's own writings that the symbolism of both Orders derived from the same sources, and if the influence upon Williams's work was not so deep as Miss Virginia Moore has shown it to have been upon that of Yeats,[5] it was nevertheless considerable—witness the symbolism used in his novels (for instance the Tarot cards, the angelic hierarchies, the talisman, all of which were important in the Golden Dawn cosmology), and the magical operations of Merlin in the *Summer Stars*. The language of the imaginary rituals which he elaborated in letters also, as I now realize, derived in part from the Order.

As to the performance of the rituals, Williams told me that most of the members (or at any rate those who were less advanced in the grades)[6] were content to read words from a script when it came to their turn, but that he himself took pleasure in memorizing what

[1] This apparently still exists, as do other descendants of the original Order, in attenuated forms.

[2] Gerald Yorke, in an unpublished lecture.

[3] C. W., in his introduction to her *Letters*, Longmans, p. 12.

[4] *Shadows of Life and Thought*, Selwyn & Blount, p. 229. Other authorities give 1917 as the date of dissolution, and Waite is not reliable in the matter of dates.

[5] *The Unicorn*, Macmillan, 1954.

[6] In the original Order, at least, there were eleven of these, but no living person had attained to the last three.

had to be said, so that he could celebrate with dignity. As he wrote in *The English Poetic Mind*: 'One of the advantages of ceremony, rightly used, is that it gives a place to self-consciousness, and a means whereby self-consciousness may be lost in the consciousness of the office filled or the ritual carried out.' No doubt it was this, as much as anything, which made the Order satisfying to him for a time.

Williams did not continue to see Waite in later years, and is not mentioned in his autobiography. However, the older man's influence had been an important one for him. *The Hidden Church of the Holy Graal* (1909) had its place among the origins of his Arthurian studies, as entries in his Notebook show, but it was *The Secret Doctrine in Israel* (1913) which interested him most—and he continued to admire it, for he recommended me to read it, when I knew him in the thirties. It is a study of a Jewish mystical work, the *Zohar*, and includes much of the lore which is found in Golden Dawn teachings, though it would be outside my scope to determine how much of it Waite owed to them. The frontispiece shows a diagram of the Sephirotic Tree[1] laid out upon the figure of a man, with the different properties related to different parts of the body—e.g. *Chesed*, Mercy, is at the right hand, *Geburah*, Severity, at the left. In this book, I believe, are the foundations of Williams's thought about the symbolism of the body, and of his lifelong attempt to develop an adequate theology of marriage—and in this last, the influence of Waite can be distinguished from that of the Golden Dawn in its original form, for the subject of sex played no part in its teachings.[2]

The need to relate our physical nature to some great principle of order exists in all of us, in some form or other, for, as Sir Kenneth Clark says, 'we still feel close to divinity in those flashes of self-identification when, through our own bodies, we seem to be aware of a universal order'.[3] And it may be that it is chiefly those who, like Charles Williams, lack any deep satisfaction in the apprehension of a visual order in painting, who turn to such a diagrammatic order.[4]

[1] Williams uses the Zodiac (also important in G.D. teachings) in the essay on 'The Index of the Body' here reprinted. But the symbolism of the Tree was familiar in his thought—see, for instance, 'The Death of Palomides' in *Taliessin.*

[2] Gerald Yorke, op. cit. The G.D. did, however, admit women as members, as the English Rosicrucian Order did not.

[3] *The Nude*, John Murray, p. 357.

[4] I am aware that Williams wrote of paintings here and there in his novels and poems: nevertheless no art besides poetry (and for music he was tone-deaf) was really important to him.

Waite had been baptized into the Roman Church as a boy, and retained his love for its rituals; his Order professedly did not compete with established Churches, and it never drew Williams from his own. The Church was the soil in which he grew; the Golden Dawn only a temporary fertilizer. Of two other members of the Order who became his friends, one was a clergyman of the Church of England, and one, I think, belonged to no Church, though he certainly believed in the deity of Love. Williams did not meet them through the Order, however, but in his capacity as a publisher, and only discovered the other connexion later on. The Rev. A. H. Lee and D. H. S. Nicholson had compiled a collection of poetry which they brought in to Amen House, and which was accepted and published in 1917 as the *Oxford Book of Mystical Verse*. It is a hotch-potch from a literary point of view, but they were primarily interested in the poems as documents of mystical experience, and it was from this point of mutual interest (which is too weak a word for it) that the friendship with Williams grew. D. H. S. Nicholson became the most intimate friend of his middle years, and the friendship lasted until Nicholson's death two or three years before the 1939 war. He was a man of lively intelligence and much fluency in argument, who could meet Williams in discussion on exactly the terms he preferred. Nicholson's books were less distinguished than his talk, though he published novels and a study of the mysticism of St. Francis.

It became a habit for the three to spend one evening together every week, and on these occasions Henry Lee seems to have filled the role which was Commander Campbell's in the early days of the Brains Trust—that of the Plain Man. He, a bachelor, would throw out remarks to the effect that it would be a sad world without the sound of the feet of little children, to be demolished by the two married men.

I have mentioned the two privately printed Masques as an extension of Charles Williams's habit of making myths for his friends. They were written for performance before 'Caesar' in the library at Amen House in 1927 and 1929; they were introduced by Charles Williams himself, and under pastoral names the chief members of the staff played parts appropriate to their several functions at the Press. It was, as Professor Lewis has so well said of his attitude to ceremony in general, at once a game and something to be taken seriously: they were acting parts and yet they were being themselves.

These relationships at Amen House were of importance in his life: in one of them he saw that Second Image of romantic love, of which he writes in *The Figure of Beatrice* (stating a truth that is hard to live by): 'we are not to pretend it is not there, or indeed to diminish its worth; we are only asked to free ourselves from concupiscence in regard to it. . . . It repeats the first, in an opposite direction. But both movements are alike intense towards most noble Love: that is, towards the work of the primal Love in the creation.'

I have already spoken of the relationship between Charles Williams and his pupils: there were some permanent pupils to whom he used to refer (again, with a style that managed to hold mimesis and reality in balance) as his Household, and who still hold themselves as of that company. One of them, Alice Mary Hadfield, worked at the Press, and became a devoted admirer of his writings. Among those whom he counted as patrons as well as friends was Olive Willis, creator of a famous girls' school,[1] and a person of princely and unselfregarding liberality. In the summer of 1918 Charles and Michal had spent a holiday in one of her cottages at the village of Aisholt in the Quantocks, and they with their son were staying there again in 1930, from which time I date my own friendship with them. I had just left school, and was staying with three friends in another of Olive Willis's cottages; she and her partner were in a third. We all heard poetry, sitting by log fires or walking in the coombes, and both Charles and his wife extended to the four schoolgirls as much interest and sympathy as if we had reached the age of expression. The holiday is commemorated in 'A Song of the Myths', in *Three Plays*: certainly the time and the place took on all the splendour of a myth for me.

The poetry which we heard was that of *Heroes and Kings*, then in proof, and *The Chaste Wanton*, then in manuscript. By the next year both were published, and the years between 1930 and the end of 1939 show an astonishing output: in that time were published (though some of the work had been done earlier) five biographies, three books of drama, and one play printed in periodical form, six novels, two theological books, three books of literary criticism, the poetry of *Heroes and Kings*, and the first collection of the *Taliessin* poems. I have not included the minor publications of the time—the Prefaces, the anthologies, the reviews—and one must remember the lectures, and the many letters, besides his daily work at the Press. Williams reviewed detective stories for the old *Daily News* and later for the *News Chronicle*; he was an occasional contributor to a number of periodicals, and a regular contributor to *Time and Tide* from 1938 onward. Yet in the summer of 1933 he was in danger of death, and underwent an operation for intussusception at University College hospital. It only interrupted for a few short

[1] Downe House. See the *Prelude* to *Windows of Night.*

weeks the flow of his pen—he was at work on his biography of James I and on his novel *Descent into Hell* at the time, and noticed, in a letter written some six weeks after the illness began, a certain disinclination to get on with them. Victor Gollancz had been an appreciative publisher of the first four novels, and his refusal of *Descent into Hell* the following year was a considerable discouragement. However, after meeting with one or two more rebuffs it found its place with Faber and Faber, of which T. S. Eliot is a director.

Charles Williams came to know T. S. Eliot as a friend through Montgomery Belgion, though they had already met briefly at the house of Lady Ottoline Morrell. They felt warm affection for each other, a feeling which in Williams was not at all touched by the slight natural envy which he felt—and laughed at himself for feeling—for Eliot's greater fame. Each poet approached the other's verse with caution and respect: in his *Poetry at Present* essay, Williams had displayed an intelligent bewilderment, which changed as time went on to a deeper understanding. He observed in a review of 'East Coker' in 1940: 'Mr. Eliot has been admired, times without number, for describing the disease. What his poetry has been always calling is the note of strange and beautiful health.' Some judges considered that the Skeleton of *Cranmer* owed something to the Tempters of *Murder in the Cathedral*; Eliot may or may not have been led to associate Shelley's *doppelgänger* lines with the destiny of a young woman (see *The Cocktail Party*) by his memory of *Descent into Hell*. But he saw Williams's importance as being, above all, in his supernatural insight, for an age which has largely lost that power. I take this opinion from a memorial broadcast which Eliot gave in 1946, in which he said also: 'Williams . . . seemed to me to approximate, more nearly than any man I have ever known familiarly, to the saint.'

Charles Williams had, if not fame, at least a share of recognition, in these years of the thirties, but it was never so wide as his gifts deserved. It was at about this time that his friendship with Dorothy Sayers began, through their admiration for each other's work. To Auden's generation he was practically unknown: perhaps even if they had come across him at that time his ideas would have made no appeal—certainly Stephen Spender, who did review his criticism, was hostile.[1] The invitation to write a play for the Canterbury Festival, which resulted in *Thomas Cranmer*, and its local success, were encouragements; so also was the enthusiasm of the Chelmsford Diocesan producer, Phyllis Potter, who commissioned *Seed of Adam* ('she says that if I don't write her a nativity play she will

[1] Auden's recognition came in the forties.

have to produce *Eagerheart* again'), and was associated with *Judgement at Chelmsford*. He was invited to lecture at the Sorbonne, and did so in January 1938.[1] But the most valuable recognition came from Oxford. In 1936 the Press published C. S. Lewis's *Allegory of Love*, and Williams was about to write to its author expressing his great admiration for the book, when he received from that source a letter in praise of *The Place of the Lion*. The friendship which followed, and the introduction to other friends at Oxford, have been described by Professor Lewis in the works I have mentioned.

When in 1939 the Second World War began, and the staff of Amen House moved to Southfield House at Oxford, the meetings with these Oxford friends became frequent, and doubtless their companionship and admiration, with the hospitality which Charles Williams and Gerard Hopkins found at the house of the Spalding family in South Parks Road (where they lodged as paying guests for the whole of the war), were the things that chiefly softened the pain of exile from London. Moreover, Williams's influence among the undergraduates was soon felt, as he began to deliver lectures and to take tutorials, and in 1943 he was given an Honorary M.A. Two more verse plays were written for Ruth Spalding's branch of the Pilgrim Players, and were acted in the University Church of St. Mary the Virgin; a third, written for her, was not acted in his lifetime. Yet Oxford, however hospitable, was still exile to him—it was exile to move from Thames to Isis, and as he wrote soon after the beginning of the war: 'Oxford is beautiful—so long as one lives in London.'

Michal Williams had remained in London for the most part, to look after their flat ('incredible woman! I don't think she *is* afraid', as he wrote after the September raids), and whenever possible he joined her there at week-ends. When apart, they wrote to each other every day. Their son was working at Blackwell's during part of this time, and also lodged with the Spaldings. In the spring of 1945 the German war ended, and on Whit Sunday Charles Williams was to have preached in St. Mary's. But he was taken ill, as a result of adhesions from his earlier operation, and although he survived the surgery, it was only for a few hours.

In a review which appeared in *Time and Tide* a few days after his death, he had written: 'Heaven is alien; we must be naturalized

[1] I have seen a typed draft of one lecture on the Augustans and the Romantics called 'The Alteration of Passion', and a typescript 'On Byron and Byronism' which must have been copied from shorthand notes taken at the time of the lecture. I thought of printing this, but decided that Williams would not have wished it to be published with its colloquialisms unchanged. An extract was printed in the *Bulletin* of the British Institute of Paris.

or die.' *The House of the Octopus* is a research into the meaning of death, and in *All Hallows' Eve* he had gone as far perhaps as any man could, in imagining the state of a soul after bodily death. It is impossible not to think that he had felt death near, though he often alluded in letters to old age and the future. But his friends were far from being prepared for his death, and the sense of bewilderment with which the Oxford circle received the news, as C. S. Lewis has described it, was common to all. C. S. Lewis has expressed, too, for all, the result that followed:

> No event has so corroborated my faith in the next world as Williams did simply by dying. When the idea of death and the idea of Williams thus met in my mind, it was the idea of death that was changed.

His grave is in the churchyard of St. Cross, which had been his parish church during his time in Oxford, with the inscription after his name of 'Poet. Under the Mercy.'

During the war years there had appeared the study of Witchcraft, and, more important, the study of Dante, called *The Figure of Beatrice*. His last novel appeared a few months before his death, and his 'missionary play' a few months after it. But his most important work, the one by which he would have wished to be remembered, was left unfinished. I mean the cycle of *Taliessin* poems, of which a further instalment had appeared in 1944. Unfinished also was his study of the development of the Arthurian myth (later published with C. S. Lewis's commentary as *Arthurian Torso*), which stops short soon after he has reached the all-important account of his own creative treatment of the myth.

I shall return later to *Taliessin*. We are now to consider the main themes of which he treated.

II

At the centre of Williams's teaching lies this dogma, that the whole universe is to be known as good. But this was a truth to him as agonizing as it was inescapable: to be grasped perhaps in such moments of ecstasy as Yeats wrote of in 'A Dialogue of Self and Soul', when

> We are blest by everything,
> Everything we look upon is blest—

but in general only to be 'believed with sighs'. The slickness of Pope's 'whatever is, is right' was repellent to him, and he had outgrown the melodramatic formulations of the Golden Dawn, where, for instance, Yeats was given the secret name of 'Daemon Est Deus

Inversus'. Williams said that he would not have hesitated to decline the gift of life if he had been offered it—though he kept a private fantasy that we might at some moment, sitting on a ledge somewhere out of Time, have been given the choice and said *Yes*. His capacity for enjoyment seemed so strong that this death-wish in him was hard to credit, but he was certainly not exaggerating in what he said. 'This gusto that everyone seems to observe in me,' he would complain, 'I am not aware of it.' (This used to remind me of a gesture of Harpo Marx, when after an impassioned performance on the harp, he turns aside with a gaping yawn at his own prolonged virtuosity.) As for immortality, Williams could not understand how Tennyson—was it?—could have lost a night's rest because he doubted it. Who would not choose an everlasting sleep, given the chance? This was not merely a personal sensation: he never lost his sense of close implication in the distresses of the world.

O Earth's body, what pain
Tightens the whole fine nervous web?

he wrote in an early poem, using the same image that he was often to use later for a heavenly co-inherence—'the web of the glory'. In this poem, ironically called 'Domesticity',[1] he recalls the history of pain which is implied in each ordinary household task:

Bathing or lighting a fire or going downstairs
What old companions crowd us, see, in our first need!

Unseen, ineluctable, those whom Morgan's blades
Pricked from the ship's side, Margaret Wilson, or they
Of France and Couthon, the stripped and bound noyades,
Floating for ever wherever water flows.

And when we set match to the fire, the small flames scorch
Something other than wood: what inaudible cry
Rends my dumb spirit! 'twas thus they put the torch
To Joan's fire or Du Moulay's—thus? no, with this.

And in one of his last reviews, of a 'Famous Trial', he thought of the fear of the victim and wrote: 'At the price of such things we live.'

He knew the relief that comes from a clear recognition of our plight—and this was one of the things that made him attractive to the young, who were driven almost to despair by being told that they were enjoying the happiest years of their lives. 'Happiest years? Think what a hell it was!' he and D. H. S. Nicholson would

[1] In *Windows of Night*. I have called the poem *early* because it seems so in relation to all that came later, but actually the book was published when Williams was nearly forty. I have found it convenient to quote in several places from these neglected earlier poems, which express certain ideas in simpler form than the later verse.

say of their youthful days. 'I did not dream I lived in pain?' says his young Duchess in *The Chaste Wanton*, and her Alchemist lover replies:

> In pain?
> The columns of your palace live in pain;
> The stones beneath us are alive with pain. . . .

Even Galahad aches 'with the fibrous infelicity of time', and Bors can only pray that his children assent to their birth, which he and God have made to be.

This acute sense of brotherhood in distress, then, gave force to Charles Williams's statement of ultimate good; his energy and capacity for delight gave poignancy to his expression of the wish for death. But the tension between opposite forces was a characteristic of his genius in other aspects too. Such was the tension between scepticism and affirmation, of which I shall speak later; and between an impulse towards violence (there is, for instance, a certain sadism in a few of the *Taliessin* poems) and a loving-kindness so remarkable that it caused T. S. Eliot to inquire of him whether he was to be called the Blessed Charles in his lifetime. So the very difficulties of his nature he made a source of strength; they became a synthesis of power. For in the realm of morals, I suppose, as in that of technique, there is no weakness that cannot be turned to good account, and we should never think that any damage or disadvantage is irreparable. It was through the courage of his own self-knowledge that Charles Williams was so entirely unshockable: 'Pride no one minds admitting,' he would say, 'but malice? . . .' Those who came to him for help felt that no experience could be outside the range of his understanding, no sin or misery could defeat his reconciling power. As the priest in *The House of the Octopus* says:

> Those who have seen their sin know sin
> And cannot be astonished.

Again, while Williams is perhaps the Christian writer of all others in our time who has restored the body to its proper place of honour, his sense of revolt against the flesh was at times very strong. He sometimes delighted to remember that the greatest poets were bound by the same physical needs as the rest of humanity, yet he was sometimes repelled by the thought of those same needs. He held that we were all of us natural Manichaeans: for as he always rejected the division of mankind into categories of varying sensitiveness, maintaining that a coal-heaver was as capable of suffering as himself, so he thought that there must be a community of distaste.

'The more remote the ratio of the parts to one another or the whole, the greater the unity if felt at all', Gerard Manley Hopkins wrote in his *Notes on Rhythm*. And it was certainly the sense of a deep division in his own nature which made Charles Williams's expression of some final possibility of union so convincing. There is a profound and difficult poem in *The Region of the Summer Stars* which expresses all that I have been trying to say. Here the Pope is celebrating Mass, with the 'heart-breaking manual acts' which are, above all, 'Acts of *Identity*', and

> The gnosis of separation in the Pope's soul
> had become a promulgation of sacred union,
> and he his function[1] only; at the junction of communion
> he offered his soul's health for the living corpses,
> his guilt, his richness of repentance, wealth for woe.

I return for a moment to Longfellow's *Golden Legend*, in which I saw a foreshadowing of Williams's grand theme. First, the romantic clash between the forces of good and evil; then the more mature insight which recognizes the Devil as being the agent of the good. For just as the Fall in each of us happens when we see good as evil, so the highest activity of love must be to transform even what we call evil into good. The apparent co-existence of good and evil (in the world, in one person) is a contradiction, an antinomy, which is the prime cause of conflict in man's soul. This is the *change and subversion* (Wordsworth's phrase) which Williams analysed in Shakespeare's tragedies, and this conflict is the mainspring of his own work. But its resolution must be not so much in the defeat of evil by good, as in a new understanding where the old terms are no longer true. In the novels, certainly, the damned are simply damned —we hardly reach the point where we could consider the fate of Giles Tumulty or of Simon the Clerk as somehow good; but in the plays and the poetry the matter is not so simple. For no judgement pronounced on sin by human righteousness will ever be wholly just, but must be judged itself by the irony of the Cross. In *Windows of Night* he had defined the antinomy.

> What are those domes? *you asked in Clerkenwell*;
> *And I*: One is the Old Bailey and one Saint Paul's,
> Sitting up there like the broken halves of the shell
> Of the egg of life, whose overspilt yolk we are.
>
> Justice is perched on one, with her sword and scales,
> And over her shoulder the ancient commentary.

[1] That is, he now exists only for the sake of carrying out his proper function; he could no longer consider that the function existed for his sake. See the quotation from Dante's *De Monarchia* at the beginning of *Taliessin through Logres*.

The cross, in huge silence that neither hopes nor rails,
Peeps,—all judgement's ironical overthrow.

. . . . .

If judges some day having uttered their judgement arose
And themselves in the doomed man's stead were drawn to the bitter
Torment of prison or death—would that cure the woes
We suffer, and quench the unquenchable fiery pang?

Not for love's sake—leave that to a god!
Not for love but only to bring the irrational in!
Madness might wander where sanity never trod
And find the secret, and strike the irony dumb. . . .

But in the late essay on the Cross, he saw beyond the irony: '. . . alone among the gods, He deigned to endure the justice He decreed . . .', therefore we can use the word justice without shame: 'God therefore becomes tolerable as well as credible. Our justice condemned the innocent, but the innocent it condemned was one who was fundamentally responsible for the existence of all injustice.'

The image of the two domes as halves of the broken egg of life is not entirely effective—rather because it seems far-fetched than because it is a mixture of the abstract and the concrete, for it was by just such a mixture that he achieved success in the *Taliessin* poems. But his later preoccupation with geometrical symbols gave him some wholly abstract images which suited this particular purpose better. The relation between the curve and the straight line, the sides of a triangle, the two lines of the asymptote,[1] is seen as the perfection of order which is so rarely apparent to us, and which, when the parts are seen without the relation, is known by us as pain and contradiction. He used these images first in some unpublished 'Euclidean' love poems, the material of which was later used for Palomides in the *Taliessin* series. Then, at the opening of *The Descent of the Dove*, his history of the operation of the Holy Spirit in the Church, he uses the asymptote to symbolize the Ascent of Christ and the Descent of the Dove, and the point of their meeting at infinity is the beginning of Christendom—that cause which is hidden to us and is therefore the cause of our distress. The asymptote also signified for him the seemingly divergent ways of asceticism and sacramentalism, as I shall later show.

'Not for love's sake—leave that to a god!' But Williams could not be intellectually content unless the solution were provided by love—he was always striving towards that point, reached at the end of all true tragedy, when we feel, not 'Justice has been done', but 'This is what must have been, and it is somehow good'. (But perhaps

[1] 'A line which continually approaches a given curve, but does not meet it within a finite distance.' *S.O.E.D.*

only poetry can make us accept it as an intellectual statement, and even there it is not always bearable.) He did not write a tragedy, but through his plays from earliest to latest there moves a Figure which acts as the instrument of reconciliation. I have sometimes thought that the first appearance of this Figure might be said to be in the person of Charles Williams himself as Introducer in his two Masques, with his 'Caesar, remember thou shalt die'. In the liturgical *Rite of the Passion*, Satan, who is finally seen as Love's shadow, is one of a pair of figures (Gabriel is the other), and for *Cranmer* Williams had at first planned a functionally similar pair. But the reconciling process was so far at work in his mind that the design became that of a single figure—or perhaps for the first time in his plays truly a person: the Skeleton or *Figura Rerum*. There is no space here to attempt an analysis of this complex character, whose many definitions of his own nature give no help to the literal-minded. Those that are most to the point here are: 'I am the Judas who betrays men to God'; and 'I am the delator of all things to their truth'; also, 'I am Christ's back. . . .' And through the Skeleton, Cranmer's apostasy is finally the source of his salvation. In *Judgement at Chelmsford* the Figure is more simply the Accuser of men to truth:

> God made me to be the image of each man's desire. . . .
> Most men when at last they see their desire
> fall to repentance—all have that chance.

In *Seed of Adam* the part of the Accuser is to some extent taken by the Third King, and his devouring wife–mother, Hell, the silent Negress, becomes midwife to the Incarnation. The Flame in *The House of the Octopus*, the last of the series of reconciling figures, is the energy of the creation, the 'uncovenanted flame of the Holy Ghost': he is not only beyond good and evil; he is at the point of equilibrium where laughter and tears are equal. For when the priest is tempted to agree with the emissary of hell to use the same word, Father, for his god and theirs, on the plausible ground that the spirit matters more than the letter, the Flame says:

> man
> must, if words mean anything, stand by words
> since stand he must; and on earth protest to death
> against what at the same time is a jest in heaven.
> Alas, you are not in heaven! the jests there
> Are tragedies on earth, since you lost your first poise. . . .

And the Flame, too, can appear as a terror—

> In the jungle my companions and I do nothing but run,
> all the forces of nature loosed on a creature.
> Only in the church we run and are still at once

—which was also the nature of the Fool in the Tarot figures, described in *The Greater Trumps.*

One last related point from this play may be referred to, though it is one of the Christian converts and not the Flame who makes it—that what seems failure to us, may in truth be anything but that:

> If God is outside time, is it so certain
> that we know which moments of time count with him . . . ?

an idea which, as we shall see, is one of the central themes of the novel *Descent into Hell.* So, when one of the girl converts breaks down and denies her faith, yet dies all the same—

> It may be that her last scream
> was no more than a cry in child-birth, when *he* was born
> piercingly in her soul, and her very death
> her first motherly awaking. . . .
> She died, even if she lied; she is still a witness.

Finally, there is Garlon, the Invisible Knight. Towards the end of the book which Williams kept in early years for notes relating to the Arthurian myths, occurs this entry:

> Garlon, invisible = the unseen attempts on Man (= Balen) Qy: must he be the enemy of Arthur and the Table just as the spirit is always the enemy of the material; although the material always regards it as far more inimical than it is.

In Malory, it will be remembered, Garlon—the Invisible Knight who stirs up strife by his unseen interference—is the cause of the Dolorous Blow that sets the world at odds, for he provokes Balin the Wild, and in the fight that follows Balin wounds King Pelles with the Sacred Spear—the spear that had pierced Christ on the Cross. But it will be seen that the idea as Charles Williams developed it, is close to his central concern. In the explanatory notes which I have printed here, he writes (I add my own italics): 'In the shape of a little viper, Garlon, the Invisible Knight—*who is Satan to us but the Holy Ghost to the supernatural powers*—provokes the last battle.' And in the final poem of his cycle—final in the chronology of the myth—'Taliessin at Lancelot's Mass':

> Lancelot and Arthur wove the web; the sky
> opened on moon and sun; between them, light-traced on high,
> the unseen knight of terror stood as a friend;
> invisible things and visible waited the end.

I have said that perhaps only poetry can make us accept as a statement the possibility of seeing evil as good, though we may accept it as a dogma by faith. Williams's development in poetry of his idea of the Invisible Knight, which should have been the most powerful of all the unifying symbols we have been discussing, was prevented by his death.

Charles Williams's analysis of an opposite state of mind, the result of seeing a good thing as evil, as it has been expressed in great poets, is probably his chief contribution to criticism. This *subversion*,[1] the sense that 'chaos is come again', follows when good is seen as evil, not—as in the Fall—because of a fault in the beholder, but because the good, the beloved person, has itself become evil. Something that cannot possibly happen, has happened: it cannot be believed, yet it must be. England has declared war on the French Revolution. Cressida is false.

> This she? no, this is Diomed's Cressida.
> If beauty have a soul, this is not she. . . .

'This is, and is not, Cressid. . . .' The lines in which Troilus describes his 'conflict of sensations' were Williams's central text, and his *English Poetic Mind* relates this crisis to Wordsworth's as described in *The Prelude*, to the 'Evil, be thou my good' of Milton's Satan, and to passages in other poets. I shall have something to say of his criticism in general in the next section.

In Williams's specifically religious writing there are several doctrines which derive from this central dogma, epitomized in St. Paul's great verse about the Resurrection: 'For as in Adam all die, even so in Christ shall all be made alive.' For all is to be known as good—*all*; nothing is to be forgotten. 'It is not conceivable that Omniscience should forget; it is not satisfactory that the redeemed should forget. If a corner of experience is to be hidden, the unity is by so much impaired.'[2] So pardon is not to involve an oblivion of the sin, but an increased knowledge, 'a knowledge of all things in a perfection of joy.'[3] 'The Communion of Saints involves the resurrection of all the past. . . .'[4] Dante uses the image of the twofold stream of Lethe and Eunoë to express this truth: he writes of the water that

> Da questa parte con virtù discende,
> che toglie altrui memoria del peccato;
> dall'altra, d'ogni ben fatto la rende—[5]

a conception which Williams reinterprets in accordance with his own thought, when he expresses it thus: 'Lethe [which] removes

[1] Wordsworth, *The Prelude*, x. 232. Simone Weil describes the effects of such a catastrophe in the soul, in those terrible pages on 'le Malheur' in *Attente de Dieu*. 'Il est tout autre chose que la simple souffrance. Il s'empare de l'âme et la marque, jusqu'au fond, d'une marque qui n'appartient qu'à lui, la marque de l'esclavage.'

[2] *He came down from Heaven*, p. 48.

[3] Ib., p. 78.

[4] *The Forgiveness of Sins*, p. 108.

[5] *Purgatorio*, xxviii. 127: 'On this side it descends with a virtue which takes from men the memory of sin; on the other it restores the memory of every good deed.' Wicksteed's translation in the Temple Classics edition.

the memory of sin *as sin* [my italics], and Eunoë which recalls the knowledge of good as good.'[1]

I have grouped the religious essays here collected under four headings which may serve to distinguish the doctrines, but they are closely interrelated. First in the natural sequence is his view of the Incarnation. He believed the doctrine that Christ would have become incarnate, even if there had been no Fall,[2] for 'In His union and conjunction with Body, God finds His final perfection and felicity.'[3]

Williams held, with justice, that even though the doctrine of the Church gives the body its true importance, the utterances of Church members on the subject are often very misleading, and that marriage still lacks an adequate theology. 'The hungry sheep look up for metaphysics, the profound metaphysics of the awful and redeeming body, and are given morals', as he wrote in 'Sensuality and Substance', which is here reprinted. No doubt the language of the Fathers about the Flesh, and the whole tradition of asceticism, arose as a necessary defence against a barbarism which is difficult for us to imagine, and as part of the civilizing mission of the Church. But its result has been that the Church too often speaks as though (as Williams put it in *The Descent of the Dove*) 'the body has somehow fallen farther than the soul'. And as to lovers:

> If you see a young couple, don't you say 'Oh, yes, of course, it is quite natural: go on and enjoy yourselves while you can—it won't last long . . . '? But what they are thinking of was defined by the great Victorian poet, Patmore:
>
> What in its ruddy orbit lifts the blood,
> Like a perturbed moon of Uranus,
> Reaching to some great world in ungauged darkness hid?[4]

Yet the language of the Church's own creeds is unmistakable, and especially 'the great humanist Ode "commonly called the Creed of Saint Athanasius"'. 'One; not by conversion of the Godhead into flesh: but by taking of the manhood into God . . . not by confusion of substance: but by unity of person.' There is to be no weakening of our conception of either nature: they do not merge, they co-inhere, however our tendency may be to blur the differences

[1] *The Figure of Beatrice*, p. 194.

[2] Duns Scotus is, it seems, the best-known exponent of this doctrine. The Rev. Clifford Williams gives me this passage among others as authority: 'The Incarnation of Christ was not foreseen as a contingent event but was seen by God directly as an end from eternity. So Christ, in His human nature, since He is nearer to the end than other things, was predestined before them.' (*Opus Oxoniense*, iii, Dist. 19. Westcott's translation.)

[3] Patmore, *Rod, Root and Flower*, p. 53.

[4] From the lecture already quoted, p. xxi.

between them. Against Williams's remarks about our ideas on the body, given here in the essay on 'Sensuality and Substance', may be set his comment in a letter of 1936: 'Those who use the term [spirit] most, mean no more than a very very thin kind of matter.' And it was the clarity and courage of his thought on this subject which enabled him to give vitality to the almost-discredited idea of chastity—see his remarks on Milton's *Comus*, here and elsewhere, and his mockery, in *All Hallows' Eve*, of the contemporary 'vague notion that if your sexual life was all right, you were all right'.

The articles here collected give the most important points in Williams's thought about the Incarnation. There is a sketch, in 'The Index of the Body', of the infinite field which he thought awaited our exploration, into the significance of the body as it is known in love. 'The Sacred Body is the plan upon which the physical human creation was built, for it is the centre of physical human creation': our own bodies, then, made in His image, are 'an index to the structure of a greater whole'.

The essays do not, however, contain any full definition of his ideas on the two complementary ways by which we may try to direct our human nature towards the goal of perfection, which he described as the Way of the Affirmation of Images, and the Way of the Rejection of Images. The terms derive from the writings of the fifth-century Greek mystic who called himself 'Dionysius the Areopagite', whose work was translated into Latin and interpreted for the Western Church by Duns Scotus. In the edition of Dionysius which Charles Williams used,[1] there is a note by the editor on one of the Neoplatonist passages, where the writer prays that we may

> attain unto vision through the loss of sight and knowledge . . . denying or removing all things that are—like as men who, carving a statue out of marble, remove all the impediments that hinder the clear perceptive of the latent image

claiming that 'this simile shows that the Via Negativa is, in the truest sense, positive'. For 'if Dionysius were open to the charge of pure negativity so often brought against him he would have wanted to destroy his block of marble instead of carving it'. Now whether or not this is true of Dionysius, the effect produced by his teaching on anyone approaching it without presuppositions is, I think, that the great negative definitions of the nature of God are more powerful than the passages where it is shown that God may be approached by means of the created world; and I understand that Scotus's interpretation for the West, though not St. John Damascene's interpretation for the East, carries this negativity to an extreme point. Add to this the writings of the mystics, especially those of St. John

[1] *On the Divine Names*, &c., ed. C. E. Rolt, S.P.C.K.

of the Cross, and it is clear that the *Via Negativa* has been made considerably more explicit than the *Via Positiva*: you must turn to the poets for any strong imagination of that Way.

The importance of Charles Williams's thought on the subject lies, I think, in his perception of the relation between the two Ways: he never divorced them, even in his manner of speaking about them. He was accustomed to use the image of the asymptote (see above) to describe their apparent division and ultimate union. Thus he wrote in a letter of October 1933:

> I do think that the double challenge of 'This also is Thou' and 'Neither is this Thou', carried into everything, probably as much as any formula, assist the soul. They are an example of my momentarily pet obsession of asymptotes, and the point at which they do meet would be the Spiritual Marriage, after which (they say) is the Beatific Vision.

In its formal doctrine the Church saw them as co-existing, almost, as he wrote in *The Descent of the Dove*, as co-inhering, 'since each was to be the key of the other'. Amplifying this, he wrote in a letter of March 1945:

> . . . the essentials of the one Way are the accidents of the other. . . . There must be, sooner or later, even in the Way of Affirmation, some sort of seclusion of the soul to the Omnipotence. It must, in some sense, be divided from all else—for ever or for a time. I think, for a time; but it will not at the moment feel this. The Rejection aims at this as a continual method; the Affirmation endures it, when it comes. As the Rejection has always to allow its debt to its parents, its teachers, its food and shelter, perhaps its loves. These are accidents of its calling; so the separation is an accident—necessary somehow and somewhere—of the Affirmation. But if all is affirmed, its past (at least) must return. Or so it seems to me. . . . It's true the Rejection a little tends to brag itself, even in some of its nicest devotees. We have known of that for centuries; it is our Mother. The Affirmation we have not so well known; it is our Beloved. But they are both (let us say) women; and there is a commonalty. The Hamlet-Macbeth period is common. We call it the Way and the other Way; but each is included in the other.

If 'the Rejection a little tends to brag itself', the reason is perhaps that this Way, once entered upon, demands an exclusive attention which the other, by its very nature, does not.

> Seale then this bill of my Divorce to All,
> On whom those fainter beames of love did fall . . .

as Donne wrote, is a recurrent cry in the hearts of all who try to reconcile the claims of the natural and the supernatural worlds by love. But in preserving this tight-rope balance, this attachment which must yet be ready at any moment to become detachment, the symbols employed by Williams can be of immense use and encouragement, helping to fill the mind with images of power. The balance is to be held not by a caution such as Raphael recommended to Adam in *Paradise Lost*—'If thou well observe The rule of not too much'—but by a courage such as Traherne's (and Traherne's *Centuries of Meditation* is one of the holiest documents of the Affirmative Way, though not quoted by Williams himself):

> That love wherewith a man sometimes doteth upon a creature is but a small spark of the love even toward all things, which lurketh in his nature. . . . There never was anything in this world loved too much, but many things have been loved in a false way, and all in too short a measure.

It was doubtless the ambivalence of Williams's own habit of mind, between belief and scepticism, which helped him to keep his poise in matters both of the intellect and the emotions. This ambivalence certainly did not come from timidity, or disinclination to commit himself to a statement, but rather from his freedom from prejudice where ideas were concerned, whatever their source. He saw that the great heresies have been a vital part of the growth of the Church; and he would have been ready to concede at least a partial truth to Bertrand Russell when he wrote[1] that 'from the Council of Trent to the present day, whatever improvements it [the Church] has effected have been due to its enemies'.

> Nasce per quello, a guisa di rampollo
> Al piè del vero il dubbio. . . .

'Questioning' is the Temple Classics rendering in these lines of Dante, but there is at least the authority of modern dictionaries to allow us to translate *dubbio* by *doubt*, and Williams would certainly have expected to find doubt growing at the foot of truth. One of his early poems was an Office Hymn (office in the liturgical sense) for the Feast of St. Thomas Didymus, Apostle and Sceptic, to whose Sodality he considered himself to belong. It ends:

> Lord God, confess we never
> Knowing not, swore we knew.

Intellectual honesty is the first necessity; but we must go farther than that: so, in a slightly later poem ('Hymn to the Protector, or Angel, of Intellectual Doubt'), he praised the Blessed Virgin for her question 'How shall these things be?', which redeemed 'The pale credulity of Eve'. In his first plans for the Arthurian poems, he had related Mary's question to the Angel, to the Question which Perceval, in the *Conte du Graal* of Chrétien de Troyes, failed to ask about the nature of the Grail, the asking of which (to over-simplify the matter) was necessary to salvation. 'The Lord demands that his people shall demand an explanation from him. . . .'[2] It was Job's

[1] *Why I am not a Christian.* [2] *He came down from Heaven.*

philosophical impatience of angry curiosity that won him his return to well-being, and as Williams pointed out, the most remarkable thing about him was that he was *not* patient. But of a curiosity that is not angry, as it is found in the great Christian sceptic Montaigne (and perhaps one might add, in Williams himself), he wrote in the *Dove*:

> It is a manner, a temperament, a nature, which may be encouraged or discouraged; it is most particularly not irony, though irony may be an element in it. It is a qualitative mode of belief rather than a quantitative denial of dogma,

and he saw it exemplified in the answer reported of the Renaissance scholar Lorenzo Valla, to those who questioned his orthodoxy, when he said that the Church 'did not *know*; She believed, and, with her, he'.

One might add, that if a question is the beginning of salvation, it is also in one sense already the end, for 'Hadst thou not found Me, thou couldst not be seeking Me': supposing only—and what an agony of search this may imply—that one has found the right question to ask.

Scepticism, then, can be complementary to belief, as affirmation and negation are complementary ways towards union with God. But in the world it is sometimes necessary to choose between them, and as Charles Williams was a poet and a married man, his life was lived along the *Via Positiva*. And as, through his belief in the Incarnation, he never ceased his effort to discover the true significances of the human body, so he perpetually related the experiences of earthly marriage to the history of the Divine Word on earth. His early poems are full of this parallelism, and it is worked out in detail in the sequence called 'The Christian Year' in *Poems of Conformity*. Later, he drafted a book on the theology of romantic love (or Romantic Theology, as he was accustomed to call it), which was not fully approved of by the authorities to whom he showed it, and was never published. I do not know whether this manuscript still exists, though I read it many years ago, but I have a copy of a lecture which must have been condensed from it, entitled 'Christianity and Romantic Love'. I had at first thought of including it in this collection, but I have not done so, for two reasons. First, because the ideas which it contains were for the most part expressed later on in chapter v of *He came down from Heaven*, and secondly, because while this lecture contains only one quotation from Dante, the later expositions use Dante as a text throughout. *The Figure of Beatrice* contains his most developed statement, and a pamphlet published by the Dacre Press (*Religion and Love in Dante*, which can still be had for sixpence) is a valuable outline. I can give no more than a brief summary here.

The experience of romantic love, then, he conceived to be capable of infinite good, and he defined that love (in the lecture I have mentioned) as 'a sub-species of love between the sexes': 'that kind in which the lover, generally by a process utterly beyond his own will, finds himself in a state of adoration'. His definition would have included love between members of the same sex, though he would have held that this was subject to the same law as that which should govern the vision of the 'Second Image', quoted above. He disliked the cautious approach of some clergy and older people, which ignores the nature of romantic love, as much as he disliked the sentimentalizing which the experience endures in a thousand films and novels. He proposed, in this lecture, four Evangelical Counsels of Romantic Theology which I paraphrase: (1) Reality—it is *true*: the Incarnation is our proof. (2) Eternity: no later defections can alter the original moment of the vision. (3) Divinity: 'The vision is a grace bestowed, not a natural right or a natural capacity'; it is true of the beloved person in his or her heavenly nature, but we must not confuse this with the beloved person in her fallen state, or deny that the vision could be seen in every human creature if we had eyes for it, or try to take possession of it for ourselves. (4) Charity: 'The beatitude of Love being seen, it briefly exists in us towards others.' So Dante describes in *The New Life* how, when he saw Beatrice, if anyone had done him an injury, he could not but have forgiven it. 'This is perhaps the cardinal point. It does not mean a vague goodwill towards Chinamen, but a definite humility towards one's neighbour. Humility is bestowed in that state of adoration, the lover—it is the cliché of sentimentality—feels unworthy. Of course he does, he is, and Romantic Love is a state of facts.'

Apart from Dante, Williams owed much to the thought of Coventry Patmore on this theme—thought which was expressed not only in poetry (at its best in *The Unknown Eros*), but also in prose aphorisms. Thus, in *The Rod, the Root and the Flower*, Patmore writes:

> There is one secret, the greatest of all . . . which is stated with the utmost distinctness by Our Lord and the Church . . . I mean the doctrine of the Incarnation, regarded not as an historical event which occurred two thousand years ago, but as an event which is renewed in the body of every one who is in the way to the fulfilment of his original destiny. [And:] Lovers are nothing else than the Priest and Priestess to each other of the Divine Manhood and the Divine Womanhood which are in God. . . .

This is the knowledge which, in the *Taliessin* poems, bursts into the paean of praise both for and from the body in 'The Vision of Empire', and speaks in the words of Bors to his wife Elayne:

> O lady, your hand held the bread
> And Christ the City spread in the extensor muscles of your thumbs.

'Romantic Love is a state of facts': so there is never any sentimentalizing of that state, in Williams's presentation of it. He never lost sight of the hard truth that 'in heaven there is neither marrying nor giving in marriage', and the end of every individual preference was to be in the words of Mary to Joseph in *Seed of Adam*: 'We said *in love*: how can one be in love with *someone*?' Or as the heroine in *Shadows of Ecstasy* came to realize: 'Love and not the beloved was the necessity; to love, and only to the beloved as the sacred means, the honourable toil was given.' One of Williams's favourite aphorisms, I think of his own coinage, was 'The vision is more than the prince'. The essence is for the sake of the function, not vice versa.

However, this is far from saying that one should cease to be aware of the individual nature of the beloved: to lose sight of this is to run into danger of destruction—the fate of Wentworth in *Descent into Hell*, who ended by preferring a succubus to any living creature. Patmore (following Plato) taught that as each human being is potentially the *entire* homo, the reflected nature of God, so 'the external man and woman are each the projected *simulacrum* of the latent half of the other, and they do but love themselves in thus loving their opposed likenesses.'[1] This idea is doubtless capable of abuse (like the statements of Augustine on Grace), yet it is allied to the realism with which Christ commanded us to love our neighbour, not better than, but *as* ourselves. Or Augustine's: 'Why may we not love that love in ourselves, whereby we love that which is to be loved?' For there is a violence of self-denigration, the result of which is to put self well in the centre of the picture. Williams's lovers may feel themselves unworthy, but they are far from that inverted self-centredness: 'Humility does not consist in thinking yourself a worm', as he often said. It is generally a woman whom he shows in his novels as having attained the complete clear-sightedness of love, though there is often a certain smugness about these heroines (to me at any rate) which he avoids with his 'good' male characters. The technique for conveying pure goodness is one of the rarest of attainment, and *the tune of Imogen* has few rivals—Hardy achieves it sometimes, and Dostoevsky, but to minds that have lost their early naïvety it is apt to seem complacent when goodness describes itself, as when Euripides' Alcestis points out to Admetus

[1] Op. cit.

what a sacrifice she is making for him. In *All Hallows' Eve*, however, we see a soul in the process of struggling towards perfection: and as we have seen the process, the final insight is entirely convincing. I describe it, as it is relevant to this brief account of Williams's thought.

At the opening of the book, Lester is newly dead, and does not yet know it. She is standing on Westminster Bridge waiting for Richard, her husband: for days she waits, and when at last he comes, in his living form, she speaks bitter words of reproach to him and he disappears. She thinks at first that it is he who is the ghost:

> Dead, and she had done it once too often. Dead, and this had been their parting.... They had told each other it [their quarrelling] made no difference, and now it had made this. They had reassured each other in their reconciliations, for though they had been fools and quick-tempered, high egotists and bitter of tongue, they had been much in love and they had been but fighting their way.

And from this moment of repentance, Lester's slow and painful purgation begins, until she becomes, as Richard sees her in a second apparition:

> More stable than rock, more transient in herself than rivers, more distant-bright than stars, more comfortable than happy sleep, more pleasant than wind, more dangerous than fire—all known things similes of her; and beyond all known things the unknown power of her.

This it is to keep the eye most firmly on the object, and yet to learn detachment from all greed of possession of the beloved. Williams never went farther in his perception of human relationships, or wrote anything more poignant, than his description of these two lovers parted by death, though it is equalled by his presentation of joy in love in *The House of the Octopus*—both books, as I have said, so close to his own bodily death, and both so clearly aware that the 'separation from the love of created things' (St. John of the Cross) has to be endured as final. 'Oh vain, all the meetings vain! ... This was it [the note of the London river] ... the small cold piercing pain of immortal separation.'

Every individual experience of love should make more vivid for us the whole human relationship. Moreover, man is made in the image of God, and God is not only a Unity, He is also a Trinity of Persons. 'It is not good for God to be alone',[1] and as there is relationship within the Deity, that 'primary act of Love' which is the Trinity, man must reflect this order in his fellowship with other men. As Augustine wrote in *The City of God*: 'then is all the whole

[1] This aphoristic misquotation from Genesis is one I heard from Williams's lips: I think he ascribed it to Belloc, but my memory may be at fault.

Trinity intimate to us in every creature: and hence is the original, form and perfection of that holy city whereof the angels are inhabitants'.

Augustine saw an ideal Rome as the likeness of the heavenly City: Virgil had seen it as the pattern of earthly order. The conception of the Roman order meant much to Charles Williams—he exulted in the lines in Chesterton's *Ballad of the White Horse* where, foreseeing his death in battle, the Roman tells his comrades to leave him where he lies—

> For all the earth is Roman earth
> And I shall die in Rome.

The idea, developed as it was by Christian thought to make the human city a likeness of the divine, was a present and living reality to Williams: he had no difficulty in both seeing and disregarding the difference between the ideal and the actual in society, just as he did in his conception of romantic love. Byzantium, Rome, Christendom, London, Amen House, and the household of the King's poet Taliessin—these were all aspects of the City: and it was an order at once hierarchic and republican. I have reprinted in this collection the Dialogue in which Williams sets out his reasons for thinking that the hierarchy and the republic are not opposed but complementary: as he put it in *He came down from Heaven*, speaking of the Vision in the Apocalypse:

> The centre is everywhere and the circumference nowhere;[1] that is, it is hierarchic and republican at once, as all good states, even on this present earth, are known to be, where everything and everyone is unique and is the subject of due adoration so, and yet all being unique, 'none is afore or after other, none is greater or less than another'.

He had expressed the idea long before, in a poem addressed to Humphrey Milford about guilds in the heavenly City:[2]

> For there in turn republican all are
> Our masters, and we theirs; so interchange
> The hierarchical degrees afar;
> Waxing and waning, dwindled or increased,
> In order as in light, all spirits range
> The whole ascent, now topmost and now least.

and in the *Taliessin* cycle the interchange is seen at its source, in the poet's distant view of the land of the Trinity

> thrice charged with massive light in change,
> clear and golden-cream and rose tinctured,
> each in turn the Holder and the Held. . . .

[1] St. Bonaventura's definition of God.
[2] *Windows of Night*: 'To a Publisher'.

I have said that Williams was accustomed to see, in any aspect of the City, what ought to be as well as what was. Sometimes, perhaps, in his judgements of people, he did not always keep the two kinds of knowledge distinct—a generous fault. But he did truly *see*; as C. S. Lewis so well described his insight: 'On many of us the prevailing impression made by the London streets is one of chaos; but Williams, looking on the same spectacle, saw chiefly an image—an imperfect, pathetic, heroic, and majestic image—of Order.' And he quotes the passage from *The Greater Trumps*, which was one that Williams himself delighted in, where the policeman's hand outstretched against the traffic is seen as the symbol of order and law—'as if Charlemagne or one like him stretched out his controlling sword over the tribes of Europe pouring from the forests'.

Williams saw, too, that in 'that common humanity whereby we are bound one to another' (I quote the words used by the eyewitness of Cranmer's martyrdom, as recorded in Foxe) there were possibilities of help beyond anything that is commonly believed. Briefly, that when Christ said 'Bear ye one another's burdens', he meant that we could really do that; that pain and fear can be borne by one person in place of another, just as though a physical weight were transferred. These ideas are set forth in this collection in the essays called 'The Redeemed City' and 'The Way of Exchange', beside which I have set his fantasy of 'The Wedding Garment'. Williams had made an earlier exposition in *He came down from Heaven*, and shows the idea in action, in several of his writings. There is the poem where Taliessin sees Virgil[1] as being, in the hour of his death, 'fathered of his friends'—saved from despair by all who have been as it were the children of his poetry. A dramatization of the idea is in *The House of the Octopus*, in the passage I have already quoted, where the priest's fear of death is borne for him by the girl convert; and there is another instance in *All Hallows' Eve* when the curse of the reversed Tetragrammaton falls upon Lester Furnival instead of upon the intended victim, merely because Lester has mentally put herself at her friend's disposal. The whole passage, which describes how Lester in her turn is saved by a substitution, upheld by the framework of the Cross, is of great imaginative power. In *Descent into Hell* the idea is central to the story: the heroine is freed from a haunting fear by allowing another to suffer it for her, and in her turn is able to reach back in Time and take the fear of death from an ancestor of hers who had died at the stake—for in Williams's books the weak who have been helped will always in their turn become strong to help others. Pauline's ancestor had gone to his death crying 'I have seen the salvation of my God', and we are to

[1] Originally, Milton, in an earlier and unpublished poem.

imagine that he was able to do so just because Pauline, centuries later, was afraid on his behalf. In August 1933, when Williams was writing this novel, he wrote in a letter:

> Rest content about substituted Love. None of us know—yet. After all, we only discovered it as an experiential fact, by chance, as it were; and I'm terrified out of my senses at the idea of going further. But even to carry what we know—what we have chosen to believe—a little steadily in the world; mentioning it now and then, if it seems desirable; and proposing it if there seems an opportunity . . . merely to do that might almost make us 'justified in our existence'. I've just tried out the chapter in the novel in which Shakespeare (so to speak) explains the idea—not very clearly . . .

and a little later he quotes this passage:[1]

> The body of his flesh received her alien fear; his mind carried the burden of her world. No doubt, the burden was inevitably lighter for him than for her, for, had there been no other cause, the rage of a personal resentment would have been lacking. He endured her sensitiveness, but not her sin; [here there is a marginal comment: 'that is—he wasn't annoyed with the conditions of her life, as she was'] the substitution there . . . is hidden in the central mystery of Christendom which Christendom itself has never understood, nor can.

'I admit', he continued, 'that the idea doesn't take us *much* farther; but perhaps it does make more credible the Christ bearing the sins of the world dogma.'

I have quoted his explanation at some length, because the idea often does not meet with ready acceptance, and is certainly harder to practise than to accept. So far as I know, Williams's experiments arose only from his reading of the New Testament, though there are hints of the doctrine to be found in other Christian writings. For instance, St. Thomas Aquinas has the following passage:[2]

> . . . since sorrow has a depressing effect, it is like a weight whereof we strive to unburden ourselves: so that when a man sees others saddened by his own sorrow, it seems as though others were bearing the burden with him, striving, as it were, to lessen its weight; wherefore the load of sorrow becomes lighter for him: something like what occurs in the carrying of bodily burdens.

I am not pretending that St. Thomas gave any central importance to the idea; indeed, he goes on to say that 'the second and better reason' why sympathy is good is that it is pleasurable to have proof that one is loved. Again, there is Cranmer's doctrine that 'Abraham and other holy fathers . . . spiritually by their faith were fed and nourished with Christ's Body and Blood, and had eternal life by Him before He was born as we have now after His ascension . . .'.[3]

[1] See *Descent into Hell*, p. 137, for the passage in its final form.

[2] *Summa Theologica*, part ii, 9. 38; article 3—on sympathy.

[3] *Defence of the Sacrament*, iii. 10. I do not think that Williams had noticed this and other similar passages when he wrote his play, but when I wrote my

Scholars argue over the meaning of Cranmer's terms, and I am certainly not equipped to enter the discussion, but at least it can be said that his words lift the idea of redemption out of all temporal limitations, as Williams tried to do.

In any case, and whatever may be the success or failure of those who attempt to put this doctrine into practice, it is surely not unorthodox. It is only an extension of the commonly held doctrine of prayer—that by our own intention of good will we may make ourselves a channel for God's grace to flow towards another soul. It is a truth implied in the construction of the words *sympathy* and *compassion*. Williams merely saw, with characteristic clarity, the full implications of the common phrases.

One of the difficulties of the doctrine in practice is that it is at least as hard, if not harder, to relinquish a mental or physical pain as to endure it for someone else—psychology tells us why. There are obvious dangers, as in all efforts to adapt something which is experienced as true in an exalted—say, a supernatural—state, to a commoner use. But one of its great rewards is the liberation which it brings from the tyranny of time as well as space, so that the sense of guilt at any temporary forgetfulness is abolished: there is no such word as *too late*; all times, like all fortune, must be good. This is also surely the justification for those efforts to share imaginatively in the sufferings of Christ, which to some have seemed a masochistic practice: if the doctrine is true, even there the Creator may accept help from His creature—a help that speeds from any point in time.

In the section of this book to which I have given the title of *Exchange*, I have included a review from *Time and Tide* of a book about the Jesuits, which speaks of the possibility of an Order, working along the lines of the 'indirect love of God' (i.e. the love of God as He is seen in His creations), as the Jesuits work in the direct. Of this Order Charles Williams says here: 'Its derivation shall be from God through others, its meditation on those indirect derivations; its aim the propaganda everywhere of that sensitive and humble knowledge.' And in his poem 'The Founding of the Company', in the *Summer Stars*, he defined it further:

> . . . its cult was the Trinity and the Flesh-taking . . .
> . . . it exchanged the proper self
> and wherever need was drew breath daily
> in another's place, according to the grace of the Spirit
> 'dying each other's life, living each other's death'.

Trial of Thomas Cranmer, I took it as sufficient justification for putting into Cranmer's mouth, as he watches from a distance the death of his companions, words that derive from Williams's doctrine.

Terrible and lovely is the general substitution of souls
the Flesh-taking ordained for its mortal images
in its first creation, and now in Its sublime self
shows, since It deigned to be dead in the stead of each man.

Charles Williams did found such a company, and it was exactly as loosely connected, as hierarchic and republican, as he here describes it:

having no decision, no vote or admission,
but for the single note that any soul
took of its own election of the Way. . . .

That is, the moment of Vision, in which the glory of God has been seen in some part of the creation—the meeting of Dante with Beatrice.

In looking through Waite's *Hidden Church of the Holy Graal*, I was struck by the following passage, with its likeness to Taliessin's Order:

. . . there is no written word to show us how its rite is celebrated: its work upon things without is a work of harmony. . . . There are no admissions—at least of the ceremonial kind—to the Holy Assembly, but in the last instance the candidate inducts himself. . . . It does not come down; more correctly it draws up, but it also inheres. It is the place of those who have become transmuted and tingeing stones.

A seed, that remained in Williams's mind from early days, to bear fruit later on? It is possible.

III

I have said that Charles Williams turned to one or other of the various literary forms which he employed, as the occasion presented itself—except in the case of poetry. This does not mean that he wrote without inner compulsion: in every instance, whether he was dealing with an unpromising subject such as Henry VII, or writing a 'missionary play', his vital themes, his burning topics, are expressed. The wood of Broceliande appears in a biography of Rochester; the hierarchy is touched on in a biography of Bacon. 'It is not always mere flattery that salutes a living prince as Caesar; is not the very word familiar and titular at once?'[1] I have already spoken of his breadth of sympathy: it enabled him to see what lay behind attitudes that our age has ceased to understand.

To say, then, that Williams wrote for money, as he himself maintained, is not to say that he would not have written without it. But it is arguable that his poetry did suffer, like Blake's, from the lack of

[1] *Bacon*, p. 143.

a stimulus not only monetary but also human. Every poet today suffers to some extent from being valued for everything except his proper work—for his reading aloud, his remarks about contemporaries, his performance at fork luncheons, and so on. But I mean something more than this: in the case of Charles Williams, the lines of communication between his poetic activity and the nourishment of an audience were inadequate. He never lacked a few appreciative readers, but these were such as perhaps enabled him to take too much understanding for granted. The influence of an audience is of course indefinable, but Daniel's line 'Each bird sings to herself and so will I' is only applicable if we imagine that the bird puts itself in a position to be overheard—rather as the great guitar-player Segovia seems to treat his audience. But a wider audience of all kinds of people, interested but not partisan, such as Williams only began to have in his last years, does tend to make poetry less obscure, less odd, more urbane in the best sense. And one thing is incontrovertible—that Williams's chief work, his cycle of poems, was left unfinished because it could not earn him money. Those sad lines about Taliessin's silence speak of a dryness that every poet knows, but Williams could not save his best energies for the work he most cared to do:

> The king's poet ached with belated verse;
> he took part against himself; his heart waited
> for his voice, and again his voice for his dumb heart.

He did something memorable, however, in all the forms he used. Much of the historical work is hack work, but at any moment the hack may become a racehorse. It is always based on careful and wide reading. The sources may be secondary, but the opinions are always original, though the best work is produced, naturally, when the subject—such as witchcraft, or Queen Elizabeth I—is one that has been of permanent interest to him.

Williams's literary criticism is 'creative criticism' of a kind that has been somewhat out of fashion since the analytical critics were in the ascendant. He did, it is true, pride himself on attending strictly to the texts: some lines in his preface to *The English Poetic Mind* define his method:

> I have been concerned with the poetry only as it exists, and with its interrelation. . . . Criticism has done so much to illuminate the poets, and yet it seems, with a few exceptions, still not sufficiently to relate the poets to the poets, to explain poetry by poetry. Yet in the end what other criterion have we? Wordsworth's poetry is likely to explain Shakespeare's poetry much better than we can, because poetry is a thing sui generis. It explains itself by existing.

The method produced some valuable results: for example, in his study of Dante (*The Figure of Beatrice*) his quotations from other great poets, and especially from Wordsworth's *Prelude*, are very illuminating. When he comes to consider Dante's exclusion of Virgil from Paradise, he is not hampered by the usual irrelevant emotional considerations, but points out that the poem could not afford to keep him in. 'The *Aeneid* has *pietas* and not *caritas*; so must its author have here.' So also, when Williams comes to consider the idea of chastity in Milton, he sees it as the poetry presents it, without the least clouding of our modern cant about this virtue. I have already spoken of his treatment of the crisis in *Troilus and Cressida*, and its relation to other passages: he sets it in its place in a description of the development of Shakespeare's genius that still seems to me to be valid and valuable: on Milton, on Wordsworth, and on the Victorians he has said much that is illuminating.

Here may be mentioned also his conception of the forest, the 'place of making', an image which belongs both to his criticism and to his poetry. There are references to it here and there in his critical writings, notably on p. 68 of *Reason and Beauty*, but the fullest description is on p. 107 of *The Figure of Beatrice*.

> The image of a wood has appeared often enough in English verse. It has indeed appeared so often that it has gathered a good deal of verse into itself; so that it has become a great forest where, with long leagues of changing green between them, strange episodes of high poetry have place. Thus in one part there are the lovers of a midsummer night, or by day a duke and his followers, and in another men behind branches so that the wood seems moving, and in another a girl separated from her two lordly young brothers, and in another a poet listening to a nightingale but rather dreaming richly of the grand art than there exploring it, and there are other inhabitants, belonging even more closely to the wood, dryads, fairies, an enchanter's rout. The forest itself has different names in different tongues—Westermain, Arden, Birnam, Broceliande; and in places there are separate trees named, such as that on the outskirts against which a young Northern poet saw a spectral wanderer leaning, or, in the unexplored centre of which only rumours reach even poetry, Igdrasil of one myth, or the Trees of Knowledge and Life of another. So that indeed the whole earth seems to become this one enormous forest, and our longest and most stable civilizations are only clearings in the midst of it.
>
> The use of such an extended image is to allow the verse of those various 'parts of the wood' to point distantly towards each other, without the danger of too hasty comparisons.

The forest stands for the primeval and wild, the part of the mind from which images are derived, the unconscious, if one adopts another set of terms. And the associations which Williams derived from Spenser, Shakespeare, Milton, Keats, and Dante (the opening of the *Divine Comedy*), enriched the idea of Broceliande which he found in Malory.[1] In his poetry it becomes a sea-wood, and the

[1] For his definition of its place in the Arthurian myth, see p. 179.

reader of his early verse will recall the sonnet in *Windows of Night*, from which I have already quoted the passage about his wife's affinity with the sea, where he says that his own preference is for the forest, with its

> innumerable trees
> Rooted and fixed and helpless; amid these
> Corners and holes of soft indwelling night.

His method has its dangers, like any other: the separate characteristics of the poets may be subordinated to the critic's determined pattern; parallels may be discovered because they were needed; the maxim of illustrating poetry by poetry may lead to a mangling of the text. This habit of dismembering great verse and mixing up the fragments with his own prose was a bad stylistic fault in Williams—no doubt the result of many years of lecturing. But he was well aware of the main danger. 'Patterns are baleful things,' he wrote in an autocriticism of his *Reason and Beauty in the English Poetic Mind*,[1] 'and more so because the irony of the universe has ensured that any pattern invented by man shall find an infinite number of facts to support it.... When, being very young I sometimes thought I knew Mr. Williams, I should have warned him to beware of his pattern; if ever, "some evening when the moon is blood", I meet him again in Holborn or on Ludgate Hill, I shall offer him the same warning.'

Certainly, a pattern that compares Patmore's verse with that of Milton as one that, 'allowing for its own peculiar genius, comes more near than that of any other English poet to the Miltonic scope and splendour', has gone somewhat askew. But Williams had the great critical virtue of enthusiasm, and the power of imparting it. Like George Saintsbury and Professor C. S. Lewis, he had read and enjoyed long poems which are commonly considered to be unreadable; he forgot nothing, and he had looked at everything for himself—there never was a critic more free from the influence of fashion. His labels were always of his own making, as for instance with Swift's lines about his own death:

> Poor Pope will grieve a month, and Gay
> A week, and Arbuthnot a day . . .

on which Williams comments: 'There is not much romantic agony about that, certainly, so we have hastily called it ironic. But it is not ironic, nor scornful, nor anything but merely actuality circumfused by poetry.'

His range of sympathy was extraordinarily wide: his studies in the moderns (*Poetry at Present*) show this quality rather than any

[1] *The Week End Review*, Nov. 1933.

remarkable justice of judgement. I do not think that Williams was deeply affected by contemporary poetry. A poet's deepest interest concerns his own creative needs, and as Mr. Heath-Stubbs has suggested, the living tradition of the time could not serve Williams's particular purpose. Hence it was Lascelles Abercrombie, who attempted the grand style and whose subject-matter was attractive to Williams, whom he boldly pronounced to be a 'major poet'. But the strongest contemporary influence on his thought and style was that of G. K. Chesterton.

On general principles of aesthetics his views were always well balanced. I set down here, since it will not otherwise be recorded, a definition of form and content in poetry which he threw off in a letter.

> Form and content are the two titles we give to two different . . . explorations of a single thing. . . . Because the words are the form, and the meaning of the words is the content; and right down at bottom there is the one thing—words —which opens out into two domains. Am I mixing metaphors? One can consider the *meaning* of 'Warring in heaven against heaven's matchless king', but to consider it properly one has to take in the sounds; and one can consider the form of the line, and I suppose to consider *that* properly one ought to pay some attention to the meaning. So it looks as if there should be a diagram—

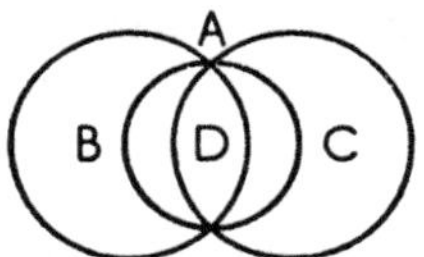

> A circle = the poem B = our consideration of its form
> C " = our consideration of its meaning.
> And the undivided bit in the middle is the unanalyzable IT.

And here is his definition of the relation between poetry and life:[1]

> We must not make poetry serve our morals, yet we must not consider it independent of our morals. It is not a spiritual guide, yet it possesses a reality which continually persuades us to repose upon it even in practical things of every day. We have only to enjoy it, but only in proportion as we enjoy it with our whole being can it be said of us that no man shall take its joy from us.

That might serve as a brief description of Charles Williams himself as critic—that he enjoyed poetry with his whole being.

In his novels Williams used the convention of the detective story to deal with a much greater range of experience than any detective story attempts—though Mr. John Dickson Carr, a writer whom Williams much enjoyed, has introduced the supernatural into tales of this type, in *The Burning Court* and elsewhere. The most obvious

[1] Preface to *Reason and Beauty*.

influence on Williams's stories is that of G. K. Chesterton. But Chesterton's effectiveness depends on his ability to evoke the surface of the ordinary world, and then to show that it is in fact extraordinary and disturbing. Williams is much more interested in psychological states, and the more he drives inward, the greater his success: his stories are least effective when they bring in the machinery of government and world affairs, as happens in *Shadows of Ecstasy*, and to some extent in *Many Dimensions* and elsewhere. It is true that, as Mr. Heath-Stubbs has suggested, he looked on his novels as entertainments: but he never made the highbrow distinction between literature and entertainment, either in his own reading or in what he wrote.

In the unfinished *Figure of Arthur* Williams has a sentence which might be an epigram of the truth which his novels convey: 'Power is not something that one has, it is something that one is.' The good characters in his books have all discovered this, while the evil characters are trying to make power into a possession. These last are not entirely credible as human beings—except perhaps Sir Giles Tumulty, the witty anthropologist of the first two books: Williams himself described Simon Magus in *All Hallows' Eve* as an 'unconvincing magician', and the reader of these books sometimes feels that, to quote a sentence from *He came down*, 'The devil, if he is a fact, has been an indulgence'. Perhaps the reader would feel more terror if he were not confident that the good is bound to triumph in the end, as the reader of Orwell's *1984* knows that it will be defeated. Perhaps also the evil is too much described—one remembers Henry James's maxim of intensifying the reader's general sense of evil: 'Make him *think* the evil, make him think it for himself, and you are released from weak specifications.'[1]

Williams succeeds in making us 'think the evil' with those characters whose selfish desires are more common to mankind—with Lawrence Wentworth in *Descent into Hell*, who wants his lover to be only a reflection of his own needs, and with Damaris Tighe in *The Place of the Lion*, who pursues learning only for the sake of fame. Each gets what he has asked for. Wentworth gains his succubus, and loses all contact with reality; Damaris discovers the power of the intellect, which she has wished to use but has not loved, and finds it the obscene thing which she has made of it. This novel (*The Place of the Lion*), in which the Platonic archetypes are imagined as having been loosed upon the world, and brought back into control by a renewal of the act of Adam in naming the beasts, is to my mind the most successful in its plot.

But it is not for the plot, exciting though this can be, that one

[1] Preface to *The Turn of the Screw*.

returns to these tales. There is a sense of mathematical rightness, of balance and necessity, about the universe ruled by love which they portray, that strikes one afresh as one re-reads them: it is not the moments of horror, but the moments of supernatural joy, which are important. One uses the word supernatural, because it is hard for men to live in such states of soul or to recognize them except in flashes, but there is nothing inhuman about them. They are to be found in all the novels, but most vividly in the last two (*Descent into Hell* and *All Hallows' Eve*), where Williams has imagined a life after death, and a transitional state between the two kinds of being. His description of the experience of the two dead girls in the last book, and the London through which they move, wonderfully combines a vivid physical reality with a sense of utter strangeness. For a comparison I turn to Cocteau's place of shades in his film of *Orphée*. But in Williams's universe there is a clear logic, a sense of terrible justice which is not our justice and yet is not divorced from love, that is beyond Cocteau's scope.

I shall say something of Williams's dramatic verse when I come to discuss the development of his poetry. I have already spoken of his treatment of the Chorus in his plays: of how he evolved a special Chorus figure of his own, at once commentator and actor. He had begun with purely symbolic figures—an early unpublished masque, for instance, has the Fool, Chaos, Earth, and Love as characters—later, he attempted naturalistic characters, but they hardly exist as individual beings. As he continued to write, however, he became able to give his symbolic figures local life, and to make his particular place and time impose themselves for the duration of the play. For although a dramatist may abolish time and space, as Williams remarked that he had done in *Seed of Adam*, he is obliged to remake them to his own specification. In that play we are made to accept the fusion of Adam with Caesar, and to see in the census-making of his soldiers an epitome of man's development, from the creation of the world to the New Creation under the order of Rome—'Now there went out a decree from Caesar Augustus that all the world should be enrolled. . . .' There is a comparable sense of scope in some of the *Taliessin* poems: it was one of the effects in Milton that Williams most admired and emulated, as in the lines:

Jehovah who in one Night when he passed
From Egypt marching. . . .

Williams's natural enjoyment of ritual, his intense apprehension of the power of symbols, gives his plays their special quality. They belong to the tradition of the morality play with its overt symbolism, and recall the origins of all drama in the liturgy. They have dramatic life, they have suspense, but the excitement derives from the clash of ideas, not of persons. Take, for example, the temptation of Cranmer, where the arguments are posed with the formality of a ritual, and at each one the Skeleton, standing 'in the attitude of a priest in procession', takes a step forward. Perhaps it would never have suited Williams's genius to attempt that further transformation where, as Yeats put it, 'gradually philosophy is eliminated until at last the only philosophy audible, if there is even that, is the mere expression of one character or another. When it is completely life it seems to the hasty reader a mere story.'[1] (It must be admitted that modern audiences are rarely content with the *mere* story, to accept it as art rather than as philosophy, but prefer to tease it to death, in *The Cocktail Party* or in *Godot*.) But one must remember that Williams had not had much time in which to practise the technique of play-writing: brilliant sketches as his plays are, it is certain that his death robbed us of something more complete.

My description of his themes has involved some discussion of Charles Williams as a religious writer, and I should not be competent to take it much farther. I therefore come now to his poetry, and in particular the cycle of *Taliessin* poems, the work by which he would have wished to be remembered.

He was unusually late in finding a style that was truly his own, and that was suited to his purpose. He began to write, naturally enough, in the conventions of the late nineteenth century in which he grew up, and as the intonation which we heard in childhood remains the natural one for us, though we may consciously alter it, so Williams's natural poetic tongue retained even in its maturity something of that diction. Three years or so before his death, when I had written a poem in praise of *Taliessin* in which I had made bold to describe the verse as 'Here and there snarled or gaudy, but still strong-fibred', he replied:

> As for 'gaudy', I never heard such nonsense; but I know what you mean—you mean 'shent' and 'kin' and 'Samarcand' and 'seraph' ('seraph'? no; perhaps you might allow that), not that I ever did say Samarcand, but I did Trebizond—O well, damn it, they were fresh when I was young; and anyhow I like 'shent'—the sound describes a purged triumph—but they all have a certain freshness to me, because of those extra 25 years.

It was an old debate between us. It puzzled me that he, whose whole critical doctrine was based upon attention to the words of which poetry is composed, who was so sensitive to the cliché and

[1] *Estrangement*, xviii.

the mortuary phrase in criticism, should ignore the deadening effect of certain words and metres. He could easily turn the tables upon me—'I do not, no I do *not* think you would let me say "heart of the world"', he commented on one of my poems, and he might, in the letter I have quoted, have gone on to defend his diction as imparting a certain remoteness to his extra-historic personages. But he used it in the first place, as I have said, because he had grown up with it, and until middle age his imitative powers were more developed than his verbal-critical. He had great facility, and with his capacious memory and extensive reading he could borrow at need from a number of poets, although, when he borrows from the seventeenth century, the verse still has a nineteenth-century air, as pastiche always has predominantly the characteristics of its own age. His sonnets show to a marked degree the influence of Swinburne; there are Chestertonian Ballades, Morris-like refrains, Miltonic inversions —'Me rather forests gladden'; 'Who could thy twinness then deny With Her, the sistered yet the sole? . . .' He came to think little of this earlier verse, but considered purely as a vehicle for ideas it is of interest—for though the style may be second hand, the ideas never are so. And in the fourth book, *Windows of Night*, there are signs of a change of style. I have already quoted some of the poems, in which are to be found many of his persistent themes, and which give us the acquaintance of a personality of great charm, tenderness, and intelligence.

A couple of the poems printed in *Poems of Conformity* (1917) were drafted in the pages of a Commonplace Book which Williams kept for notes in connexion with the Arthurian cycle, and which he gave me many years later. It is one of those binder's dummies which are useful perquisites of all who have any access to a Press, made for the *Concise Oxford Dictionary*, of which the first edition came out in 1911. The first newspaper cutting pasted into the book is dated 1913, but some 27 pages of notes have been filled up before that: 174 pages (about a third of the book) have been numbered and completed. Underneath the title of the *C.O.D.* on the spine, he has written 'The Holy Grail'. I find the title-page very moving: a facsimile of it is printed opposite this page. The first line is quoted from Tennyson's dedication of his *Idylls* to the memory of the Prince Consort, and the piece from the Vulgate contains the words which he intended as the motto of the whole of his work: 'Ecce nova facio omnia.' The passage from the *Vita Nuova* describes Dante's self-dedication to a life's work, which Williams wished to renew for his own part.

Into the book went everything—every idea, every scrap of

His exec, his thine Arthur, some twelve books.

'Ex umbris et imaginibus ad Veritatem'

Cardinal Newman.

After writing this sonnet, it was given unto me to behold a very wonderful vision: wherein I saw things which determined me that I would say nothing further of this most blessed one, until such time as I could discourse more worthily concerning her. And to this end I labour all I can: as she well knoweth. Wherefore if it be His pleasure through whom is the life of all things, that my life continue with me a few years, it is my hope that I shall yet write concerning her what hath not before been written of any woman. After the which, may it seem good unto Him who is the Master of Grace, that my spirit should go hence to behold the glory of its lady: to wit, of that blessed Beatrice who now gazeth continually on His countenance *qui est per omnia sæcula benedictus.*[1] *Laus Deo.*

[1] 'Who is blessed throughout all ages.'

Et dixit qui sedebat in throno: Ecce nova facio omnia. Et dicit: Scribe, quia haec verba fidelissima sunt et vera.

~~Rev.~~ xxi 5.
Apoc.

First page of the Commonplace Book

knowledge—that might conceivably be of use in the making of his life's work, from quotations about the Papacy to a description of various kinds of armour, from the account of the Delphic Oracle given in F. W. H. Myers's *Classical Essays* to a discussion of the use of the second person singular in epic, and the question whether there could have been 'bears, wolves, deer, wild oxen, ditto cats' in Arthurian England. There are several sketches of possible general plans, showing a characteristic elaboration and ingenuity: 'Division, vertically into books of Love (cf. Athanasian creed as a song of love) . . . horizontally, into the "secular" and "religious"'; or again, he thinks of making a trilogy: 'Three volumes—Tristram, Lancelot, Galahad. Each divided into, say, four or five books; the general name of each only holding them rather loosely together, and describing the circumstances of Love in each—Love overpowered, Love in error, Love triumphant. Three circles having one centre, the Achievement of the Grail.' Or later: '?divide into "branches" (after Sebastian Evans's pattern) not into books.' And near the beginning he writes: 'Love, as God, and as the Way, to dominate the poem.'

He discusses epic styles:

> ?the 'romantic', meaning the use of all sorts of common things and words for images and expressions—as distinguished from the classical remoteness of, say, Milton. It would be possible to mould this to what restraint or swiftness or lucidity was desired. The very stuff of mingled light and darkness should show in the poem. [Many readers of *Taliessin* might echo this phrase about light and darkness.] ?Is this what Dante did. Cf. also the A.V. '. . . ?Abercrombie's suggestion (*The Epic*) of great Odes.'[1] And: 'The whole point of plainsong is to decorate the unimportant syllables.' ?is this a principle of Art? . . . ?Turn into 'Never decorate except in unimportant parts'.

The book has the fascination of all still-potential things—a fascination which we feel strongly at the present time, with our cult of the informal, the landscape drawing, the rough torso. The fragments of composed verse (which include the lines with which he intended to close his epic) show how far, as yet, his powers were from matching his intention. But the book contains a number of the ideas which, later developed, were his own contribution to the great Arthurian myth; besides a number of promising ideas which had only a beginning. It will be more convenient to describe some of these in a

[1] Abercrombie's ideas about the future of Epic, set forth in his short book, must certainly have influenced Williams's thoughts about form. He suggests there that in modern times we must dispense with the story because we have not enough formal belief to introduce the supernatural (which he thought essential) and retain credibility and *solidity*. He suggests separate poems based on a single idea, as in Hugo's *Légende des siècles*, or a sequence of odes, toward which Meredith's *Song of French History* points the way.

separate short article, preceding the Arthurian prose fragments which are here collected.

During the nineteen-twenties Williams began to compose the cycle in earnest, though he ceased to make entries in his notebook. He completed some fifty poems, a number of which were printed in *Heroes and Kings*, in *Three Plays*, and in an anthology edited by Lascelles Abercrombie called *New English Poetry*. There are some successful things, in the old pastiche style, among them: the influence of Chesterton upon the stanzaic poems is very marked, and that of *The Ring and the Book*, among others, on the long blank verse epistles. The poems are diffuse, and make free use of exclamations to eke out the rhythm; the reader is inclined to echo the words of Kenneth Mornington in *War in Heaven*: 'A little minor, but rather beautiful. . . . Better be modern than minor.' So Williams himself came to think, and he began experimenting with new versions of some of the poems.

His main scheme remained the same: the poem that had originally been planned as an epic has emerged as a cycle, a series of poems in varying metres in which there is at least as much of meditation and commentary as of narration. The theme, to use his own words from the preface to the *Summer Stars*, is

> the reign of King Arthur in Logres and the Achievement of the Grail. Logres is Britain regarded as a province of the Empire with its centre at Byzantium. The time historically is after the conversion of the Empire to Christianity but during the expectation of the Return of Our Lord (the Parousia). The Emperor of the poem, however, is to be regarded rather as operative Providence.

The complexity of the idea of Byzantium had greatly increased since the first series, as Williams developed its identification with the form of the human body. In the earlier series Percivale had identified the persons of the Table with the parts of his mistress's body, but the symbolism seems somewhat forced, especially when after an elaborate recital he demands: 'Is there not something for those feet to be?' and discovers that they are Tristram and Palomides, with more knights for the toes. I mention this to show that Williams did purge his symbolism of much that was merely fanciful, before he came to the more powerful idea of the whole Empire as a single organism, with the head in Logres (where Taliessin the king's poet makes it articulate for us), the hands in Rome (where the Pope performs his 'manual acts'), the navel—the centre—in Byzantium, the genitals in Jerusalem where Christ was crucified. The reader is referred to Williams's own remarks in the all-too-brief essay on the making of his poem which is here reprinted, and to the end-paper map of *Taliessin through Logres*. The poems of that book deal with most of the main themes, and the eight long poems of the second book, the *Summer Stars*, are in a sense a filling out, a commentary on the earlier ones.

The change in his style which we must now consider, coming more suddenly than the change between the early and late poetry of Yeats, is a remarkable one. I was lucky enough to see it happening, and by the mere chance of things can claim some small share in the development, for although Williams knew many distinguished men of letters at that time, none of them happened to be both interested in his poetry and concerned with the problem of how to write in a contemporary idiom. I, belonging to a generation whose inheritance had been fought for by Eliot and Pound, probably overemphasized the importance of the colloquial, but as I intensely admired what he was doing, I provided—within the limits of my capacity—a useful testing-ground for the new versions, as letters of the time recall to me.

The change was partly the result of maturing taste; no doubt also the fact that Williams had edited the second edition of Gerard Manley Hopkins's poems, which appeared in 1930, had a greater effect than he himself realized. In the review which I have here reprinted, he speaks of having read and enjoyed Hopkins's poems when they first appeared in periodicals, and there is a quotation from 'The Habit of Perfection' copied into the Commonplace Book, but they had no influence on his own writing at the time, and he used to say that the only line of Hopkins which he could quote was 'And to-fro tender trambeams truckle at the eye'. We have seen all too much of the influence of Hopkins on poets who reproduce his mannerisms but have none of his passion: on Williams the influence was more fruitful and more elusive. One can only see that he had re-read Hopkins at the right moment—the moment when he was able to make use of certain technical effects which were much better suited to his needs than the elaborate stanzas and the too-well-used blank verse forms which he had been employing. He took from Hopkins, for one thing, a habit of rhythm, of breaking up a statement into short segments linked by rhyme and by paired stresses, which Hopkins had adapted from early English poetry. Williams remarked that Hopkins's 'sprung rhythm' was not new, but the use made of it was new, even though the formulation may have been at fault. And a comparison of *The Wreck of the Deutschland* with the *Taliessin* poems does show some striking similarities of cadence, especially in the long line that ends the *Deutschland* stanza. I take a few examples—first of whole lines:

> Burden, in wind's burly and beat of endragonèd seas. . . .
> To the shrouds they took,—they shook in the hurling and horrible airs.
> Tarpeian-fast, but a blown beacon of light.

And Williams:

> The red track of the back was shown in a front of glory. . . .
> Balanced the line of the spine and reached for the gain.

And for the *blown beacon of light*:

> Everywhere the light through the great leaves is blown. . . .

Besides the obvious similarity in the closely following interior rhymes and dissonances (in Hopkins: 'the goal was a shoal', 'the gnarls of the nails'), there is a general sense of the pressure of words which cannot be illustrated without more extended quotation. There is also the (visual not verbal) colouring:

> Hopkins: 'For lettering of the lamb's fleece, ruddying of the rose-flake. . . .'
> Williams: 'Golden fleeces, and gardens of deep roses. . . .'
> 'Flashing flaunts of snow across azure skies . . .'

and some of Williams's compound epithets—'light-sprinkling, flaked-snow-sparkling'—are also reminiscent of Hopkins.

I do not mean to suggest more than that Hopkins gave him a key to unlock resources which he already had. But something was needed to break the too-facile cadence of his earlier verse. Theoretically, it would have been possible to write freshly in the old stanza forms, but except with a poet of exceptionally critical ear, their hypnotic effect is too great, and one word leads to another, as a shrew-mouse runs blindly along habitual paths. As I have said, Williams had not a keenly critical ear in this respect, though he was quick to notice a weakness of stress, remarking of Tennyson's blank verse that it 'oozed', and of Addison's

> For ever singing as they shine
> The hand that made us is divine—

that anything would have been better than to end on such a weak accent, even

> For ever singing as they plod
> The hand that made us IS OF GOD!

After some twenty years of pondering on the myth, then, and after writing a quantity of poetry more than twice the extent of the later cycle, he began to re-form his work. The first series had the general title of 'The Advent of Galahad';[1] the second makes the

[1] He christened it thus in later years.

king's poet the focal point, and (in December 1935) he wrote of the new title, 'Taliessin through Logres': 'I love that title; why? O it sounds romantic and vague and is almost classically exact.' The new drafts were begun during the second half of 1934—the first one that I can date definitely is 'Taliessin's Return', September 1934. I think that he had been working on the 'Prelude' before this, but there were so many versions of it, that he wrote later on: 'Pretty soon I shall abolish the Prelude altogether. Or else leave any odd stanzas I like with no care for any intellectual co-ordination.' In any case, he would be working on several different poems at one time.[1]

In 1935 Williams was invited to write the play for the Canterbury Festival of the following year, and in September he sent me the opening speeches of his *Cranmer*, followed by a letter in reply to my comments on these, in which I had urged him to abandon the blank verse of *Three Plays* in favour of the new *Taliessin* rhythms:

> [You have observed] what I myself had acutely and peevishly remarked: viz. the curious Abercrombianness of some of it. If you ask me, Cranmer's own very first line was far too Lascellian: I can't think why. . . . let us do anything but be Influenced. Largely I feel with you about blank verse, but I don't quite know what to do: irregular speeches and stanzaic arrangements are awkward. I tried Cranmer again, and I will take another sheet and write it down now.

The fragment that followed, a speech of Cranmer's about Communion, was never used, but it has imagery that is reminiscent of some of the *Taliessin* poems, with 'monstrous mountain paths' and 'granite of charity', and from then on he abandoned the pseudo-Shakespearian line as a basis in his prosody. The play and the poems proceeded together: by the end of 1935 *Cranmer* was all but finished, and he looked to see the poems collected during the following year. Instead, 1936 brought *Seed of Adam*, and it was not until 1938 that some two dozen of the new *Taliessin* poems were completed and published.

All that was most valuable in the imagery of the old material was kept, with unerring choice, in the new versions. To take a couple of examples: the original 'Prelude' has as its second stanza:

[1] Other dates, deduced from letters which enclosed versions, are: 'The Vision of Empire', Oct. 1934; 'Taliessin in the School of the Poets', Nov. 1934; 'Percivale at Carbonek', Feb. 1935; 'The Crowning of Arthur', Apr. 1935; 'The Star of Percivale', July 1935; 'The Departure of Merlin', some time in 1936. A list made late in 1934 called 'The Poems of Taliessin' gives a dozen of the old poems which he had thought of combining with the new: in addition to those which I have mentioned as dating from 1934, this list gives 'The Last Voyage', two Palomides poems, and 'Taliessin's Meditation'—not 'The School of the Poets', but a draft which was later used in 'The Coming of Galahad'.

I have called to the dark to hide,
  to the hills to cover me,
lest I should see in the starlight ride
  the lord of charity:

and this is practically the only part that is retained in the new Prelude:

Call on the hills to hide us
lest, men said in the City, the lord of charity
ride in the starlight, sole flash of the Emperor's glory.

Then, the original 'Mordred's Song of the Kingdom', which was very long, described

  that strange Emperor
far beyond Christendom
of whom the mad tales come . . .
who sits in a house of jade
which slant-eyed goblins made . . .
and he deigns a rare caress
to his tiny-footed wives . . .
around his empery
beats a wide yellow sea.
Even so strange will I grow
To all men else below.

Not only was this passage used, with a much more macabre effect, in 'The Meditation of Mordred' (*Summer Stars*, 1944), but the idea was developed more fully in the headless Emperor of 'The Vision of Empire'.

The ability to refresh and refashion poetic material so long after its first appearance is surely very unusual. There were, however, two drawbacks to it. First, that the cycle does not achieve entire unity of style: the old has not always been quite transformed into the new, and in such a poem as 'Taliessin at Lancelot's Mass' the traces are visible. Second: while the tightening of the form in the new versions was all to the good, the poet came to presuppose a certain knowledge in the reader which has nowhere been conveyed, and to leave out some necessary links in the story, simply because he had given them once. For in the original cycle some essential narrative had been included—as, for instance, Taliessin's account of the Table and of the striking of the Dolorous Blow[1] in his 'Letter to the Princess of Byzantium'.

To 'tell a story' was admittedly no important part of the plan. The blurb to *Taliessin through Logres*, drafted by Williams himself, puts it very clearly. 'The poems do not so much tell a story or describe a process as express states or principles of experience. The names and incidents of the Arthurian myth are taken as starting-

[1] The wounding of King Pelles with the spear that had pierced Christ.

points for investigation and statement on common and profound experience.' And it is certainly true that, as Waite puts it in a passage which might also serve to describe Williams's poem, 'the history of the Holy Graal becomes the soul's history, moving through a profound symbolism of inward being, wherein we follow as we can, but the vistas are prolonged for ever, and it well seems that there is neither a beginning to the story nor a descried ending'. Therefore the chronological sequence of the poems, helpful though it is at first to have them arranged in a tentative order as Professor Lewis has done, is not finally important. But the poet's scheme does demand that some part of the history be expressed, and his tendency, as he worked on his poem, was to take more and more of it for granted. He disliked the idea of extensive notes: it was in vain that I asked him to print the explanations of puzzling passages that he gave in talk or in letters. Some letter might throw off an elucidation such as this:

> And do you think the Pope, who is young, with white hair, brilliant, the image of Merlin (only M. has black hair), might be Merlin+loss? If you get me. The Pope (let us say) is time losing its beauties (by deprivation or will, not by mere passing change) but affirmatively. O I write it badly . . .

and I could not see how any reader would be able to guess the significance of the Pope's white hair or understand why he is said to be *rich* in loss without such a hint. But all that he would concede was the small collection of notes at the end of *Taliessin*: it is fortunate indeed that C. S. Lewis has given us so much, and the Arthurian essays in this book add something to our understanding.

One piece of the narrative that would have been included in the new cycle, if Williams had lived, was the account of the central catastrophe. In March 1941 he wrote: 'I think, on and off, of our Taliessin and the Dolorous Stroke—the method of the Invisible Knight evades me still.' Yet he had pondered on this from the beginning. I have already quoted the passage about Garlon from the Commonplace Book, and the notes which explain how it could be that 'The invisible knight of terror stood there for a friend', and it is one of the best examples of the way in which his mind worked on a mere hint from Malory, expanding it, as living cells divide, into the tissue of the myth. What he did achieve was a description of the *result* of Garlon's action and its final solution in mercy; and in 'The Prayers of the Pope' (the last of the poems we have) there is a drawing together of the separate events: we are given not the *why*, but the *how*, of the schism and redemption. I have already quoted from this poem, where the Pope (rich in *voluntary* loss) celebrates the Christmas Eucharist, and in that action takes upon himself the heart-break of the division in Man, in the kingdom, in the world.

He felt within him the themes divide, each
dreadfully autonomous in its own corporal place,[1]
its virtue monopolized, its grace prized, in schism,
and the little insane brain whimpering of pain
and its past; before the Parousia, before the Redemption,
all his unredeemed deeds and words
rose as once they had been. . . .
Such is death's outrage; so the Pope
died in a foretasting. . . .

While he prays, we see the wars in Logres, the breaking up of the Empire, the necromancers (gnostics who deny the Incarnation) raising up the bodies of the dead to fight; and then, the Grail taken to the land of the Trinity, the tentacles of hell (P'o-l'u) caught and held fast on the ocean bottom by the primal matter, 'the roots of Broceliande', Taliessin's Company disbanded, but only that it may be centred more directly upon God, the defeat of the heretic necromancers and the saving of all:

the Body salvaged the bodies
In the fair, sweet strength of the Pope's prayer.

It is a most difficult poem to grasp, because it has to express, in the sequential form of poetry, happenings which require to be held simultaneously in the mind.[2] It is the same difficulty that we are in when we use the words *repetition* or *recalling* for the action of the priest in the breaking of bread—words which tend to separate his action from Christ's sacrifice, made 'once for all' and yet here *happening*. So the Pope's Christmas Eucharist gives us the *happening* of the division and reconciliation, which have been the subject of the whole cycle.

I have sketched, as far as I could in the available space, the development of this work: so long laboured at; great in conception; often splendid in execution. Good judges have held that its appeal is to the mind, and only remotely to the senses. Perhaps it is a special taste, but to those who have that, its beauty is as evident as its truth. It creates its own sense-world, one of primary colours and often harsh sounds, and part of its effect of strangeness, as of a world that is slightly different from that of our usual sense impressions, is gained by the close linking of abstract and physical terms: 'times variously veined', 'the fine air of philosophical amazement', 'mystical milk', 'hair bleached white by the mere stress of the glory', and so on. A line of his own describes it: 'Intellectual art arm-fasted to the

[1] As in cancer.

[2] Williams had felt the difficulty: see the extract from his Notebook on p. 171.

sensuous.' And natural images in Charles Williams have almost always been mediated through books. To give a typical example of this I will quote from a letter of October 1939:

> I wished however to remark that I want to do a longer poem—the one about Lancelot and Helayne, and that the Encyclopaedia Britannica helpfully assures me that there is a kind of rose which is derived 'from a district of the Caucasus'. Most charming![1] It is, it seems, the cabbage-rose. And what marks the cabbage-rose? It is a dark red colour, and, unlike most roses, it has a heart under its petals! Does not that seem to you attractive? And do you not think that Blanchefleur might walk in the rose-gardens of the king when she talks with the lord Taliessin before she goes into a convent at Almesbury—thus doing in the lord Taliessin completely? and then we could sweep on to the tournament at Lonazep, or Caerleon?

So, in 'Taliessin in the Rose-Garden', the king's poet

> turned, at a path's end, between two bushes
> of cabbage-roses, scions of Caucasia, *centifoliae*,
> hearts folded strong in a hundred meanings.

Or to give another instance—there are some beautiful lines in 'The Departure of Merlin':

> grace ungrieved
> floating through gold-leaved lime or banked behind beech
> to opaque green. . . .

I do not know whether Williams could have distinguished between an actual lime and beech; I do remember that he was delighted when someone told him that a lime tree let the light through and a beech tree held it back—an observation which does not seem to me to be accurate. The point, however, is that for the purpose of his poem he only needed to see it with the eyes of his imagination. As C. S. Lewis puts it: 'he is in one way full of images: but where he is most himself each image is no sooner suggested than it fades—or, dare I say? *brightens*—into something invisible and intangible.'

In trying to describe and appraise the sound-effects of this poetry, I recall the words of Gavin Bone about Anglo-Saxon, in the essay which was posthumously published with his translations:[2] '[it is] a nice strong vigorous language for writing poetry. The words are stony and have character, and there is the great advantage that it is impossible to be neat.' This is just the effect of the *Taliessin* language, and there is a further passage which is relevant:

> It is the vowelling of a line, far more than the bundling of the consonants that makes it sound good or bad. A thousand things have to be considered in

[1] This because the Caucasus stood, in the poems, for the pure physical sensation, when it is in communication with the rest of the Empire; when it is cut off, it becomes non-Caucasian, 'undistinguished, aboriginal, Antipodean'.

[2] *Anglo-Saxon Poetry*, Clarendon Press, 1943.

poetry. There is the requirement that the line should be a pleasant variation from its predecessor; that the syntax should fit naturally into the space to be filled; that the stresses of the line should support the meaning; and when all these requirements are fulfilled it would be worth considering whether certain consonants or clusters of sounds which are thought cacophonous may be rearranged. . . . The Anglo-Saxons seem unaware of this cacophony, yet they pay very careful attention to vowelling and many of their lines are heavily sonorous.

Many of Williams's best musical effects are gained by his vowelling, as in the lines about 'grace ungrieved' already quoted, or in 'Presaging intelligence of time climbed', or (from *Seed of Adam*) 'And angels on the way delayed us . . .'; though the consonants and sibilants have at least an equal share in the beautiful 'The stones of the waste glimmered like summer stars'.

In the matter of the syntax fitting naturally into the space to be filled, and even of the stresses supporting the meaning, I think he is often at fault—there are still instances of those unnatural inversions, the result, I suppose, of his love for Milton, which I have commented on in the early poems:

'Nor wist the crowd, he gone, what to do'; '. . . and it she.'

I have already remarked that he used, via Hopkins, the 'extremely short segments' which are a characteristic of Anglo-Saxon verse; and where, in Hopkins, the packed interior rhymes carry on the rhythm, rather as waves carry a boat, in Williams they more often seem to check it, so that the poem proceeds in jerks:

Any may be; one must. To neighbour
Whom and as the Omnipotence wills is a fetch
of grace; the lowest wretch is called greatest
—and may be—on the feast of fools. The God-bearer
is the prime and sublime image of entire superfluity.[1]

However, the 'stony' words produce the desired effect of some outlandish and primitive world—

Hued from the livid everlasting bone
The queen's hewn eyelids bruised my bone;
my eyes splintered, as our father Adam's when the first
exorbitant flying nature round creation's flank burst—

but there is also the sonority of Latin, which he had always loved, in this poetry:

[1] 'The Founding of the Company'. See also the line 'the ejection to the creature of the creature's rejection of salvation' which he quotes (in 'The Making of *Taliessin*') as having been brought about by the rhymes, without seeming to think it a bad line.

> Doubtfully stood the celestial myrmidons, scions
> of unremitted beauty; bright feet paused.
> Aching with the fibrous infelicity of time,
> pierced his implacability, Galahad kneeled.

And he achieves his monstrous or unearthly effects by means of the sound as well as the association of his chosen words: 'The glittering sterile smile of the sea that pursues.'

Yet when all praise has been given to his strongly individual use of words, it is here, I think, in the region of the 'auditory imagination', that Williams's poetic equipment shows deficiency. Miss Helen Gardner, in her very interesting discussion of Mr. Eliot's term,[1] speaks of it as the 'special feeling for the connections of words in sound and meaning', which makes Chaucer a greater poet than Langland, even though 'he might well be called a less profoundly serious one'; it is, as she further defines it in speaking of Dryden, the 'power to compel words to serve his particular purpose while respecting their general meaning'. This instinctive power, I think, Williams lacked, though he was successful in some of his attempts. Take the word *salvaged*, which was a favourite of his, as he used it in the lines quoted above—'the Body salvaged the bodies'. He chose it, rather than the commoner *saved*, I should suppose, to gain the greatest possible contrast between the saviour and the castaway stuff which he redeems, but the contemporary associations of the word, with its suggestion of Municipal Councils and patriotic citizens, are too strong. It could have been done, no doubt, but 'the Body salvaged the bodies' does not succeed in doing it. Or take technical terms of various kinds. When, in *Seed of Adam*, Mary exclaims 'Parturition is upon me', the effect is not magnificent, but odd: the medical textbook association has not been overcome. It is very difficult to say *how* it is that success in such usages is achieved: one can only see that in a few poets—of whom W. H. Auden is a contemporary example—the instinct is unerring. 'It is the vice of distinctiveness to become queer', as Hopkins wrote: 'this vice I cannot have escaped.'

Yet in that great duty of a poet towards his language, of respecting and enriching its intellectual coinage, Williams was among the most honourable: he never lessened the intellectual power of any word he used, and some, such as 'kingdom' and 'glory', he left more powerful because of his use.

If the musical design in the poems is not always equal to the argument, that argument is of a splendour and an intellectual scope which makes itself felt even when the verse is at fault, and which

[1] *The Art of T. S. Eliot*, Cresset Press. For Mr. Eliot's definition, see *The Use of Poetry*, Faber, pp. 118–19.

is certainly beyond my own powers of understanding. The scope is to be seen in the work as a whole, but if it be argued that we can make no final judgement on something that was not completed, it may be profitable to look at one of the long poems, where the poet's power of controlling a complex movement of ideas can be seen. 'The Son of Lancelot' is in some sense a parallel poem to 'The Prayers of the Pope', since it also draws together a number of important events in the history, showing at once disaster and salvation. It describes the madness of Lancelot after he has begotten Galahad by being unknowingly false to Guinevere,[1] the birth of Galahad, and the bringing of the child from Carbonek to Almesbury on the back of Merlin, who is in the shape of a white wolf, while Lancelot in his wolf-madness seeks to devour his son. The scene moves between Rome at the time of the Lupercal, the wolf-month, revolt and restoration in the Byzantine empire, and the events in Logres; the actions of the Lancelot-wolf and the Merlin-wolf interchanging with the rest, in an elaborate and ordered movement. The sense of distance and simultaneity, of moving through both time and space, and the bringing together of vast natural and supernatural events, is magnificent, and the visual images, all of a winter landscape, are equally fine:

> he saw
> over the Empire the lucid flash of all flesh,
> shining white on the sullen white of the snow.

and Merlin as a wolf—

> a silver shape in the moonlight changing to crimson,
> A line of launched glory.

The burden or refrain of the whole cycle is that clear note of joy which I spoke of as sounded in the novels, a burden in two senses, heavenly and therefore scarcely supportable, yet in no sense inhuman; an emotion which is more often conveyed by music than the other arts—as, to give only modern and English examples, by the high piercing *Amens* of Holst's *Hymn of Jesus* (a work whose intellectual beauty seems to me to have an affinity with *Taliessin*), or the antiphonal *Alleluias* of the two choirs at the close of Walton's *Belshazzar's Feast*.

[1] His madness is lycanthropy, an addition of Williams to Malory. For its significance, see C. S. Lewis in the *Torso*, pp. 159–60, but it seems to me an over-simplification to call Lancelot's madness an expression 'of the dangers of concupiscence'. He falls mad because he has been false to Guinevere, as Williams makes clear in 'Malory and the Grail Legend' here printed; nor do I think Williams would have spoken of going '*down* to the world of D. H. Lawrence' in the way that Professor Lewis means it.

Fierce in the prow the alchemical Infant burned,
red by celerity now conceiving the white;
behind him the folded silver column of Percivale,
hands on the royal shoulders, closed wings of flight,
inhaled the fine air of philosophical amazement;
Bors, mailed in black, completing the trine. . . .
By three ways of exchange the City sped to the City;
against the off-shore wind that blew from Sarras
the ship and the song flew.

and

Jupiter rode over Carbonek; beyond Jupiter,
beyond the summer stars, deep heaven
centrally opened within the land of the Trinity;
planetary light was absorbed there, and emerged
again in its blissful journeys. . . .

Wordsworth, in his famous encounter with the power of Imagination in *The Prelude*, speaks of the moment

when the light of sense
Goes out, but with a flash that has revealed
The invisible world. . . .

I cannot think of any more exact definition of the effect of Williams's poetry at its best: it is at just such a moment of almost hallucinatory vision, held in the senses but on the point of reaching beyond them, that his images must have been made. It is not a poetry for all moods; it is one, also, to which you must wholly submit in order to enjoy it. But I am sure that his cycle has its place in the tradition of English visionary poetry. The figure of the burning Infant and the silver column of Percivale, the High Prince riding into Logres 'small and asleep And warm on a wolf's back', the land of the Trinity seen 'as from a high deck upon tossing seas' with its 'moving rocks and granite voices', or again

tiny, dark-rose, self-glowing
as a firefly's egg . . .
the entire point of the thrice co-inherent Trinity
when every crown and every choir is vanished,
and all sight and hearing is nothing else—

these images, once known, become for us one of the means by which we touch reality.

I have already explained the headings under which I have grouped the religious essays in this book, all of which were written during the last six or seven years of Charles Williams's life. I have tried to preserve some sequence of thought, though this was not wholly possible, and each was chosen because it illustrated or amplified some important idea. The section which I have called *Literary*

Subjects is the most heterogeneous: some of the pieces in it were chosen because of their serious value, and some because they were entertaining. In a few cases the titles of essays are my own: their origins can all be discovered from the sub-headings and from the bibliography. As an Appendix I have given a series of collects which Charles Williams composed for a marriage, in the hope that they may find a more general use, for he was rare among modern writers in his ability to create language for prayer that is alive and strong.

Anne Ridler

I · LITERARY SUBJECTS

VICTORIAN NARRATIVE VERSE

An introduction to a selection, 1927

ONE of the most interesting things about the Victorian age, which is at last taking on the full aspect of the past, is the honour paid to, and the terms used of, George Eliot. A novelist, ranking certainly very high among the writers of the period, was ranked by them with the greatest names of antiquity, with Sophocles, with Homer, with Dante. So general an agreement argues that all found in her something they recognized and admired. Is it to epigrammatize too recklessly to call that quality nobility?

All genius, at the moments of its full exercise, becomes symbolical not so much of the age in which it is produced as of the universal life of man. It is not therefore in the greater but in the lesser writings of the Victorians that their characteristics are most clearly seen, in *Romola* rather than in *Adam Bede*. It is still more in the casual phrases of a hundred novels, of minor verse and almost unnecessary essays, that the aim of the period is to be most clearly discerned. Between the two romantic ages which preceded and followed it the Victorian seems to aim, like the thirteenth century and the Augustan age, at establishing a sort of stability. But where the thirteenth century sought to base its stability on an assumed supernatural basis, and the eighteenth within accepted rational limitations of the mind, the Victorian seems rather to have settled its stability upon conduct. To Matthew Arnold, certainly not the most Victorian writer, 'conduct was three-fourths of life'; to Tennyson and Carlyle and Thackeray, to Froude and Trollope and Gladstone, it was almost the whole. George Eliot, far more than the Queen who gave her name to the period, symbolized that preoccupation, and was unconsciously recognized as so symbolizing it.

Since conduct was to be the basis of their desired stability a particular kind of conduct was their aim. The Victorian age, like the Augustan desiring a balance of the forces of the world and a steady possession of their mental selves, retired from and disliked extremes. Sanctity and sadism were words alike unknown to it. Enthusiasm, in the earlier technical sense of the word, was an abnormal and alarming thing, a thing as alien to, say Kingsley, as to the author of that eighteenth-century tract which was entitled *The Twelve Apostles not Enthusiasts*. The famous quarrel between Kingsley and Newman might almost be described in the terms of 'enthusiasm'. To Newman a man who always had to tell the entire truth was an extremist of a dangerous and impossible kind. But though in practice Kingsley would have agreed with him, in theory he differed. For telling the truth was exactly a part of that nobility of conduct which Kingsley with all his heart admired, and from which he would not allow that there could be any diversion. He was endeavouring, in vain, to include an enthusiastic and romantic extreme of theory in a balanced and classic stability of conduct, and it was the ill-constructed bridge between them which the guns of Newman shattered.

If Romola is a manageable type of high nobility of conduct, Tennyson's King Arthur is an example of nobility become unmanageable, and wavering between nobility and mere pomposity. No great poet has ever been betrayed into a more disastrous episode than that in which Tennyson presented Arthur deploring and exhorting the prostrate form of Guinevere; and this, not because what Arthur seems to mean is necessarily wrong or stupid or selfish, but because it is nobility become conscious of itself, and nobility cannot afford to be conscious of itself. The mortal pathos, the immortal symbolism of Arthur are lost in such words as 'I am thy husband, not a smaller soul', and others wherein the King 'mouths out his hollow o's and a's'. Tennyson recovered himself in those great and famous lines which describe the King's departure, but it was because Arthur had left off being noble, and was in process of doing something. He had forgotten conduct and was occupied with action.

For perhaps the chief trouble about Victorian literature—and certainly the chief trouble about those now somewhat underrated poems of Tennyson, the *Idylls of the King*—was that its metaphysic could not present nor its withdrawing poetic imagination conceive an end sufficient to the means. To do one's duty was a noble thing, but the only reason for doing it was that it was one's duty. This indeed is a great enough theme for a great poet, if such duty is unmistakable and if tragedy follows upon its fulfilment. But the Victorian mind, though it accepted the first condition—the subtleties of exploration, the illusions of which duty is prolific, were not for that age—rejected the second. Duty faithfully followed and therefore inevitably producing tragedy—interior as well as exterior—would have been one of those extremes of the imagination from which ages which desire a stable mind instinctively recoil. The optimism of the Victorians was an accidental result of their desire for balance; it was certainly a subdued optimism, by no means so hearty as is sometimes thought, but cheerful enough to exclude intense tragedy, though not pathos. A few witnesses—the *Mill on the Floss*, and pre-eminently the *Ring and the Book*—testified against optimism; and the *Ring and the Book* even abandoned nobility. Pompilia and Caponsacchi in that very great poem are too young, too innocent, too helpless, too 'enthusiastic' to be called noble; the black household of Guido and the slavering obscenities of the Fisc are too vile even to be called ignoble.

But in the *Idylls* Arthur is presented as the soul; and the purpose, the end, of the soul is to do its duty. The King does not reject the Quest of the Graal merely from an artistic necessity, but from the necessity of an inadequate metaphysic. The high Prince Galahad passes across the stage and is gone, and the poem is uneasy in his presence. In that pursuit all the ordinary rules of conduct seem to be left behind; the bridges break down behind the chosen knight as he runs on to the city far out on the waste. It is merely apart from Camelot and the Table; it is merely apart from Arthur and the soul of man. Conduct without any adequate end, duty without interior and eternal significance, morals without metaphysics—these are the guardian angels of the Victorian chivalry and of the King. Lancelot mourns in Tennyson, 'not knowing he should die a holy man'. But in the end of the older story he dies, not necessarily holy but priestly; 'and a twelvemonth he sang mass', and so is assumed into mystery.

The weakness therefore of the Victorian age, as of the *Idylls*, is not in its concern with conduct but its failure artistically to suggest an adequate significance in conduct. When, however, it had subjects which came within its scope, when the centre of a poem became no longer an exhortation but a story, when, in short, conduct became simply action, the weakness was no longer felt. Then the greatness of the time appeared, and a score of figures in high moments of triumph or disaster were presented in poignant or exalted verse. Hardly since Chaucer had stories been so well told, and our own period, though in some things it surpasses, in this has scarcely rivalled its predecessor. Mr. Kipling, Mr. Masefield, Mr. Chesterton—these and a few others—have told us stories, and told them well, but many contemporary poets are too agitated or too dull for the art. In demanding significance they set out to impose significance; Mr. Hardy and Mr. Chesterton answer one another from opposite hills of doctrine, and are equally eclectic in their choice of tales, though perhaps Mr. Chesterton would admit the eclecticism more willingly than his peer.

The poems which follow are drawn from that great period of narrative, and are all concerned chiefly with one thing—telling a story. In one or two of them a flavour of exhortation or instruction is to be distinguished—Browning's *Donald* is the worst example. But the moral there is worked into such an admirable verbal climax that it may easily be excused. Apart from such moments the poems suggest themselves as being at once the continuance and the close of a great tradition. Here, by the chance of the selection, are many of the names of the heroes—Arthur and Olaf, Balder and Rustum, Perseus and Tristram; of dukes and kings, princes of faery and of fact, myths to which the Victorians willingly submitted themselves. Nobility in action and unconscious of itself, seems to be visible in most of these poems; and where it is not, the variations are characteristic of all that which eventually broke up the Victorian repose. The two possibilities which chiefly disturbed it were malice and ecstasy (say Samuel Butler and Francis Thompson); and except in the *Witch's Ballad* of William Bell Scott, neither of these appear until the admirable Christina's *Goblin Market*. Their presence determines the departure of nobility which is, in itself, incapable of either. The 'noble' hero cannot be rapt out of himself into a supernatural abandonment or betrayed into a sub-human hate. Lok, in Arnold's *Balder Dead*, is hardly convincing in his hostility; he is part of the necessity of a story which is defended by its sub-title of 'An Episode'. The old duchess in Browning's poem is not so much malicious as tyrannical and greedy; and apart from these two figures the catastrophes with which the heroes variously contend are rather of the nature of inevitable destiny. The day on which the Round Table was dissolved in battle and death was a day of thick mist; the fatal duel between Sohrab and Rustum is a strife between two unknowns; Balder dies by the destined forgetfulness of his mother as well as by the hate of Lok; in *Conary* the faery minstrels mislead the king's men who leave their lord to his doom; the vengeance of the gods pursues Andromeda, as the love of a goddess for Perseus saves her. The gipsy woman who lures the duchess from her home is 'of another nature' than she at first appeared. In Morris's *Son of Croesus* the doom which Croesus labours in vain to avert from his son is foreshown in a dream. 'The sea hath no king but God alone', is the refrain of Rossetti's *White Ship*.

For at its best the nobility of the Victorians contended with great adversaries, with time and the nature of the gods and fate. Around it existed, as it very well knew, 'darkness and cruel habitations'. It was heroic and steadfast, and when at last, as in the *King's Tragedy* or *Heather Ale*, its doom came to it, it passed as strongly as it had lived. To explore the darkness, whether in philosophy or poetry, it did not primarily hold to be its business. Herbert Spencer called those other modes of being 'the Unknowable', but the name was rather an indication of the Victorian temper than philosophically sound. In the *Witch's Ballad* and *Judas Iscariot* some sort of imaginative exodus into the unknown is attempted, something of the strangeness of the magical dance or the seas above the sky is conveyed, as in *Goblin Market* is something of the sub-human malice of the elves.

The only incomplete poem in the book is the extract from Swinburne. Swinburne was nearly incapable of telling a story directly; in this, and almost in this alone, he differed from the other great Victorians. It is true that he reversed their code of conduct, and praised the things that they blamed; physical love and revolution and tyrannicide. But this reversal did not alter his central concern, which was as much conduct as George Eliot's was, and lacked a satisfactory metaphysic as much as did Tennyson's. He did however, reversing the code, reverse the attitude, and nobility is not the virtue which chiefly distinguishes his characters. They are praised for the abandonment with which they give themselves to their experiences; they are praised for their conduct, but the significance of conduct is not greatly conveyed. The opening of *Tristram* is magnificent, but it does not suggest the intense interest and importance of love as much as certain Jacobean lyrics. So the magnificence of the lines given here does not succeed in presenting Palamede as the strange and exalted figure which moves through Malory. Mark lets Iseult go rather, it seems, from a sense of helplessness in the recollection of his promise than from a mad and passionate loyalty to it. But, perhaps by accident, there is also in this episode a suggestion of something beyond the Victorian age. For Palamede refrains from kissing Iseult, not only because of honour and nobility, but because

> More grace might come of that sweet mouth unkissed
> Than joy for violence done it.

There flashes for a moment in those lines the silver chastity of Britomart and the Lady in *Comus*.

Nobility is at the moment an unfashionable virtue in literature. Subtlety is preferred to it, and irony, and bitterness; just as allusiveness and the lyric are preferred to the direct narrative style. But as the Victorian age recedes it is taking on the strangeness of any past century. The side-whiskers of Arnold are no more ridiculous than the long curls of Prince Rupert or the formal beards of the Pharaohs. So their characteristic attitude, for all its dangers of pomposity and insincerity, is seen to be a real method of dealing with the crises of experience, whether interior or exterior. These poems are a tribute to its endeavour and its success.

Also, of course, they can be read as stories.

LORD MACAULAY

Contributed to Six Short Biographies, *ed. R. C. and N. Goffin, 1933*

To name Macaulay is to awaken one's own youth. To enjoy Macaulay is to be able to enter into the enjoyments of youth: the rich colours, the sounding drums and trumpets, the direct tales and the simple explanations of youth. As one grows older one finds that neither are tales so direct nor explanations so simple as Macaulay, in his history, his politics, and his criticism, tended to make them. Even his poetry errs, if it errs, by taking on a certain false simplicity; even to die for one's country is a little more complicated than the jingle of his rhymes and the clangour of his lines make it seem. But, though we can agree that entire truth is not in him, yet flaming colour and echoing sound are triumphantly in him; and the wise mind, adult or child, will enjoy those things, and all else that it can find, as thoroughly as it can.

He was born on 25 October 1800, the 385th anniversary of the Battle of Agincourt. It was the kind of battle and the kind of victory which was peculiarly suitable to him; and the bravery of the verse in which Shakespeare in *Henry V* embodied it, was peculiarly suitable to his imagination also. He was not really so simple, nor was Shakespeare, as to suppose that the 'ten thousand French' of that remarkable bulletin were slain at the cost of only twenty-nine English. But though his own pictures were more life-like, yet he loved to paint after that great example; the relief of Londonderry, the battle of Killiecrankie, in the *History*, or the cry of Aulus the Dictator in the *Lake Regillus*—'The foe begins to yield'—are examples. And if, as he grew older, he enjoyed his birthday, he also enjoyed those other things that he was afterwards to use so effectively—words. He took that double pleasure in their sound and their meaning which writers of any worth always have, and though his ideas might be limited the instruments which expressed them were not. He gathered them and enjoyed them; the longer the words the better, for there was more sound and colour. Lying on the hearth-rug in front of the fire, from the age of three, he read passionately, and what he read he used. Hannah More, calling one day, was received with an invitation to have a glass of 'old spirits'; *Robinson Crusoe* had supplied the enchanting drink. A maid moved a border of oyster-shells which he had set to mark his own plot of ground. He went into the drawing-room where his mother was entertaining company, and declaimed solemnly: 'Cursed be Sally, for cursed is he that removeth his neighbour's landmark'; the Bible had given him that magnificent denunciation. From a more general reading came the phrase in which, when a servant had upset hot coffee over his legs, the small child thanked a kind and anxious hostess; exquisitely courteous, he said solemnly: 'Thank you, madam, the agony is abated.'

His memory was prodigious; it retained words, poems, facts, and as many ideas as his mind could contain. He remembered the history of the world, and it was for him expressed in two mediums, (i) knowledge, (ii) belief. Those two capacities all his life contended unconsciously within him. He believed that the world, all by itself, was growing better; that civilization was spreading, and inevitably, and almost inexorably, conferring benefits on humanity; that humanity's business, generally speaking, was to let it alone to spread; that, in consequence, the age in which he lived was the best, but that the next age would be automatically better; and that, of that present age, the constitutional and social arrangements of England were the finest expression. His father and his father's friends had belonged to what was called the 'Clapham sect'—a group of devout Evangelicals who beheld in history the expression of the immutable judgements, mercies, and decrees of God. It might be said that Macaulay toned down God but kept the immutability of progress. They had fought for the Abolition of the Slave Trade and the freedom of the slaves, thus removing what was apparently the last fixed legal barrier to a universal advance towards felicity. That Macaulay identified positive felicity with the removal of positive ills was, no doubt, his error. It may, however, be added that, even so, the removal of positive ills is a matter of some importance to mankind. Many people have blamed Macaulay who are less vivid in their sense of the ills and no more vivid in their imagination of spiritual felicity.

School, Cambridge, the Bar, journalism, the House of Commons followed, and on them followed Holland House. 'The chief turn of nineteenth century England', says Mr. Chesterton, 'was taken about the time when a footman at Holland House opened a door and announced Mr. Macaulay.' Macaulay himself describes the event in a letter to his sister:

Take it dramatically in the German style.

Fine morning. Scene, the great entrance of Holland House.

Enter MACAULAY *and* TWO FOOTMEN *in livery.*

First Footman.—Sir, may I venture to demand your name?

Macaulay.—Macaulay, and thereto I add M.P.
  And that addition, even in these proud halls,
  May well ensure the bearer some respect.
Second Footman.—And art thou come to breakfast with our Lord?
Macaulay.—I am: for so his hospitable will,
  And hers—the peerless dame ye serve—hath bade.
First Footman.—Ascend the stair, and thou above shalt find,
  On snow-white linen spread, the luscious meal.

[*Exit* MACAULAY *upstairs*.

In plain English prose, I went this morning to breakfast at Holland House. The day was fine, and I arrived at twenty minutes after ten.

It was, in fact, the union of the great Whig families which had throughout the eighteenth century been as much the Families as the Tories, with the middle classes. For another alliance so memorable, and this time on the Tory side, history had to wait ten years, from 1831 to 1841, when Mr. Disraeli became a Tory. The aristocratic government of England had then on all sides allied itself with those who would have been its conquerors, were it not that both they and it were, before the grand progressive advance towards freedom and comfort had been properly begun, to be dominated by the extremely wealthy groups which arose within it. The advance towards comfort has, on the whole, continued; the advance towards social freedom has, on the whole, stopped. Spiritual freedom has remained as it was and always must be—an achievement only gained by intense labour and discipline.

In the eighteenth century great place was the patron of talent, and talent—even genius—had to find patronage in order to work and even to exist. But talent was now beginning to have a little money of its own, and the terms of that ancient alliance were altered. Johnson had written, years before:

But mark what ills the scholar's life assail:
Toil, envy, want, the patron and the jail.

But the young Mr. Macaulay was in no danger of want or the jail; toil he thoroughly enjoyed, and envy was negligible. The patron had to change his tone. Genius in England has always resided in the smaller houses of the middle classes and it was genius—especially journalistic genius—of which the great families were now in growing need. The time had not yet arrived when it would be their fate either to fear or to own the newspapers; indeed, the newspapers, as yet, were not. But the great Reviews were—the *Edinburgh*, the *Quarterly*, *Blackwood's*; and Mr. Macaulay was a valued contributor to the *Edinburgh*. He was invited, and he went, to breakfast at Holland House. Lord Russell, of another great Whig family, was there. They gave him 'very good coffee, and very good tea, and very good eggs, butter kept in the midst of ice, and hot rolls'. Lord

Holland (in a wheel chair) showed him the pictures; Lady Holland showed him more; Mr. Luttrell, a wit, a scholar, a poet, and an intimate of the house, showed him the gardens.

The connexion so happily begun prospered. By 11 July Macaulay was dining and sleeping at Holland House, 'a very agreeable and splendid party'. He met the Duke and Duchess of Richmond, and a greater than they—M. de Talleyrand, who had been First Minister to Napoleon and to the Bourbons who supplanted Napoleon. He was driven back to London by Lord John Russell, another scion of the great house and a future Prime Minister. Macaulay's personal appearance about this time was described by a friend, a political enemy, and a spectator. The friend wrote: 'A short, manly figure, marvellously upright . . . a massive head, and features of a powerful and rugged cast.' The spectator said, 'He has a good face,—not the delicate features of a man of genius and sensibility, but the strong lines and well-knit limbs of a man sturdy in body and mind. Very eloquent and cheerful. Overflowing with words and not poor in thought. . . . He seems a correct as well as a full man.' The enemy wrote (in *Blackwood's Magazine*, a Tory organ): 'A little, splay-footed, ugly dumpling of a fellow, with a mouth from ear to ear.' Macaulay's own controversial habits were finer; he fought hard, but he fought the mind with the mind, and he never used insults instead of argument—even to anyone whom (as he said of one opponent), 'I detest more than cold boiled veal.'

He was by now a power in journalism; he was becoming a power in politics. In 1832 he was given a minor office under the Whig Government, and took part in the final passage of the Emancipation of the Slaves. Meanwhile a new India Bill, to regulate the affairs of the East India Company, had been passed, and had decreed that one of the members of the Supreme Council was to be chosen from outside the servants of the Company. The Directors of the Company appointed Macaulay by nineteen votes to three. He determined to accept, and made his arrangements. He inquired from a returned Anglo-Indian about the mosquitoes. 'Always contrive', was the answer, 'to have at your table some flashy blooming young writer or cadet, just come out, that the mosquitoes may stick to him, and leave the rest of the company alone.' He arranged with the editor of the *Edinburgh* to be paid for his articles, while he was away, not in money but in books. He bought and read books on India—and (as always) on everything else. Lady Holland went into hysterics; Lord Holland rebuked her for selfishness. He sailed in February 1834.

On the way out, he said, 'except at meals I hardly exchanged a word with any human being. I never was left for so long a time so completely to my own resources; and I am glad to say that I found them quite sufficient to keep me cheerful and employed.' It was one way of putting it; his resources were the reserves of his mind and the preserves of his books. He read 'the *Iliad* and *Odyssey*, Virgil, Horace, Caesar's *Commentaries*, Bacon's *De Augmentis*, Dante, Petrarch, Ariosto, Tasso, *Don Quixote*, Gibbon's *Rome*, Mill's *India*, all the seventy volumes of Voltaire, Sismondi's *History of France*, and the seven thick folios of the *Biographia Britannica*'. So burdened and bursting with the West's vital enjoyment of the West he descended on India and on the Supreme Council. But he brought with him what perhaps the Supreme Council lacked rather than India; an immense feeling for the authority of the past and of the great men and things of the past, and an immense feeling for high achievement. His correspondence is full of that apprehension: 'I was enraptured...', 'I was enchanted...', 'I never enjoyed it so much...'. There is a vignette of him in one of his later letters which deserves to be remembered. In 1849 he was going to Ireland. Between London and Bangor he had read the lives of the Roman Emperors, but on the boat at night he could not see to read. There was magnificent starlight; he sat on deck and repeated to himself *Paradise Lost*. 'I could still repeat half of it, and that the best half. I really never enjoyed it so much.' When Macaulay is remembered for blame, that scene should be remembered also to his honour: the short stocky figure, wrapped in a greatcoat, sitting alone on deck under the glory of the stars, and abandoning himself to the unutterable other glory of the most sublime verse that the English genius has ever made.

In India he carried on his picturesque veneration—races, States, writings, and buildings offered themselves to him; and travelling in the subdued pomp of a Member of Council he admired the antique pomp which he now so nearly neighboured. But he also threw himself into affairs. Over a question of legal administration he was violently attacked by the Calcutta Press. He wrote that 'We know that India cannot have a free government. But she may have the next best thing—a firm and impartial despotism.' Into the last five words went all his historical knowledge and all his real intelligence; he meant despotism, but also he meant impartial. The opposition which he met with seemed to him to come from 'two or three hundred people' who wanted 'to domineer over millions'. He, and the Government, remained firm, and the opposition failed.

He was appointed President of the Committee of Public Instruction, and found the Committee divided—five against five—on the secular question of the kind of education which was most desirable. Five wanted to encourage Sanscrit, Persian, Arabic; five wanted

English. Macaulay adopted the view which has generally prevailed in the history of Europe: that the culture of the ruling class is made the doctrine of the ruled. He wrote a Minute such as no one else could write, throbbing with his own sincere belief in the civilization of the West, enlarged by his extraordinary knowledge of that civilization, shaped into the coherent and lucid sentences which are one of the chief gifts of that civilization to its obedient children. It swept the Government and the Governor-General away on its own intensity of conviction. It was determined that 'the great object of the British Government ought to be the promotion of European literature and science among the natives of India'. The Indian millions were to become millions of Indian Macaulays—at best and with necessary variations. But they were to be the best Macaulays; they were to be alive with all the vitality of European imagination, not merely frigid with European pedantry. *Robinson Crusoe* 'is worth all the grammars of rhetoric and logic in the world'. Macaulay, revisiting the glimpses of his Indian moon, might not be very satisfied—a hundred years after—with our results. Our slightly sardonic comfort is that he would have been even less satisfied with results in England. Somehow the automatic machine of progress has functioned to strange and different ends.

He was President of the Law Commission, and had much to do with producing the first draft of a Penal Code which was greatly admired by lawyers. He left India in 1838, having profoundly affected its future, and having also—the famous incident must be mentioned—provoked the whole of the circle of the Governor-General one rainy season in the Nilgiris to read *Clarissa Harlowe*. 'The Governor's wife seized the book; the Secretary waited for it; the Chief Justice could not read it for tears.' But Richardson without Macaulay might easily have left that supreme circle at Ootacamund uninterested. He was infectious; he invigorated taste by his mere contact.

English historians are roughly divisible into two classes: those whose style is thrilled through and through by their subject and those whose style remains unmoved by it. Accuracy and inaccuracy are as likely to occur on one side as the other; the picturesque is not necessarily opposed to learning, and where exaltation and learning are mingled the result is far more likely to correspond to truth than the more pedestrian journey along a flat road of unvaried statement. The uninflected statement of fact, in history as in everything else, may be sometimes necessary. But it avoids any reflection of the emotion which accompanied the original fact. The flight of James II is in that prose more placid than ever in reality; the death of Dundee is sedater than any death could be, let alone one that followed on the charge of the Highland clans. It is the vibrating truth of the fact which the historian with a sufficient style recaptures. Even if it is a fact which he hates and denounces, still the denunciation itself brings the reader by its fervour nearer to history than uninterested frigidity. Certainly we need accuracy and impartiality. But impartiality does not mean a failure to understand anybody so much as a capacity to understand everybody. So great a sympathy Macaulay hardly possessed, but he thrilled, and his prose thrilled, to heroism, magnificence, honour, and magnanimity.

He returned to London in 1839. He re-entered public and parliamentary life and was made Secretary for War. In 1846 he became Paymaster-General, but in the next year he was defeated at Edinburgh and retired into 'private life'. His private life was to become the field in which grew the harvest of the *History of England*—private is hardly the word for a field in which generations have gathered grain.

In 1842 he had published the *Lays of Ancient Rome*; Leigh Hunt, then nearing sixty years, wrote to him, 'asking me to lend him money, and lamenting that my verses want the true poetical aroma which breathes from Spenser's *Faerie Queene*'. There is perhaps no English poem which the *Lays* are less like than the *Faerie Queene*, unless it were that other poem which a young friend of Leigh Hunt's had fashioned at Hampstead, while Macaulay was still at Trinity—the *Ode to the Nightingale*. They have no poetic depth and no poetic significance. One reviewer wrote that Macaulay 'robbed in the face of day'. From whom? From Homer. It is merely silly. The comparison, for good or evil, of the *Lays* with the great poetic achievements is like comparing Macaulay with Caesar or Thucydides. His verse has no more depth of passion than it has subtlety of movement. It is the verse of poetic childhood. But in becoming adult in poetry we need not leave childhood behind, and we can enjoy flagrancy, gusto, and splendid names without either persuading ourselves that they are, or lamenting that they are not, more.

In 1838, looking forward to his return to England, he had looked forward also to beginning his *History*. On 9 March 1839 he wrote in his Journal: 'I began my *History* with a sketch of the early revolutions of England. Pretty well; but a little too stately and rhetorical.' In 1841 he had settled to it. He was shocked to think that some people could not repeat the names of the prime ministers of England from 1688 to 1789 in order; he aimed at producing something 'which shall for a few days supersede the last fashionable novel on the tables of young ladies'. These are the two elements of Macaulay's mind. He did know all about the prime ministers, and he saw no reason why they should not be as exciting to the young ladies as they undoubtedly were to him. He gave up time and energy to making them so, and he succeeded. The first two volumes appeared at the end of 1848; within four months 13,000 copies had been sold —even nowadays it would not be a poor achievement. Congratulations poured in on him. The Duke of Wellington admired it. The Quakers objected to the treatment of Penn; Macaulay received a deputation and maintained his case. He walked in Fleet Street and saw in a bookseller's window an edition of Hume's *History* marked 'highly valuable as an introduction to Macaulay'. 'I laughed so convulsively that the other people who were staring at the books took me for a poor demented gentleman.' But they did not know him. Where he was known he became a spectacle, he who loved spectacles. But as he loved them with humour and intelligence, so he laughed at himself.

> I have seen the hippopotamus, both asleep and awake; and I can assure you that, awake or asleep, he is the ugliest of the works of God. But you must hear of my triumphs. Thackeray swears that he was eye-witness and ear-witness of the proudest event of my life. Two damsels were just about to pass that doorway which we, on Monday, in vain attempted to enter, when I was pointed out to them. 'Mr. Macaulay!' cried the lovely pair. 'Is that Mr. Macaulay? Never mind the hippopotamus.' And having paid a shilling to see Behemoth, they left him in the very moment at which he was about to display himself to them, in order to see—but spare my modesty. I can wish for nothing more on earth, now that Madame Tussaud, in whose Pantheon I hoped once for a place, is dead.

Some such public admiration, with its disadvantages, was his for the rest of his life. Palmerston in 1857 made him a peer. Less famous persons continually pestered him for money or with verses and other work. An unknown painter wrote to him, 'adjuring me, as I love the fine arts, to hire or buy him a cow to paint from'. An unknown writer offered to bring up the manuscript of his novel from Scotland if he were sent £50. In 1859 Macaulay went to Scotland for a fortnight; from where he wrote:

> I went the day before yesterday to Grasmere Churchyard, and saw Wordsworth's tomb. I thought of announcing my intention of going, and issuing guinea tickets to people who wished to see me there. For a Yankee who was here a few days ago, and heard that I was expected, said that he would give the world to see that most sublime of all spectacles, Macaulay standing by the grave of Wordsworth.

His labour, his fame, and his enjoyment, went on till the end of his life. Toward the end of that same year 1859 he was working regularly, having reached the year 1700, but by the December his health was breaking. The last entry in his journal is on 23 December, a comment on Dickens; on the 28th he signed his last letter, to a poor curate, sending him £25; on the same day late in the evening he was found dead in his library, the latest *Cornhill* open on the table by him. He was buried in Westminster Abbey; it was perhaps excusable.

He remains one of the stumbling-blocks of criticism. He is liked yet disapproved, and read a little shamefacedly—except in prose anthologies. The austerer part of the reader's mind deprecates at once his style and his convictions, not altogether unwisely. One remembers that Arnold was scornful of the *Lays*, and willing to make them a test of good judgement in verse; and as it is clear at once that Arnold had a finer mind than Macaulay it is difficult not to regret liking them. But it remains a little difficult not to like them—and the *Essays*—and the *History*—and, in short, everything.

His only real instrument was the trumpet; his only good colour purple. But he had a great instinct for knowing how long to blow the one and how much to put on of the other: a single blast or a fanfare, a delicate pattern or a magnificent sweep. He admired spectacles, and his style is spectacular. It is directed, not by intellect, not by profound emotion, but by proper names and heroic admirations, and while it is in action it subordinates if it does not impress us. The poem on the Armada takes us through England with the glare of the beacons and the ringing of bells. The *History* takes us through the Revolution to the marching of mobs and the defeat of kings. Even when he disapproves he pays tribute—to the death of the Jacobite Dundee or the splendour of Louis the Sun-King. And between these multitudinous moments he is always active. His proper names are facts, rather than myths. Even the gods in *Lake Regillus* are champions rather than deities; they create an unholy, but hardly a holy fear, in the hearts of their enemies. It may be that he does not stop to think, but it must be admitted that his movement prevents us also from stopping. He compels us to say Ah ha! among the trumpets, and we say it even to his own. There is no single page in him where he can give any food for his reader's mind. But also there are few pages during which the reader does not forget that he is hungry.

LANDOR

An introduction to his Imaginary Conversations *(selected), 1934*

WALTER SAVAGE LANDOR was born in 1775; he died in 1864. He was born, that is, before the Romantic Revival in letters had begun; he died, fourteen years after Wordsworth, long after it had ended. In the year of his birth there appeared Johnson's *Journey to the Western Islands of Scotland*; in the following year the first volume of Gibbon's *Decline and Fall of the Roman Empire*. Round about the date of his death appeared *Romola* (1863), *Our Mutual Friend* (1864), *Enoch Arden* (1864), *Dramatis Personæ* (1864), and *Atalanta in Calydon* (1865). Between those two periods in literature lay all Wordsworth, Coleridge, Blake, Byron, Keats, Shelley, Beddoes, Darley, and Hood. With any of them all Landor had as much alliance as with any other—which is to say, very little. There were two writers who, being neither Augustan nor Victorian, remained singularly aloof from the Romantic affairs of their time in letters; one was Landor, and one was Jane Austen.

It is perhaps their only resemblance, except in the sudden flashes of insight of which they were both capable. They could both be tender; they could both be devastating. In general, however, Jane's was the more universal genius. Her style was more subdued and less noticeable, though no less effective; her concern was with men and women in their daily affairs. But Landor in his books made himself a colonnade of marble to walk in, and though he admitted to it all who came, his guests were usually men and women introduced on high affairs of state. He superbly withdrew himself to his art, and his art has ever since remained superbly withdrawn.

It was an age of imagined perfections. Human perfectibility and human freedom were the watchwords of the great political Romanticists. 'Man was born free and is everywhere in chains', Rousseau had written; and men had believed the great half-truth. Freedom was man's prerogative, and perfection his possibility. He had been robbed of the one and cheated of the other. By whom? By tyrants; more exactly in their dreams (and less accurately in the facts), by kings and priests. Shelley declared it to the world; so did Landor. Kings and priests—and the intelligence of their genius compelled them both to add mobs—were responsible, and must be destroyed or changed. They both attempted, in different ways, to change Oxford as a start, and they both failed. Landor fired a gun at the windows of a man he disliked; Shelley fired an intellectual gun at the windows of the university by publishing a pamphlet on the *Necessity of Atheism* (1811). The authorities refused to allow the necessity of the material or the mental gun, and sent down their owners. With a high sense of an injured heart each young poet went out into the world, and abandoned himself to a life in which, however surely perfection was on his side, he was continually to find a great deal of imperfection around him.

Landor, indeed, spent his life in continual personal quarrels of the most violent kind. He was enraged by his father (while alive), by his neighbours (wherever he was), by his wife (when in 1811 he married), by his comrades on an expedition to fight against Napoleon in Spain (1808), by English, Spaniards, and Italians, by his relations, his friends, and his enemies. During almost the whole of his life he was at war personally and intellectually. And during almost the whole of his life, amidst that tumult of frenzy, he was producing prose and verse of the most stately kind, illuminated sometimes by touches of an almost supernatural delicacy. Yet the two things were not so greatly opposed as they seem. For his personal behaviour had in general a high dignity; he felt and expressed passion in the loftiest sense of the word, and the power of his imagination which could not keep bitterness and anger out of his life was able in his writings to order and harmonize the lesser passions into his proud style.

That imagination owed something to a personal prejudice. He was of good birth; he knew it, loved it, exaggerated and exalted it. Almost by birth, certainly by belief and by preference, he was among the aristocrats. It was not for him to treat the English language lightly. It was the vehicle of an aristocratic mind, which recognized in it its own verbal aristocracy of long descent and high vocation. He recognized and obeyed its traditions, and he had recognized them early. He had been at first under the influence of the Greek and Latin classics; later he came under the influence of *Paradise Lost*. 'My prejudices', he wrote, 'in favour of ancient literature began to wear away on *Paradise Lost*; and even the great hexameter sounded to me tinkling when I had recited aloud in my solitary walks on the seashore the haughty appeal of Satan and the deep penitence of Eve.'

No one who has so come under the influence of that sublime verse can ever be the same again, but in Landor it did but encourage him upon his own proper way. He composed *Gebir*, a long poem, which he published in 1798. It opens:

> When old Silenus call'd the Satyrs home,
> Satyrs then tender-hooft and ruddy-horn'd,
> With Bacchus and the Nymphs, he sometimes rose
> Amidst the tale or pastoral, and shew'd
> The light of purest wisdom; and the God
> Scatter'd with wholesome fruit the pleasant plains.

It was in this semi-Miltonic spirit that he separated himself with gladness from the Romantic literature of his day: 'I claim no place in the world of letters; I am alone and will be alone as long as I live, and after'; 'It has been my fortune and felicity, from my earliest days, to have avoided all competitions'; 'I shall dine late, but the dining room will be well lighted, the guests few and select'; 'He who is within two paces of his ninetieth year may sit down and make no excuses; he must be unpopular, he never tried to be much otherwise, he never contended with a contemporary, but walked alone on the far eastern uplands, meditating and remembering.'

Such notes are not frequent in the critical confessions of English writers; as a rule from Chaucer to Chesterton they have been content to write and live among their fellows, and only the greatness of genius set even Shakespeare alone. Milton in the seventeenth and Patmore in the nineteenth centuries made comments on their solitude, if not claims to it; but there was all but a boast in Landor's which was not in theirs. He was well-born, in letters as in life; in both he seemed to himself of loftier rank than serious truth can allow him.

To say so is to be unfair to Landor, yet it is an unfairness which all but the most fanatical Landorian will excuse. It is not merely by accident or by the dullness of our critical taste that so much of Landor's prose remains unread. The *Imaginary Conversations* . . . began the publication of their five volumes in 1824 and closed them in 1829. For our modern and feebler minds the title is itself misleading. In our contemporary novels we are used to realistic conversation, to slang and hesitation, to dashes and dots, to all the tricks, verbal or typographical, by which the incapacity and folly of our daily speech is made clear. We do not expect the lofty exchanges of conscious art, the arranged modulations of careful thought in careful utterance, stately rhythm and proportionable, if undecorated diction. And this is what we find in Landor. Nor is it wholly our daily habit of life that has left us unprepared; it is the habit of our literature. From Malory to Fielding, from Smollett to Dickens, from Thackeray to—Galsworthy, let us say, lest we should be invidious, there are few prose writers who imagine conversations so. Milton's archangels, had they ever condescended to prose, might have managed it, but the speech of archangels seems to need the wings of poetry and the humanity of Milton's all but universal mind to carry it. These others are the conversations of great men; we are purified and instructed, we are humbled and dwarfed by them. It is very well to be humbled; it is more tiresome to be dwarfed; and there are pages of Landor where he dwarfs us with his exalted art, without humbling us by his profound and intense passion. We weary of those halls and colonnades of style, of that solemn air of recollection and declamation, and we begin to find Landor dull.

It is folly again, another example of the fatal folly of asking from a writer what he neither will nor can give. One might as well ask for good priests or good kings in Landor as for colloquial phrases. His aristocratic republicanism forbade him to present the one or to use the other. With the dreams of royalty or orthodox religion he had little sympathy, and we miss in him the vivid concerns of a large part of mankind. It was his limitation, and in so much prose that limitation becomes monotonous, if we permit ourselves to be aware of it. But if we confine our attention to the substance contained within that limitation, we shall find ourselves of a different mind. He said of his own style: 'I have resigned and abandoned many things because I unreasonably doubted my legitimate claim to them, and many more because I believed I had enough substance in the house without them.' The substance which he has, and communicates, is the nourishment in every soul of the wise and generous Best, of an aristocracy of spirit capable of and manifested in a noble heroism. One feels sometimes one needs to be something of a hero to read all Landor. But it is wiser to remark how heroic is his style and how heroic his spirit. The *Conversations* contain many examples of extraordinary crises and of commonplace experiences. They maintain towards them all that magnanimity which Landor, despite all his faults, profoundly believed to be a condition of any tolerable life of the soul. His prose has a ceremony about it but not a profusion. Its disposed order is conscious, but only by conscious effort can a continual level of virtue possibly be obtained. Virtue, magnanimous virtue, is the quality Landor demanded of man; his prose at its greatest communicates sacramentally that nobility and severe beauty of life to its reader. It is shown in *Elizabeth Gaunt* and *Joan of Arc* as it is in *Marcellus* and *Blake*. It is a quality which, for all its severity, has about it a capacity of lovely and swift tenderness, and for all its limitation a universal sense of man and his doom. There are, no doubt, greater writers than Landor, but it is certain that if we underrate his greatness we shall never be able to appreciate theirs. He is, in that sense, a test of our own art, in life as well as in letters, and the extremer experiences of prose and (more usually) of poetry lie on the yonder side of his stately barrier.

He attributes an overheavy part of man's burden to the deliberate machinations of wicked men, mostly tyrants. He was himself (as his first biographer, Forster, remarked) apt where he had power to become tyrannical—with the highest motives. The motives of other tyrants did not seem to him nearly so high. Where he had no power he was apt to become rebellious; and in general the motives of all rebels seemed to him not only high but exalted. But there is a tyranny of Life itself against which rebellion is futile and foolish. Against that tyranny there are but two defences—heroism and love. Landor knew of them both. He accepted life—at least, in literature—as he accepted literature itself, on the conditions which he understood them separately to impose. He understood Fate, and from the workings of Fate he could extract the last drop of sweetness.

The two dialogues of Aesop and Rhodope contain as exquisite examples of this as any; balanced and restrained as the prose is, there are phrases which contain the passion of abandonment or dereliction. But the fullness of that passion is apt to be felt only by the fullness of adult knowledge; no easy acquaintance with letters will fathom the depth of such a sentence as: 'There is no name, with whatever emphasis of passionate love repeated, of which the echo is not faint at last.'

This solemn music of a consciousness of death echoes down his prose and sometimes in unexpected places. To the obsequious Chancellor in *Peter and Alexis* is given one climax: 'The hand of death; the name of father'; to Bossuet, in the not quite worthy presentation of the great bishop during his dialogue with the Duchess de Fontanges: 'Duchess de Fontanges, think on this! Lady! so live as to think on it undisturbed.' For Death, to one so full of the gusto of living as Landor, was the only opponent he could not despise. Even magnanimity of spirit could there give no more than cheerful memories and peace at heart.

THE NEW MILTON

From The London Mercury, *July 1937*

Two alterations have taken place recently in our views of Milton—alterations not yet sufficiently received, but likely soon to justify Milton's ways to us much more than we have hitherto realized. Of these, one is a series of minor alterations—and one major—in our knowledge of his biography; the other, and inevitably the more important, is a similar series of alterations in the reading of his verse. It is the more important because his verse is the thing that, primarily and profoundly, affects us; his life is of interest only because of that, and not that because of his life. Each series can be exemplified by a single instance: first, the change in the date of his marriage; second, the realization that Milton imagined Satan as silly. The colloquial word is the best for the moment; it presents the whole neglected element of comedy in *Paradise Lost*, and it prepares the ear for that change in the sound of *Paradise Lost* which is the result and summary of the new realization and our very great gain. For by this we do not lose the old style, either of Milton or of *Paradise Lost*, but we enlarge and complicate them. Milton becomes less like one of his own detestable pagan deities, and *Paradise Lost* becomes a poem of immediate importance to our own daily experiences.

It has been, on the whole, though there are exceptions, the habit to regard Milton as a proud Puritan—having at best a certain nobility and at worst a noxious inhumanity. Every incident of his life has been interpreted on this basis. His irritations and his faults have been petrified into a great range of mountains down which no rivers of living waters rushed. He must be always granite, and at that not the granite of charity but of solitary haughtiness and hate. He could perhaps show us how to endure, but not how to love. One might think he had gone blind on principle and with an august masochism perversely preferred the return of the Stuarts. It is true he preferred his principles to his sight, and that he made great poetry out of the defeat of his cause. But he never forgot that sight was normal, that good was somehow victorious beauty, that romantic love was a wonder of grace and authority and delight, and that laughter was one of the divinest virtues allowed to man.

On the biographical side the most important change has been in our knowledge of the date of his marriage. It used to be said that he wrote the tract on the *Doctrine and Discipline of Divorce* during, as it were, his honeymoon. Miss Darbishire has shown us that his marriage with Mary Powell more probably took place a year before, in May or June 1642. His wife left him in about a month; the tract was published in 1643. She returned about August 1645, and within a year afterwards, by August 1646, her father and her family followed her. Milton's own father had come to live with him soon after Mary first left him in 1642.

The marriage was, at best, a dreadful and deplorable mistake, and Milton produced from his own experience what he regarded as a principle of religious and civilized life—the principle of divorce. He was not alone in that among poets, nor, indeed, among men. But even the force and fervour of the divorce tract is due rather to his genius than to himself. The militant epigrams were no more than expressions of emotion felt by many; but they are infinitely more effective than the stammerings of those unused to words. Mary Powell has had, and justly, a good deal of sympathy. But at least it seems that her husband was not busy on his repudiation of the marriage before her departure, and that therefore his repudiation had been preceded by hers. One can hardly repudiate a thing more effectively than by abandoning it. His genius enabled him to denounce their joint effort for centuries, but at least she had denounced it first. The centuries have condoled with her, as with John Keats. But Milton and Fanny Brawne had also their mortal and intimate wounds.

It is precisely such a stress as has been varied by the altered date of the marriage that has been neglected in the arrival of her family. She had lived with him for a month and then been two years absent —with her family. In a year after her return her family followed her, and her husband received them. It was, no doubt, his duty. But they were a Cavalier family, supporting the King, and ruined in the King's cause. They were noisy and loyal. The father 'was compounding for his delinquency'. Milton must have known the state to which the house in Aldersgate Street would be brought. His own father was then living with him as well; he had come soon after Mary had fled. Milton, writing to Diodati in Italy, complained of the general upset—they 'stun me with their noise and waste me with vexation', while those with whom he had an intense sympathy of 'manners, tastes, and pursuits' were either distant or dead. He then, like Wordsworth after him and Dante before him—he midway between the two in genius as in time—was already distressed and harassed by the actions of the Government of the day. But, troublesome as the Powells no doubt were to him, he not only received but endured them, nor is it likely that the awful greatness of Mr. John Milton was able, or hoped, or perhaps intended, to crush the domestic riot of his 'in-laws'. His behaviour then provides a neglected stress on his goodwill and generosity.

Another, and notorious, stress upon the 'stormy egotism' of Milton (the thrilling phrase is Miss Rose Macaulay's) lies in the tale of his compelling his daughters to read to him in languages of which they understood nothing. This, in its simple monstrosity, is quite inconceivable. That the fastidious ear of Milton should have been offended by Deborah plunging through an uncomprehended vast of Virgil, or that Deborah should have been able to learn to read the Latin correctly, and yet not to understand anything of the meaning—both are alike impossible. The solution of the problem lies, it may be suggested, in the actual day-to-day needs of the blind. A blind man has an intense wish to *remember*, and he finds his memory failing unless continually refreshed. A blind man who has known much verse finds that little fractions—words, phrases—escape him. He remembers, for example, 'Dusk faces, with white silken turbans . . .' and cannot remember the last word—'decked'? 'topped'? 'crowned'? 'backed'? he knows none of these are right. His only hope is to get someone to look up the line, and that someone has first to find the line. He has to search for it among a mass of others, for the blind man will only be able to say, at best, *about* where it comes: in what connexion, or in relation to what figure. He hunts, he finds, he reads—'Dusk faces, with white silken turbans *wreathed*', and the blind man is released for a little from that intense state which Milton described.

> So much I feel my genial spirits droop.
> My hopes all flat, Nature within me seems
> In all her functions weary of herself.

But this research is, often enough, over-troublesome to the assistant. A blind man once said to me: 'People are willing to read what they want, not what you want, and they are rarely willing to look things up.' It is a dull business, if one is not interested. It is a much duller business if the desired reference is in a foreign language. Boredom on the one side, expectation on the other, irritation on both, make the grasshopper a burden. No wonder it seemed to Deborah Milton that she had read Virgil aloud to her father, but we may be permitted to guess that we know Milton as well as she and that he could not have stood it. What, above all, he did need were those minutes, so tiresome to her, in which she supplied the hunger of his memory with the true words.

The probable right adjustment of these and other stresses in Milton's life may not make him as affable as Shakespeare, and may leave him as passionate as Dante. But they help a certain consistency. The young man who said of the Muse and Love that 'Both them I serve and of their train am I' retains something of his doubly divine vocation. He did not, it seems, rush quite so quickly to demand freedom from a marriage which was no marriage; he did not ask for its civil annulment until his wife had already annulled it for a long period in practice. He re-established it on her request, and he gave hospitality for months to her family in their distress—a family of whose politics he profoundly disapproved and whose noise distracted him from his work. He did not make his daughters read to him in tongues unknown to them; though he did, against their will, demand that they should supply the accuracies of which his evil fate was slowly robbing him. He had, that is to say, in his life that natural scope of humanity which many readers have refused to see in his verse.

Even there, perhaps, they are wrong. Milton's fame has been petrified by phrases, and one of the most damaging has been 'organ-note'. He has been compelled to be the organ all the time. *Paradise Lost* has been called sonorous, and sonorous it has been made to be, in season and out of season. Yet the very first book contains the account of a music which might have made us pause in so universal an attribution. The perfect phalanx moves 'to the Dorian mood of Flutes and soft recorders', which have power

> to mitigate and swaye
> With solemn touches, troubled thoughts, and chase
> Anguish and doubt and fear and sorrow and pain
> From mortal or immortal minds.

It is time that we mitigated the organ with the 'soft pipes' of that passage; and the chief of them is laughter, honest and pleasant laughter at solemn folly.

It would not, perhaps, be true to say that *Paradise Lost* is a comedy, but it is certainly true to say that there is an element of comedy running all through *Paradise Lost*. The traditional view of the poem as a sonorous organ and the traditional view of its author as a supreme egotist have supported each other. The Milton who could do nothing natural or loving and the verse which has no relation to man's contemporary life have reflected each other, and in neither original nor mirror is there any hint of a smile. Yet in fact both the poem and the poet do smile. They do not laugh loudly, they are as opposed to that as was Dante; they, with him, 'laugh with becoming restraint'. But the laughter in *Paradise Lost*—and perhaps that too was in Milton's own life—is like the laughter spoken of in almost the loveliest passage of Dante's *Convivio*: 'The soul shows herself in the mouth almost like colour under glass. And what is laughter but a scintillation of the soul's delight, that is, a gleam showing itself without no otherwise than it exists within? . . . O wonderful smile of my mistress of whom I speak, which never is seen save in her eyes!'

That Lady was, under one semblance of her identity, Philosophy; and the scintillation of the soul's delight which exists in *Paradise Lost* is also philosophical. It is the admirable laughter at the idea, at the vision, of any created thing attacking for its own profit the adorable omnipotence of Love. It is seen in the sympathetic and philosophical eyes of the poem when it contemplates Satan in hell. It allows, it even admires, Satan's real powers and virtues; it does not desire to lessen them or him. But it insists on seeing all of him. Now one element of Satan in hell is his apparently quite sincere belief that the revolting angels have endangered the Omnipotence:

> His utmost power with adverse power opposed
> In dubious battle on the plains of heaven,
> And shook his throne.

At the moment we may believe that. But presently it becomes clear that Satan is merely wrong; the facts laugh at him. The facts are that he never came anywhere near shaking the throne, that the utmost power was never called on, and that the divine Son (having acceded to the wish of the rebel angels,

> since by strength
> They measure all, of other excellence
> Not emulous)

had to check himself in mid-volley lest he should destroy them: the Son who is himself the laughter of heaven at egotistic folly—

> calm aspect and clear
> Lightning divine, ineffable, serene.

Such lightning, having all foes of Love in heavenly derision, is not unlike the purest scintillation of the soul's delight, exalted into greater places.

The comprehension of this lucid accuracy revolutionizes our first view of Satan, and therefore of the poem. Milton, it has been said, had no sense of humour, and indeed there are not many jokes in *Paradise Lost*. But there is this element of soft and joyous comedy, and its existence is much more universal than is often supposed. It directs attention to another matter—the vocalization of the poem.

The austere Milton, sonorously sounding the august art of his verse, has been generally made to begin with an organ prelude. But the opening is much more like softness than sonority; it is almost shy. 'The Lady of Christ's' possessed still, so many years afterwards, a kind of maidenly modesty in beginning his high task. That humility, the lack of which causes such laughter in heaven and such misapprehension of the facts in hell, is present in the first twenty-six lines of invocation. The Muse and the Spirit are not commanded but implored. The proof is chiefly in the words 'Dove-like' and 'pregnant':

> Thou from the first . . .
> Dove-like sat'st brooding on the vast Abyss
> And mad'st it pregnant.

A sonorous reading of those opening lines will completely ruin those two words, and make their sound devoid of meaning. A reading which gives them their proper value restores to the rest their sense of delicate and gracious awe. Milton's own dove-like mind, freed from its carrier-business in the conflicts of the day, brooded on the abyss where, as another poet said, Imagination dwelt:

> Imagination—here the Power so-called
> Through sad incompetence of human speech,
> That awful Power—rose from the mind's abyss.

There is no space here to develop in more detail the dim picture of a lovelier—and not less lordly—Milton, which begins to emerge out of the dark shadows of his life and his poetry. He has been presented so often as a defiant, a tragic, a proud, and angry figure that it must take some time before this other figure can be accepted. It is not without defiance nor pride nor anger, but it has other things also. The young poet who was a follower of the Muse and Love (and whose love-poetry shocked Charles Lamb because it was too Dantean) does not lose all his beauty in his mature life. He was a human being and he wrote about human beings. He compressed into a line the hopeless misery of a man fighting for the sake of his own profit against inevitable Love—

> Warring in heaven against heaven's matchless King.

But he knew something of what the war and the abandonment of the war were like in his own soul. The reception of the Powell family into his house may not have been unconnected with the abandonment of the war. He has been blamed, not without justice, for his continual insistence on the subordination of women to men. We have changed all that. Yet even in that the subordination is to be within Love—and love. Eve's submission is but part of her passion. When she is not in love she loses the submission; when she recovers passion she recovers obedience. Milton may have erred, as we all err, by formulating for everyday life laws only tolerable in rare paradisal states. But it was the passion of Paradise, and its comedy, which is the heart of his verse.

To believe that, about both his verse and his life, will take some time, so accustomed are we to the organ-throated egotist. We have made Milton's controversial prose the measure of his natural and his poetic breath, but it is not so. His controversies were his duty; he surrendered to them what we must not call too much because he never thought of it so—his time and his sight. As a reward he has been turned into their image. It is to be admitted that there was a good deal of their image in him; he enjoyed fighting, he had a pride, he formulated laws too easily, and too hastily supposed that the people with whom he disagreed were wrong rather than himself. But his youth had been bright with shyness, chastity, and love; and as he came through the dark 'bottom of the monstrous world' the light of that youth was still about him. His sonorous battles were perhaps more sonorously abusive than we like because he felt them as his arduous business rather than his passionate joy. He exhibited and practised goodwill; he put up with things. He has been bravely thanked; he has been given three centuries of compulsory misplaced admiration to put up with. We have been educated on him long enough; it is almost time that we read him, which, it seems, we have hardly yet begun to do.

JOHN MILTON

An introduction to the World's Classics edition of his poems, 1940[1]

We have been fortunate enough to live at a time when the reputation of John Milton has been seriously attacked. The result of this attack, which has come from various sources otherwise not noticeably sympathetic with each other, has been to distract the orthodox defenders of Milton, and to compel the reconsideration everywhere of his power as a poet. This reconsideration of poetic glory has now reached everyone but Shakespeare—and, it seems, the metaphysicals and W. B. Yeats. All these, it is true, are united by one general tendency—the tendency to suggest, by one means or another, 'the feeling intellect' of which Wordsworth spoke. It has been because of his supposed lack of that intellect that Milton has been chiefly repudiated. He has been supposed to be a heavy and, if resounding, yet, one might say, a comatose poet. He has been called, personally, a bad man. Mr. Middleton Murry has said so in so many words: 'On the moral and spiritual side I find it easy enough to place him; he is, simply, a bad man of a very particular kind.' But Mr. Murry went on to profess himself puzzled: 'The difficulty is . . . that a poet so evidently great in some valid sense of the word, should have so little intimate meaning for us. We cannot make him real. He does not, either in his great effects or his little ones, trouble our depths.'[2]

The success of such an attack—I do not suggest that that particular demonstration was confined to Mr. Murry; I quote him because those sentences form a convenient and compact epigram of the Opposition—lay chiefly in two things: (i) the lack of power in the orthodox party; (ii) the chance that Mr. Eliot had, about the same time, defined certain weaknesses in Milton. The orthodox Chairs of Literature, it must be admitted, had for long professed the traditional view of an august, solemn, proud, and (on the whole) unintelligent and uninteresting Milton. Professor Oliver Elton had already committed himself to the hint that Milton's subject could not concern us. 'What is made of the central myth? Does it in Milton's hands embody some enduring truth that speaks to the imagination? I doubt it.'[3] The great academic teachers confined themselves to analyses of his diction and his rhythm. Remote from us (they, in fact, declared) was his pre-empted Eden; the pride of his Satan was his own pride, and he approved it. They argued over

[1] This essay repeats a point or so from the previous article, but in general the two are complementary. A. R.

[2] *Studies in Keats*, second edition.

[3] *The English Muse.*

his Arianism or his Calvinism. They confined his instrument to the organ. They denied him cheerfulness and laughter (he who, it is said, used to sing while he had the gout!). They gloomed over him, as (they supposed) he, in his arrogant self-respect, gloomed over the world.

In the midst of this monotonous and uncritical praise, there emerged the calm voice of Mr. Eliot commenting on their subject —already admitted by them to be, to all intents and purposes, poetically alien from us. The present writer, disagreeing firmly with the effect of Mr. Eliot and indeed with some of Mr. Eliot, may admit his gratitude to Mr. Eliot for one or two critical statements. But 'the corrupt following' of Mr. Eliot went to lengths which Mr. Eliot (so far as I know) never suggested. Some writer—I have forgotten whom and I certainly will not look him up—said that Mr. Eliot had 'destroyed Milton in a parenthesis'. In fact, it might be permissible to say that no critic of Milton ought to be uninformed of Mr. Eliot's article, 'A Note on the Verse of John Milton'.[1] I shall not discuss it here, because, frankly, I wish to discuss Milton; it is why other distinguished critics must also be ignored.

The general opposition resolved itself into four statements: (i) that Milton was a bad man; (ii) that Milton was, especially, a proud man and was continually writing approvingly about his own pride (Blake's incorrect epigram—that Milton 'was of the devil's party without knowing it'—was generally used here); (iii) that Milton's verse is hard, sonorous, and insensitive; (iv) that Milton's subject was remote and uninteresting. This being almost exactly what the orthodox party had been, for centuries, saying with admiration, they were quite helpless when they found it said with contempt. The solemn rituals in praise of Milton were suddenly profaned by a change of accent, but the choruses had not altered; what then were the pious worshippers to do?

There had been, of course, another possibility all along; it may be put very briefly by saying that Milton was not a fool. The peculiar ignorance of Christian doctrine which distinguished most of the academic Chairs and of the unacademic journalists who had been hymning Milton had not prevented them from arguing about the subtle theological point of the Nature of the Divine Son in *Paradise Lost*. The peculiar opposition to high speculations on the nature of chastity felt in both academic and unacademic circles had prevented any serious appreciation of that great miracle of the transmutation of the flesh proposed in *Comus*. And the peculiar ignorance of morals also felt everywhere had enabled both circles to assume that Milton might be proud and that yet he might not at

[1] *Essays and Studies*, 1937.

the same time believe that pride was wrong and foolish. It was never thought that, if he sinned, he might repent, and that his repentance might be written as high in his poetry as, after another manner, Dante's in his. Finally, it was not supposed, in either of those circles, that Satan could be supposed to be Satan, and therefore a tempter; that Christ (in *Paradise Regained*) could be supposed to hold human culture a poor thing in comparison with the salvation of the soul; or that Samson, in the last great poem, could in fact reach a point of humility at which he could bring himself occasionally to protest like Job against the apparent dealings of God with the soul.

I have said nothing here against the explicit denial to Milton of any drama or of any humanity. Those denials, as well as the others, had been consecrated by custom and a false *pietas*. Yet there was no need for them. The great and sensitive poetry of that august genius had escaped his admirers. 'Milton', said Landor, 'wrote English like a learned language'; no one had thought it worth while to learn it as a living language. All *Paradise Lost* was supposed to be an image of pride; and yet much of *Paradise Lost* can be felt to revolve, laughingly and harmoniously, round the solemn and helpless image of pride. To discuss this in full would need a volume. All that can be done here is to dwell on a few chief points in the discussion of *Paradise Lost*, with one or two comments on the other poems. And we may begin with *Comus*.

Comus is a kind of philosophical ballet. Comus himself is, no doubt, a black enchanter, but he talks the most beautiful poetry, and he does not seriously interrupt the dance of the three young creatures opposed to him, with their heavenly attendant: there is a particular evasion of violence (when Comus is 'driven in'). But what is this ritual ballet about? It is about an attempted outrage on a Mystery. The mystery which Comus desires to profane is the Mystery of Chastity. It is no use trying to deal with *Comus* and omitting chastity; *Hamlet* without the Prince would be an exciting melodrama compared to the result of that other eviction. Chastity (not only, though perhaps chiefly, that particular form of it which is Virginity; it will be observed that Sabrina, the chaste goddess, is particularly favourable to herds and shepherd life) is the means, in *Comus*, by which all evils are defeated, the flesh is transmuted, and a very high and particular Joy ensured. It may be true that we ourselves do not believe that to be so, but our disbelief is largely as habitual as our admiration of *Comus*. That is why it has been possible to admire *Comus* without any serious realization of the mystery of chastity, in spite of John Milton.

> To him that dares
> Arm his profane tongue with contemptuous words

> Against the Sun-clad power of Chastity,
> Fain would I something say, yet to what end? . . .

And that, as one may say, is that. Comus is a fool in these matters, and

> worthy that thou should'st not know
> More happiness than is thy present lot.

But the Lady and her brothers and the Attendant Spirit and Sabrina do know. They know that Chastity is the guardian and protector of fruitfulness, that Temperance is the means of intense Joy. In their eyes Comus, by refusing to admit the general principle of things and to be obedient to it, is foolishly and sinfully limiting the nature of Joy. He prefers drunkenness to the taste of wine and promiscuousness to sensitiveness. He knows nothing about that other power which can make the flesh itself immortal; he prefers to sit about in sepulchres. Let him, cries the whole lovely dance.

Obedience then and Joy are the knowledge, in their degree, of those three Youths of *Comus*. And *Paradise Lost*, following long after, did not forget its prelude. It dealt with the same subject, but differently. Obedience, in the longer poem, is no longer that of a particular devotion to a particular law; it is the proper order of the universe in relation to a universal law, the law of self-abnegation in love. This, like chastity, is a mystery, but a mystery so simple that only the two sublimely innocent figures of Adam and Eve—beautiful, august, pure, and lucid—are able to express it; they, and the glowing fires of the celestial hierarchy; they, and beyond them the passionate deity of the Divine Son. It is not only a law—something that ought to be obeyed—but a fact—something that obeys and is obeyed. There remains, nevertheless, the possibility of disobedience to the law, of revolt against the fact. That disobedience depends on choice; and it is that choice on which the poem concentrates.

Comus had not gone so far. There is challenge there but no analysis of choice. Indeed, that is a problem which has been very rarely attacked in English verse. Generally the poets have confined themselves, sooner or later, to showing the decision; and certainly the actual motion of the will in its pure essence is inconceivable by the human imagination. Even Shakespeare, in *Macbeth*, when he reached that point, disguised it; Macbeth is half-determined; he asks if he will be safe; and when he is assured of safety he finds that he is wholly determined. But the actual decision is not there. Twice in *Paradise Lost* Milton attempted that problem: the first effort is contracted into Satan's speech on Niphates (iv. 32–113); the second is expanded into Eve's temptation, which begins with her dream (v. 8–135) and ends with the sensual degradation of her and Adam, so that the two of them, in another sense than *Comus* had foreseen, are 'lingering and sitting by a new-made grave'. Her temptation certainly is greater than that of her younger sister, the Lady, though it depends on the same method of flattery. To be praised and lured aside by such lines as 'love-darting eyes or tresses like the morn' is well enough; but Eve needs a lordlier and more subtle, even a more metaphysical, attraction:

> Wonder not, sovran Mistress, if perchance
> Thou canst, who art sole Wonder.

This flattery is, however, of the same kind as Satan has previously, one may say, offered to himself; and, in a lesser degree, to the angels whom he persuades to follow him, in that speech (v. 796–802) which is the nearest thing in English poetry to Antony's speech in *Julius Caesar*, though Milton's lines are perhaps even more highly wrought, as they had to be, the speech being shorter. Every word echoes another; each accent is calculated—'magnific titles . . . merely titular', and so on. The aim in all three instances is the same; it is the awakening, in Satan, in Eve, in the angels, of a sense of proper dignity, of self-admiration, of rights withheld, of injured merit. This, it is asserted, Milton himself felt about himself. Perhaps; but if he did, then he certainly also thought it foolish and wrong. We need not fall back on any exterior evidence for that nor on any exposition of Christian morals; the evidence is in the poem itself. Satan thinks himself impaired, and what is the result? 'deep malice thence conceiving and disdain'. He is full of injured merit; what is the result? 'high disdain'. He is the full example of the self-loving spirit, and his effort throughout the poem is to lure everyone, Eve, Adam, the angels, into that same state of self-love. His description of himself in the first two books is truthful enough—

> that fixt mind
> And high disdain from sense of injured merit
> That with the mightiest raised me to contend. . . .

But it is also ironical. Certainly Satan has this sense; only this sense has landed him in hell—and in inaccuracy. Hell is always inaccurate. He goes on to say of the Omnipotence that he and his followers 'shook his throne': it is only afterwards that we discover that this is entirely untrue. Milton knew as well as we do that Omnipotence cannot be shaken; therefore the drama lies not in that foolish effort but in the terror of the obstinacy that provoked it, and in the result; not in the flight but in the fall. The irrepressible laughter of heaven at the solemn antics of 'injured merit', of the 'self impair'd', breaks out. Love laughs at anti-love.

> 'Nearly it now concerns us to be sure
> Of our Omnipotence' . . .
> To whom the Son, with calm aspect and clear

> Lightning divine, ineffable, serene,
> Made answer: 'Mighty Father, thou thy foes
> Justly hast in derision.'

In fact, the rebel angels only get as far through heaven as they do because God precisely suspends their real impairment—

> What sin hath impaired, which yet hath wrought
> Insensibly, for I suspend their doom.

So much for Milton's approval of the self-loving spirit. He thought pride, egotism, and a proper sense of one's own rights the greatest of all temptations; he was, no doubt, like most people, subject to it. And he thought it led straight to inaccuracy and malice, and finally to idiocy and hell. Milton may sometimes have liked to think of himself as proud, but it is extraordinarily unlikely that he liked to think of himself as malicious and idiotic. Yet it is those two qualities he attributes to Satan as a result of his energy of self-love. When Satan sees Eve:

> Her graceful Innocence, her every air
> Of gesture or least action overawed
> His malice . . .
> That space the Evil one abstracted stood
> From his own evil, and for the time remained
> Stupidly good.

It is not, however, Eve alone who is the image of some state of being opposite to Satan's. It is all the rest of the poem, but especially it is the Divine Son. Precisely as the mark of Satan and the rebel angels is that they will not consent to be derived from anyone else; he will have it that he was like Topsy and grew by himself; so the mark of the Son, of the angels, of Adam, of Eve, is that they derive, and take delight in deriving, from someone else. Their joy is in that derivation-in-love. The Divine Son carries it into the highest state—

> this I my glory account,
> My exaltation and my whole delight,
> That thou in me well pleased declar'st thy will
> Fulfilled, which to fulfil is all my bliss.

So Eve, in a state of passionate and pure love, to Adam:

> My author and disposer, what thou bid'st
> Unargued I obey.

Milton had his own views on the relation between the sexes, which (like almost any other views of the relation between the sexes) were probably wrong. But this last quotation does not spring from that only; it springs from the essential fact of things; which is everywhere this derivation-in-love. The Son is the Image of that, as Satan is the Image of personal clamour for personal independence. The casting-out of the rebel angels from heaven is the result of the conflict between the two Images—in so far as there can be any conflict between the state which is in utter union with Omnipotence and the state which is only in union with itself—if that, and the Niphates speech suggests that it is not even that. The obstinate figure of Satan does but throw up the intertwined beauty and lightness of the universe beyond him, the universe (and more than the universe) which understands, enjoys, and maintains, its continuous derivation, lordship, and obedience.

In this sense, therefore, the poem is concerned with a contrast and a conflict between two states of being. But those states are not only mythological; they are human and contemporary, and thus the poem has a great deal of interest for us. The overthrow of the rebel angels is the overthrow, spiritually, of all in whom that deriving and nourishing Love is dead. The very blaze of eyes from the chariot in which the Divine Son rides is the spectacle of a living and stupendous universe rolling on the 'exhausted' rebels. There needs no battle; the exposition of the Divine Nature is enough.

> Sole Victor, from the expulsion of his foes,
> Messias his triumphal chariot turned.

It is we who are involved, one way or the other: it is not only to Adam that the Archangel's word is addressed—'Remember, and fear to transgress'.[1]

Paradise Lost then is chiefly concerned with the choice between these two states of being, with the temptations which provoke men and women to that sense of 'injured merit', as Eve and Satan are provoked, and with the terrible result of indulging that sense. It is true that John Milton was not a man for compromise. When Adam, in the fullness of his passion for Eve, really does abandon heaven and his knowledge of God for her, Milton denounced his act. But it was, after all, Milton who imagined his passion so intensely as to make us almost wish that it could be approved. There and elsewhere *Paradise Lost* is full of the senses—even Shakespeare hardly made the human hand more moving. This would perhaps be more obvious if we were more attentive to the tenderness of some of the verse. It is no doubt as a result of the long tradition of the organ-music of Milton that the shyness of some of his verse passes unnoticed. The famous prayer to 'justify the ways of God to man' is a prayer of humility. This is seen by considering the lines that lead up to it. Milton, invoking the Holy Spirit, says:

[1] 'The self-loving man', wrote Pascal about the same time as Milton wrote *Paradise Lost*, 'conceives a mortal enmity against that truth which reproves him. . . . He would annihilate it, but, unable to destroy it in its essence, he destroys it as far as possible in his own knowledge and in that of others.'—'Warring in heaven against heaven's *matchless* king'; *matchless* is the whole point.

Thou from the first
Wast present, and with mighty wings outspread
Dove-like sat'st brooding on the vast Abyss
And mad'st it pregnant: what in me is dark
Illumine . . . .

And so on. Now the point is that 'Dove-like' and 'pregnant' are words which cannot be sonorous and tremendous; it would make nonsense of them emotionally. The passage is daring in its hope, but shyly and modestly daring, palpitating with its own wonder at its own audacity. Milton may have been proud on earth (and repented of it), but he was not proud in his approach to heaven.

There is another word, at the other end of the poem, which is another example of a certain misreading. The renewed and repentant passion of Eve for Adam expresses itself.

In me is no delay; with thee to go
Is to stay here, without thee here to stay
Is to go hence unwilling; thou to me
Art all things under heaven, all places thou,
Who for my wilful crime art banished hence.

This again is derivation (she from him and he from her), and the knowledge of derivation. After which outbreak of human love, the lines sink again into a shy softness of hope.

This further consolation yet secure
I carry hence; though all by me is lost,
Such favour I unworthy am vouchsafed,
By me the promised Seed shall all restore.

'The promised Seed' is, of course, Christ. But Milton did not choose to use any such august title. He preferred, there, the word Seed, and the literal meaning is not to be forgotten in the metaphorical. The metaphorical refers back to the glorious, devoted, self-abandoned figure—glorious because self-abandoned—which has again and again been deliberately contrasted with Satan throughout the poem; I need name only the pause in heaven and the pause in hell (ii. 417–29; iii. 217–26), the two progresses through Chaos (ii. 871–1033; vii. 192–221; and the Chaos is not only exterior; it is also the interior chaos of the human soul); and, of course, the conflict in heaven. But the literal meaning of 'Seed' is of the new, tiny, important thing, the actuality of the promise, the almost invisible activity upon which all depends. So small, so intimate, so definite, is the word that the line becomes breathless with it and with the hope of it. That breathless audacity of purpose towards the beginning of the poem is answered by a breathless audacity of expectation towards the end. And at the very end humanity has its turn in the hand again, the hand which has meant so much at certain crises of the poem: at the separation, as if symbolically, of a derived love from its source—

So saying, from her husband's hand her hand
Soft she withdrew;

and in the sin (the derived love working against its human and Divine sources):

So saying, her rash hand in evil hour
Forth reaching to the fruit, she plucked, she ate;

and so now in the rejoined union of that penitence and humility which Milton knew so well:

They hand in hand with wandering steps and slow
Through Eden took their solitary way.

There are no linked lovers in our streets who are not more beautiful and more fortunate because of those last lines; no reunion, of such a kind, which is not more sad and more full of hope. And then it is said that Milton is inhuman. The whole of our visibility, metaphysical, psychological, actual, has been increased by him.

It is the word 'solitary', however, which looks forward to the last two poems—to *Paradise Regained* and to *Samson*. The first is completely different from *Paradise Lost*. The verse is, on the whole, less infinitely sensitive than that of the earlier poem; it is already changing to something else. There are few personages; in the earlier there had been many. They are brooding rather than active. And whereas in *Paradise Lost* everything had been exposed from the beginning, now the chief thing is hidden. The centre had previously been a spectacle; now it is a secret. The Blessed Virgin is in a state of expectation:

his absence now
Thus long to some great purpose he observes.

Christ himself waits:

to what intent
I learn not yet, perhaps I need not know.
For what concerns my knowledge God reveals.

The urgency is in Satan, but even he is here haunted by the unknown: 'who this is we must learn.'

It is the discovery of this nature, which Satan does not know, and which Christ only half-knows, that is the theme of the poem. Christ's answers to Satan's efforts to find out are, in a sense, riddles, for they are given half in his own terms and half in Satan's. Food; glory; kingdoms; earthly wisdom—these are the temptations; through all of them, in Milton's phrase,

the Son of God
Went on and stayed not.

He goes on—or in ('into himself descended'). It is precisely into his

Nature that the argument plunges to seek its discovery, but the moral trials are hardly enough; at the end Milton used something else. He came to the mysterious 'standing'; moral temptation is lost in what lies behind it. 'Stand or cast thyself down': be whatever you are. But the answer is still a riddle; it has precisely the lightness, almost the happiness, certainly the heavenly mockery which is always the answer to the hellish sneer. Satan is as hopelessly foolish as ever, and Jesus speaks to him, in the technique of this poem, as the Divine Son had spoken of him to the Father in the *Paradise Lost*:

> To whom the Son with calm aspect and clear
> Lightning divine, ineffable, serene,
> Made answer.
>
> To whom thus Jesus: Also it is written
> Tempt not the Lord thy God; he said and stood.
> But Satan, smitten with amazement, fell.

He and his had been in the same case before—

> They astonished all resistance lost,
> All courage; down their idle weapons dropped . . .
> Exhausted, spiritless, afflicted, fallen.

'So, strook with dread and anguish, fell the Fiend.' Heaven is always unexpected to the self-loving spirit; he can never understand whence it derives, for he has himself renounced all derivation, as do those who follow him. It was this great and fundamental fact of human existence which Milton very well understood; it was this which his genius exerted all his tenderness and all his sublimity to express; it was this which is the cause of the continual laughter of *Paradise Lost*, and it was because of this that Milton invoked that Spirit which Itself derives from the co-equal Two.

It is not possible in the remaining space to discuss *Samson*. The verse again has changed, and I doubt if we have yet properly learnt its style. 'A little onward lend thy guiding hand'—to what? To the 'acquist Of true experience from this great event'. What then is our true experience from the poem? Much every way; perhaps not the least is the sense of the union of Necessity and Freewill. That had been discussed in *Paradise Lost*, as an accompaniment to the spectacle and analysis of man choosing. But there the actual stress had been a little on the choice; here it is a little on 'dire Necessity'. Here 'the cherub Contemplation' is allowed even fuller view. The persons, if they do not exactly accuse God, at least indicate to God the unanswered questions. There is no humility in refraining from asking the questions; the humility consists in believing that there may be an answer. Both asking and believing are desirable, and both are here. In the earlier poems the sense of a full comprehension had been chiefly felt in the Figure of the Divine Son—and therefore either in heaven or (if among men) then prophesied for the future. But in *Samson* there is more than a hint that the great satisfaction of all distresses is already there. It is perhaps not by a poetic accident that here and there in the poem Milton wrote like Shakespeare; in other places, like himself with a new song. The modest and appealing courage of the opening of *Paradise Lost*—'and justify the ways of God to man'—becomes an angelic beauty of victory—

> Just are the ways of God,
> And justifiable to men,
> Unless there be who think not God at all.
> If any be, they walk obscure,
> For of such doctrine never was there school
> But the heart of the fool,
> And no man therein doctor but himself.

That is precisely Satan—and men and women. But 'Nothing is here for tears' is here no Stoic maxim, but something beyond—something 'comely and reviving'.

The phrase would cover most of Milton. So far from being granite, his verse is a continual spring of beauty, of goodness, of tenderness, of humility. The one thing he always denounced as sin and (equally) as folly was the self-closed 'independent' spirit, the spirit that thinks itself of 'merit', especially 'of injured merit'. It does not seem a moral entirely without relevance to us. All things derive in love—and beyond all things, in the only self-adequate Existence, there is the root of that fact, as of all. It is known in God; the Father speaks—

> and on his Son with rays direct
> Shone full; he all his Father manifest
> Ineffably into his face received,
> And thus the Filial Godhead answering spake.

'Filial . . . answering.' Milton has been too long deprived of half his genius. He did his best to make clear what he was saying. But then, as his admirer John Dryden wrote:

> Dim as the borrowed beams of moon and stars
> To lonely, weary, wandering travellers
> Is Reason to the soul.

TWO BRIEF ESSAYS ON SHAKESPEARIAN TOPICS

1. Time and Tide *review of* Shakespeare and the Popular Dramatic Tradition, *by S. L. Bethell, 1944*

Two things in Mr. Bethell's book warmed me egotistically to it. The first was that I once wrote a line of verse:

> Let the hazel
> of verse measure the multifold levels of unity.

It is a similar experience of what he calls 'multi-consciousness' in dramatic art of which Mr. Bethell is writing. The second thing was that his book to some extent discusses the relation of the cinema to our dramatic tradition, about which I once wanted to write a different book. In a sense, the awareness of this relation itself constitutes a minor example of multi-consciousness. It is agreeable, while watching a gangster film, to be aware of Kyd and Tourneur; or, to be exact, since Kyd and Tourneur had more to them, let us say of *Titus Andronicus*. If Aaron in that youthful melodrama is not a cinema villain, who is?

The central theme of Mr. Bethell's book is, if not new, yet interesting and valuable. He asserts 'that there *is* a popular dramatic tradition, and that its dominant characteristic is the audience's ability to respond spontaneously and unconsciously on more than one plane of attention at the same time'. Thus, an Elizabethan audience enjoyed being reminded that it was only watching a play, whereas our convention is to be persuaded that we are watching something actual. Similarly with the ladies who disguise themselves as youths—'probably the situation of "boy playing girl playing boy" pleased in its suggestion of multiple planes of reality'. Similarly, Touchstone is to be regarded as both 'fool and wit'; the 'audience is required to . . . keep the two strands of attention separate', as it is with Claudius when he suddenly changes from a villain to a royal hero in the Laertes scene.

These are small instances. Mr. Bethell proceeds to larger. He might almost be commenting on the relation to Shakespeare of a famous passage of Keats: 'Coleridge would let go a fine isolated verisimilitude caught from the Penetralium of mystery, from being incapable of remaining content with half-knowledge.' Some such verisimilitudes are everywhere in Shakespeare, and were (to a greater extent than we realize) apprehended by the audience. Where we should think a play's characters inconsistent, the Elizabethans did not worry. They were not thinking first of psychology, but of poetry. Thus Prospero 'seems to represent divine providence', but he has 'human imperfections'; 'the audience needs to attend to two diverse aspects of the same character: the representational and the symbolic'.

With this instrument Mr. Bethell proceeds to open the oysters of certain plays, and produce the secreted pearls. Here his multi-consciousness leaves me dubious. But even before that I find myself asking whether it is necessary to denigrate the other tradition, the naturalistic play, quite so severely. Why may we not enjoy ourselves in two different ways at two different times? I do not suggest that, in fact, Mr. Bethell denies this, but he rather leaves a low impression of the naturalistic play. Surely we may sometimes enjoy a play with several aspects and sometimes a play with one aspect?

I doubt if the wildest supporter of the dramatic unities ever fundamentally intended to persuade his audience that a play was not a play; he wished for that particular delight which arises from compressing the whole representation into one action at one time in one place. I particularly enjoy a murder story which does the same thing—when crime and solution happen in the same room in the same two hours. The Renaissance writers discovered that this was in fact as delightful as the Greeks had known it to be, and they were delighted. And in the *Tempest* Shakespeare liked it himself. The more pleasures the better.

Mr. Bethell, however, having been haughty with the Renaissance, proceeds to be firm with the Victorians. He writes: 'Hotspur would "pluck bright honour from the pale-faced moon". Although in the last century considered poetical, this line is meaningless rant.' Overlooking the fact that what Hotspur really says is that he *feels* as if it would be easy to . . . and so forth, what is the matter with the line? And as for Prince Henry 'not taking Hotspur seriously', because he makes fun of him—

> I do not think a braver gentleman . . .
> More daring or more bold is now alive
> To grace this latter age with noble deeds.

Mr. Bethell has overlooked this as an example of 'multi-consciousness'.

The difficulty, of course, between Mr. Bethell and myself is that he sees significance where I do not, and I see greatness where he does not. He says that the verse spoken by Caesar in *Antony and Cleopatra* is 'dull, flat, and impersonal'. Perhaps a little impersonal, but dull and flat? And 'calculating meanness' in Caesar, in him who represents the domestic virtues and the world-peace for which we now are longing? I allow certainly that the verse of the lovers is more magnificent; I doubt if it is more moving. It is because Caesar is what he is that I feel Mr. Bethell's multi-consciousness of the play does not go far enough; Rome may be opposed to Egypt, but to say that 'the good life may be built upon the Egyptian but not upon the Roman values' is denying the very synthesis the play requires. It is Caesar who speaks of Antony—

> my brother, my competitor
> In top of all design.

And, if it comes to multi-consciousness, there is a profound metaphysical meaning in this. Of the two, it is Caesar and the universe who have a place for Antony, and Antony who has no place for Caesar and the universe.

So with even deeper problems. The trouble about Shakespeare is that he is both Christian and non-Christian, and it is fatal to call him either. The transcendental note in *Lear*—in 'the gods', in Cordelia, and in Albany—is of things happening; the words 'clear' and 'rare' which are scattered over the later plays have the exquisiteness of fact and not of doctrine. It has been said that Shakespeare expressed supernatural values in natural terms; it is as far as we ought to go. When Mr. Bethell says that 'it is quite evident that the paganism of *King Lear* is a deliberate reconstruction, planned for comparative appraisal in relation to the Christian world', he is dragging the whole thing into other terms of reference. Let us—O let us leave that great ambiguous figure, his own ambiguity! 'It seems more than likely that, in this constant association of Cordelia with Christian doctrine, Shakespeare wished to suggest the foreshadowing of Christ in pure natures before His coming.' I cannot but feel (asking Mr. Bethell's pardon) that we are in grave danger when we talk so; we do better to confine ourselves to Shakespeare's own line—these are 'the unpublish'd virtues of the earth', and their publication in him had better be left to his own terminology. Mr. Bethell may retort that they were 'unpublish'd' before Christ, and that 'it seems more than likely' that Shakespeare meant it so. I do not like to suggest that 'it seems more than likely', on page 60, has become 'it is quite evident' on p. 61; but that is the dreadful danger. In Dante, no doubt, Beatrice is an illustration of Christ; it would be truer to say that, while reading Shakespeare, Christ is an illustration of Cordelia—and out of the 'Penetralium of mystery' at that. We ought to remain content with 'half-knowledge'; the 'irritable reaching' after identity of doctrine is as dangerous on one side as on the other. The plays are the cloudy frontier where much meets, and their definitions are always and only in themselves.

2. Time and Tide *review of* The Fortunes of Falstaff, *by John Dover Wilson, 1943*

QUITE the most astonishing thing about Dr. Dover Wilson's book is that it should be necessary. I had thought that criticism had long since abandoned the high view of Falstaff and the low view of the Prince; that it had accepted the culmination of *Henry IV* to be where Shakespeare put it—in the appearance of King Henry; and that—sad as we might feel at the line 'Go, carry Sir John Falstaff to the Fleet'—we recognized it as inevitable, as we might if our personal friends were involved; that we knew the greater romanticism of duty must overthrow the lesser romanticism of dalliance, and the greater poetry of the citizen the lesser prose of the individualist. But Dr. Dover Wilson says it is not so. He declares that most critics are still misled by their own 'idleness', and we must believe him. His book, in that case, is not only instructive but important, and all of us true believers should warmly welcome it. The following remarks are meant rather in support than in review.

One of the original critical errors was to underrate the importance of the Prince throughout. It is not always observed that it is the Prince who keeps Falstaff possible to us in the freedom of intellectual enjoyment. It is the Prince, for example, who prevents the Gadshill robbery from being too serious. 'The money shall be paid back again with advantage.' It is the Prince who 'procures this fat rogue a charge of foot', and in the battle blames him for idleness—'What! is't a time to jest and dally now?'—but (for all the Gadshill episode) raises no question of bravery, and thus in the swift crashing passage prevents us raising it. It is, in short, the Prince who, through all the First Part, prevents us receiving the full realistic impact of Falstaff's behaviour.

It might be argued that it is unfair in Shakespeare to manage his play so, and then to demand of us a full apprehension of that behaviour. But it is more likely that we do not wish to live up to the energy of Shakespeare's own imagination. He could do more than one thing at once. The first great speech of the Prince defined the situation:

> I know you all, and will awhile uphold
> The unyoked humours of your idleness.

The phrase is precise. Falstaff is 'unyoked'; he is 'idle'. It is his idleness, and the Prince's idleness, and our idleness, which enjoys the 'unyoking', the putting off responsibility (especially when the Prince secretly makes himself responsible for seeing that the 'unyoking' does no great damage). And had Falstaff understood the limitations of this, there need have been no terrific rejection. Other favourites might have understood, might have kept quiet and waited to be sent for, might have refrained from thrusting themselves on to 'formal majesty' at its most explicit moment. But Shakespeare did not choose to let Falstaff be so intelligent. He raised vulgarity to its highest pitch and loosed it straight at the 'golden rigol' of the Crown. What is Henry supposed to do? Did *he* ask Falstaff to come and shout at him? He promises him an income and (if possible) promotion. The scene (if Shakespeare chose) was inevitable; that he did choose shows only that he was more daring in poetry than we.

It is perhaps worth remarking that Falstaff and his company are not the only 'unyoked humours' in the play. Hotspur is another. The 'honour' about which Hotspur makes such a song and dance is his own 'humour'. He unyokes his humour everywhere. Worcester rebukes him for 'defect of manners, want of government'. The State can no more afford to have Hotspur loose than Falstaff. It is their looseness which is the danger; it is (like it or not) the responsibility of government—say, of behaviour—which lies on the King. 'How characteristically muddle-headed', Dr. Dover Wilson justly observes, 'it is that a generation which has almost universally condemned a prince of its own for putting private inclinations before his public obligations should condemn Hal as a cad and a prig for doing just the opposite.'

Dr. Dover Wilson follows the fortunes of Falstaff in detail through both Parts, and shows how consistent the whole thing is. He points out how much juster an estimate Johnson held than many later critics—particularly Morgann and Bradley. But of course Johnson never forgot that all we have is the play. If we think of Henry as a cad and a prig, we either mean that Shakespeare deliberately drew a cad and a prig, or that Shakespeare did not know a cad and a prig, or that the Elizabethan notions of caddishness and priggery were different from ours. The first is impossible, on the evidence; the second is possible, but unlikely; the third is (in this particular) not very likely. We have too much used his characters to make nonsense of Shakespeare; the poor fellow might have been, like any modern novelist, the helpless victim of his own people. Imagine Burbage saying: 'But, Bill, why have Falstaff at the Coronation at all?' And Bill replying: 'I can't help it; he would do it. We creative artists are the servants of our creations.' Fortunately there is nothing to show that Shakespeare thought of himself as a creative artist or that he would not have stood up to the responsibilities of his own work.

Every reader will be instructed by Dr. Dover Wilson according to his own needs. The two points which I have myself found notable are (first) the relation of Falstaff to the old Riot of the Interludes and of Henry to the traditional Prodigal Prince. It was, of course, always clear that the situation and the characters were ancient enough, but it is worth having our memories revived. The second point is the suggestion that the Prince, gilding the lie 'with the happiest terms I have', supported Falstaff's claim to have killed Hotspur. Dr. Dover Wilson claims that this imposture explains Sir John's increased prestige as a soldier and courtier in Part II. I am not entirely convinced, but I willingly allow the ingenuity of the suggestion; only I should have expected Shakespeare, as usual, to have made clear what was happening. What is certainly true is that the Prince is much less of a blanket in Part II; the deeds of Falstaff are covered only by his own wit. But it is the deeds and not the wit that break out in 'Let us take any man's horses; the laws of England are at my commandment'. It is with this in its brain that, in Dr. Dover Wilson's phrase, 'the great red face breaks in upon [the King's] "white celestial thought"'. But the phrase must not weaken Henry; it is our fault if we misjudged Shakespeare's writing. The rejection, wrote Lascelles Abercrombie, 'reveals Henry to us as formidably as Odysseus was revealed to the suitors when he stript off his rags and shot Antinous'.

ALEXANDER POPE

Time and Tide *article on the centenary of his death, reviewing the Twickenham edition of his Poems, 1944*

He died on 30 May 1744, a man of fifty-five, and with his death the great effort at strong control began to cease. When he was born, poetry had not long emerged from what had been, to him and his peers, the Gothic world of the Elizabethans; when he died, there was approaching, though fifty years off, the alien enthusiastic world of the Romantics. There were, certainly, to be other barriers—notably, the *Vanity of Human Wishes.* There the couplet was to be still strong and ordered. But the central effort was over. Its champion, himself bitterly describing the triumph of his more foolish enemies, died, though his reputation was still a standard for those of his own kind. Seventy years afterwards, Byron looked back to him as the last of the poets.

Byron, when he finally decided no longer to try and lose his head, but to keep it and allow it the scope it undoubtedly deserved, had some justice in his belief. The most extreme serious Romantic is bound to read, not only with respect and admiration, but even with a slight sense of danger and guilt, the great conclusion to the *Dunciad*. It is unfortunate that it is not only under the rule of Dullness that 'unawares, Morality expires'. Many unwise followers of strange stars have seen their meteors fall. The superstitious is too apt to accompany the supernatural. In the fervour of their new discoveries, the poets of the Romantic age were inclined to talk a little unfairly of their predecessors. They were wrong, though they had some excuse. Delighting in their own abandonment, they mocked at the self-possession of the earlier age. It has taken a long time before we can be equally fair to both poetic vocations. Our own age has seen De Selincourt's Wordsworth and this noble edition of Pope. He could himself have desired no greater tribute, nor any reader a more ample grace of scholarship and production.

The division between the two styles—in poetry and in the spirit—is no longer pressed too far. Passion must feel both abandonment and control. The Romantic beginnings have been traced so far back into the Augustan age that in fact they have ceased to be beginnings; there is merely continuity. The Earl of Rochester, who died in 1680, was already protesting—''Tis below sense, they tell you to admire'—against precisely what Pope was to say—'For Fools admire, but men of sense approve'; and again

> Whether we dread or whether we desire,
> In either case, believe me, we admire.

The approval of Pope might indeed be worth more than the admiration of Rochester. Yet Rochester voiced the protest of the Romantics more than a century later against the refused admiration:

> To an exact perfection they have brought
> The action Love; the passion is forgot.

In spite of this protest, the change had been necessary. The dream 'of Paradise and light' lasted long into the Augustan age; it is in Dryden's line 'A milk-white Hind, immortal and unchanged', and something of it is even in Pope's own lesser:

> —and hardly flows
> The freezing Tanais through a waste of snows.

But even this light had its dangers; enthusiasms sprang up in it, and the results of enthusiasm can be deadly, as we have every reason to know when an Enthusiast of our time has ruined Germany and another Italy. Control and Good Sense were necessary.

Pope was the climax of Good Sense—but meaning *Good* and meaning *Sense*. The image of it is the rhymed couplet. All great verse implies and exhibits a control of passion and intellect, but all verse does not exhibit it so clearly as the couplet; there one sees and hears it in full and apparent force. The couplet has been misunderstood. Miss Sitwell has justly said of it that 'the reason why, to an insensitive ear, the heroic couplet seems monotonous, is because structure alone, and not texture, has been regarded as the maker of rhythm'. Even its structure has been scamped. Thirty years ago, our teachers encouraged us to hurry to the rhyme. Correct that error, allow the lines to have their proper length, and therefore their interior distance, and the superb mastery becomes clear.

> Yet let me flap this bug with gilded wings,
> This painted child of dirt that stinks and stings—

hurry *that*, and the dreadful accuracy of power is lost. So with the softly breathed terror and defiance of

> She comes! she comes! the sable Throne behold—

or that couplet on the dunces which precedes the attack on Addison, and is only not quoted because it is not in the anthologies:

> How did they fume and stamp and roar and chafe,
> And swear, not Addison himself was safe.

The rhyme ordered, composed, and measured the distance; the two words of it are the eyes through which the reader sees the length. But the world seen there is not a narrow world, and is a dangerous.

> Thus good, or bad, to one extreme betray
> Th' unbalanced Mind and snatch the Man away;
> For Vertue's self may too much Zeal be had;
> The worst of Madmen is a Saint run mad.

No doubt this wise balance omitted much—Blake's Tyger, and the horrible churchyard of Cyril Tourneur, and Wesley preaching to the miners, and Christopher Smart writing 'Rejoice in the Lamb'. But saints had run mad too often, and had been followed by more madmen than saints, and by even more dunces—by 'all that on Folly Frenzy could beget'.

Pope knew precisely the danger, and defined it.

> Most Critics, fond of some subservient Art,
> Still make the Whole depend upon a Part:
> They talk of Principles, but Notions prize,
> And all to one lov'd Folly sacrifice.

Dunces do, and Romantics are apt to, fall into this serious error; everything must depend on their own gospel, and their gospel is mightily unwilling to be but a Part. It is true that when Pope followed St. John (the politician, not the apostle) into philosophy, he made no very good job of it. He explained that God, having ordained the laws of nature, could not stop a landslide because 'blameless Bethel' was in the way. It did not occur to him that when

God ordained landslides he must have foreseen Mr. Bethel's propinquity, so that the problem remains. Even Metaphysic leaning for aid on Sense is not perhaps so chaotic as Pope thought. No doubt also he was wrong in other things—in his 'notion' of Theobald, in his too-careless attack on scholars. But he had always the whole generalization in mind; he meant the universal as well as, and more than, the particular. He revised in that sense. Mr. John Butt points out that he omitted from his final version of the Addison lines two which were applicable only at the moment:

> Who, if two Wits on rival Themes contest,
> Approves of each, but likes the worst the best.

Not only does the removal do him personal honour, but it shows at what he was aiming. He meant to 'keep good humour still'.

'The life of Pope', Mr. Geoffrey Tillotson once wrote, 'is that of one who suffered intensely and yet was master.' He was perhaps occasionally betrayed into a 'dismal and illiberal' phrase. But the length of his lines gives scope for tenderness as well as taunts. The dying Narcissa sighs:

> One would not, sure, be frightful when one's dead:
> So—Betty, give this cheek a little red.

The lines are not merely ironical. Pope was one of the most realistic of poets; his couplets are felt in the blood and felt along the heart. It is this which backs, strengthens, and counteracts his satire.

> Yes, I am proud; I must be proud, to see
> Men not afraid of God afraid of me—

that is half-justified by his realism. There is something terribly like despair in him—

> Life can little more supply
> Than just to look about us and to die.

His battle for lucidity has the sense of a forlorn hope, and even there despair hovers. Literature was being destroyed. '"Art after Art goes out and all is night". Pope was exaggerating magnificently and he must have known it', says Mr. Sutherland, 'but the danger threatened.' Infinite dullness always threatens; our own duncehood always threatens.

He held down despair, dullness, folly, and enthusiasm by that wonder of his style, of which the rhymed couplet is a notable part. Both Miss Sitwell and Mr. Tillotson have praised his sense of beauty. The *Dunciad*, Miss Sitwell wrote, 'is just as beautiful in its own way, and just as strange, as the *Ancient Mariner*'; and Mr. Tillotson: 'No other poet has found his sense of beauty so closely and continuously allied to his sense of human values.' He died on 30 May 1744, but he was born on 22 May 1688; it is after all what matters.

REJOICE IN THE LAMB

Time and Tide *review of W. Force Stead's edition, 1939*

'THE manuscript [of this new work of Christopher Smart] consists of three folios, written on both sides, making twelve pages, and ten single sheets, written on both sides, making a further twenty pages, or thirty-two pages in all.' Mr. Force Stead says that the present owner, Colonel Carwardine Probert, 'believes they were left with the Reverend Thomas Carwardine (1734–1824) at Colne Priory by William Hayley'. They have remained there ever since until the courtesy of Colonel Probert and the editorial care of Mr. Force Stead made their contents available to the general public.

It is a little disturbing; what else may be hidden in the treasures of English country houses? We have enough great poetry to keep our poor minds busy, much more than we can do with, if truth were told. But there are a number of lines here one would be sorry to have missed; and at least one illumination: 'I bless God for two visions of Anne Hope's being in charity with me.' Lady Anne Vane, with whom Smart, at the age of thirteen, had proposed to elope, was then married to the Hon. Charles Hope Weir; Smart was also married, and poor, half-crazy, intermittently confined. Mr. Force Stead suggests, with probability, that the attachment to Anne counted for most in his life; he thinks that perhaps it was her marriage in 1746 which drove him, at the age of twenty-four, into a reckless dissipation. At least, fifteen years afterwards, he could write that line; it is as much as could be hoped between any two mortals. Plotinus four times experienced ecstasy, and Christopher Smart in the madhouse saw perfection twice.

The poem (so to call it) is a litany or *Benedicite* of the universe, interspersed with remarks, some accurate and some witty, and with private prayers. It wanders off at times into what seems nonsense and recovers itself suddenly into poetry and more. I take a few lines at random from different places:

> Let Jude bless with the Bream, who is of melancholy
> from his depth and serenity . . .
>
> Let Paul rejoice with the Seale, who is pleasant
> and faithful, like God's good Englishman . . .
>
> For in my nature I quested for beauty, but God,
> God hath sent me to sea for pearls . . .
>
> For to conceive with intense diligence against
> one's neighbour is a branch of witchcraft . . .
>
> Let Chloe rejoice with the Limpin—There is a
> way on the knees to the terrestrial Paradise . . .

I cannot remember any other document in English—except perhaps the manuscripts of Keats's poems—which so clearly shows poetry in a state of becoming. It lacks, of course, the necessary relationships within itself, and in that it falls below the Prophetic Books of Blake which are bound to occur to everyone as the nearest comparison. Their myth is consistent with itself, even if the figures of it are rarely convincing to us. But if the young Milton had become mentally distracted through one of his love affairs he might have produced something like Smart's verses. It will be remembered that in the *Midsummer Night's Dream* Hippolyta described poetry as 'something of great constancy, But howsoever, strange and admirable'. (I am aware that the preceding definition of Theseus is usually preferred, but as Theseus is completely wrong in his remarks about the lovers of the *Dream*, I have never understood why he should be supposed to be right on other points.) This draft poetry is strange and admirable; it lacks constancy, as is natural enough, considering the mental state of its author. But it recalls to the mind the great necessity of that virtue in Letters—the virtue at which the other, and greater, part of the eighteenth century was aiming; more than consistency—a power of holding all opposites together, 'constant to keep them so'.

The verse of that greater part, for example, civilized and moralized the menagerie of English poetry; they left it to Smart and Blake to be at once realistic and fantastic about the various animals of that menagerie. Pope would have been, even in an asylum, incapable of writing of the Beetle—'whose life is precious in the sight of God, though his appearance is against him'. But the two schools—the sane poets and the mad poets—to some extent enlighten each other; Pope's slain birds, who 'fall and leave their little lives in air', are the stranger for Smart's insects. And Smart's farrago of admirable wonders draws nearer to the point of 'constancy' through the constancy of the *Essay on Criticism.* It is pleasing to see that Smart wrote: 'For I bless the Lord Jesus for the memory of Pope, Gay, and Swift.' He had not apparently fallen into the mistake of the later Romantics who despised the Augustans because their passion was *different.*

The 'constancy' of the *Song to David* is noble but limited; the 'strangeness' of these lines is wider than that of the *Song*. Greek and Hebrew, inventions and philosophies, 'the immortal soul of Mr. Pigg of Downham in Norfolk' and 'Spica Virginis' (which is 'the star that appeared before the Wise Men in the East and directed their way before it was yet ensphered') and the Antarctic Pole which 'is not yet but shall answer in the consummation'—all these shoulder each other. Mr. Force Stead has traced with a marvellous industry as many as possible of these allusions to their source. Their effect will be felt in the future. There is about this verse a sense of significance; no doubt, if Smart had been able to make his poem constant, he might have straitened as well as straightened the significance. The desirability of that is the real argument between the schools today; one side prefers an insane strangeness, the other a tedious constancy. Smart, like the greater poets to whom, frustrated, he almost belonged, desired both; it was not his fault that the union was removed, unless indeed Mr. Force Stead is right, and he had allowed himself to be less than 'constant' in his recollection of the Lady Anne Vane, unless her departure overthrew him, and, escaping to recklessness, he betrayed, as men do, the power and the vision that should have come. Even so, his God was merciful; he had two visions of her 'in charity'.

GERARD HOPKINS

Time and Tide *review of Dr. Gardner's study, 1945*

... [THIS] is quite the fullest and most valuable of the books that have appeared about Hopkins. Its seven chapters deal with (i) The Two Vocations—which expounds, among other things, the effect of Scotist thought on his poetry; (ii) *The Wreck of the Deutschland*; (iii) Sonnet Morphology; (iv) Diction and Syntax; (v) Themes and Imagery; (vi) Critics and Reviewers; (vii) Hopkins and Modern Poetry. The second volume, which is expected in the New Year, will deal with his rhythmical origins, his criticism, and with certain particular poems. The complete work will certainly for many years be a necessary accompaniment of the poetry for any serious student.

But how it, as they say, 'takes the mind back'! Dreaming, an aged creature, by the fireside if not the fire, I grow aware how unreliable memory is. It hurries to persuade us and I would not too rashly be persuaded. Yet it does seem to me that when I first saw the name of Hopkins, it was on two or three pages torn from one of those little red volumes known as the *Poets and Poetry of the 19th Century*. Dr. Gardner says it was Volume VII; I am almost sure that it was called 'Bridges to Kipling'. A friend had lent them to a friend, who lent them to me. We were all round about twenty—young and poetasters; we read, we admired, we were thrilled. Yet I do not remember that we were so extraordinarily surprised. English verse, to our minds, was unlimited; it could do anything. This was beautiful and exciting, but it was native to verse. We could even smile while we admired. The line which, with a sigh of pleasure, I remember from that time most clearly—'Or to-fro tender trambeams truckle at the eye'—gratified us at once with joy and comedy. One did not laugh; one even wished one could write like it—in a general way. But one did not try to.

Then there came a copy, transcribed (I suppose) from one of Beeching's anthologies, by the same friend, of the *Blessed Virgin Compared to the Air we Breathe*. This was not so striking then, nor has my feeling for it grown stronger. It would sound arrogant to say one could do it oneself, but one could do something rather like it oneself—of the same kind, if less well; it had not so strong a sound of alien and superior genius, though it had, of course, Hopkins's own kind of power.

And then, for another twelve years or so, we waited. The *Poems* came in 1918. Bridges introduced them with a sonnet—

> Amidst our chaffinch flock display
> Thy plumage of far wonder and heavenward flight.

Nouns and adjectives seemed to us then entirely justified. We might disagree with some of Bridges's prose comments, but we knew very well and we felt strongly that we owed the whole of Hopkins—both preservation and publication—to his care. It had not then occurred to us that his care could be supposed to be jealousy or his devotion envy. Since the letters had not been published, we could not measure the patience with which (as we now know) Bridges endured to be instructed, corrected, and rebuked—not only on matters of poetry. 'There was a centre of humility in that haughty soul', and it is evident in every thing we can gather of the whole relationship. Dr. Gardner himself is, I think, a little hard on Bridges's Notes. It is one thing to see now; it was another to decide then. They were in small type at the end of the book, and even today as one re-reads 'a stalwart stallion, very-violet-sweet . . .' Bridges was more right than we then thought. But we did not think him very right.

The poems were a literary sensation. All the papers reviewed them; everyone who was anyone talked of them. Yes, but the papers had had review copies, and everyone did not buy them. The edition was of 750 copies; it took eleven years to sell—five or six copies a month. There is nothing surprising in this, but it is a fact to be remembered. Not till 1929 did the need of a new edition arise. Bridges was then busy on the *Testament of Beauty*, yet he wished something more done. It was, of course, impossible to suggest altering his own work, even had I wished. I agreed to prepare an Appendix of other poems not in the first edition, and to write a brief introduction for the general public.

One odd fact became clear. Before I went down to Oxford to see Bridges, I spent some time getting well into Hopkins's own preface —expecting and fearing that he would be talking lightly about Sprung Rhythm. At the end of the Preface was an equation. Hopkins's Note read 'Nos. 13 and 22 are Curtal-Sonnets, that is, they are constructed in proportions resembling those of the sonnet proper, namely 6+4 instead of 8+6, with however, a halfline tail-piece (so that the equation is rather

$$\frac{12}{8}+\frac{9}{2}=\frac{21}{2}=10\tfrac{1}{2}).\text{'}$$

As I read, I became confused.

$$\frac{12}{8}+\frac{9}{2}=\frac{21}{2}\,?$$

I reckoned and re-reckoned. Could it be that Hopkins had slipped and that we had not marked the slip? Could it be that none of those ardent admirers, those sedate inquirers, those scorners of Bridges or explorers into the new, had noticed it? Or, noticing, had been silent? The possibility of deliberate silence I dismissed then and dismiss now; some experience of publishing had taught me better. Humbly and fearfully I submitted the problem to Bridges. 'There seems', I faltered, 'to be something wrong. . . .' The dominating eyes turned on me; the dominating voice said: 'Wrong?' I explained. He stared and broke into laughter. 'And no one', he said, 'has seen it.' In the second edition we really did tamper with the text; we printed $\frac{12}{2}$. But the incident remains a pleasant memory.

The Introduction, on the whole, has been perhaps as fortunate as it deserved. It seems now a slender lyric thing as one looks at the four pages of bibliography devoted by Dr. Gardner to 'Books, Essays, Articles, etc.'; 'G. M. H. and Associative Form'; 'G. M. H.: A Study of Influences'; 'On Approaching Hopkins'. (In those other far off days, we did not have to 'approach'; we merely came across him.) Whenever I look at Dr. Gardner's own stateliness alone, I blush. I have every hope that my small effort may be removed from future editions; what should such a daisy do in these woods of Westermain?

The word reminds me. As a corrective to an over-sensitized apprehension of 'influences' let anyone who has not read Dr. Gardner yet open at the first page and read the three lines quoted. When I did so, my mind said 'Meredith'; it took me a moment to recognize them as Hopkins. Mr. Eliot has commented on the likeness between the two. We may come to see that Hopkins does not belong to our time (in so far as we can properly talk about 'time' and poetry) as much as we had supposed. The more the Victorian age is examined, the more native to it Hopkins seems. He was indeed, in some sense, its corrective, but every age carries its own corrective within it; as the Augustans carried Charles Wesley, and the Romantics Byron. Dr. Gardner's second volume proposes to discuss Hopkins's 'real status as a poet'. The sooner the more welcome. He prepares Hopkins so for posterity. But the one thing we cannot do instead of posterity is to *remember*. I will permit myself to say that those of us who in our youth came across those poems and fragments are more like posterity than the great students of the *Poems*. Tradition lives in such moments, and Hopkins was now, in that verse, part of our own poetic youth.

SOUND AND VARIATIONS

Notes on the Way

Contributed to Time and Tide, *September 1938*

THE distinguished and brilliant lady with whom I was dining said, speaking with a peculiar bitterness out of a pleasant silence: 'Television!' She went on, in answer to a silent inquiry: 'I hate television. It will rob us again of sound—just when we might have begun to listen, when we might have begun to break the tyranny of the eye.' 'Wordsworth', said I, 'had the same view—he called the eye "in every stage of life the most despotic of our senses". But he went on pampering it—with daffodils and clouds and what not. A Lost Leader. Tell me more.'

She said: 'I like to think that once we could *hear*, when almost everyone composed their own songs, till printing came in and persuaded them to prefer other men's. But the air that was given for the senses came and helped us afterwards, for on the air we depended entirely on sound, until the jealous eyes revolted against their neglect. O noise, yes; there is noise everywhere, but that is not the point.' 'There is', said I, 'music—as you allowed.' 'Music', she said, 'is expected nowadays; you hear it in an accepted manner. The B.B.C. were teaching us the value of sound, even if it were usually representational sound. And now television is coming in, and we shall all fall back on doing what we could do originally—on seeing.' 'We shall see', I ventured, 'contemporaneously. You do not perhaps think it a gain?' She said: 'Even now you could see your Test Match or what not by nine in the evening—but no! you must have it at once while it is happening. Greedy, indelicate children!'

It is, in fact, I thought, walking home much later, more so than I had supposed. The eyes have been encouraged and the other senses depressed. Smell has almost entirely gone, and sound very far. Not noise—sound. The B.B.C. themselves have been at a difficulty. There are, of course, the series of mysterious sounds in *Monday Night at Seven*; there they grasped their nettle. Two thuds, a squeal, and a long vibrating wail—what was it? A sheet of brown paper split by a poker. It is true that few of us habitually tear brown paper with a poker. But more familiar sounds—marmosets chewing bananas or fountain-pens writing leading articles—were as alien. I must have heard the faint sound of pen on paper or fingers on paper a million times, but is it possible to recognize them casually, as I should in a casual glance recognize the pen, the paper, or the finger? No.

Take a more obscure point. In plays and such things on the air certain sounds are introduced dramatically. Thus in Mr. Pudney's interesting arrangement of *Three Men in a Boat*, someone, if I remember right, fell into the Thames. We heard the splash. But could the splash be said to be helpful? Alas, we had been so prepared for it that the very climax was an anticlimax; the sound of the splash did nothing. That was not Mr. Pudney's fault; if he had not prepared us, the sound would have been unrelated to the other sounds and there would have been no climax at all. It lost, either way, its importance; it only worked because it was conventional, and convention, if it is not ritual, tends to be dull. The only ritual sounds we know are bands. The secularization of ritual has spoiled it; look at the celebrations of our only new feast—January 1st!

The more I listen to plays on the air, in which the sound effects are, more or less, illustrative of the voices, the more I wonder if we have begun at the right end. Much, of course, may have happened that I have missed; and anyhow I do not quite see what else can be done. Few of us are prepared to give up time to having our ears trained to experiments with sound. Yet drama in sound must demand some such training, unless sound effects are to consist wholly of doors shutting, horses galloping, trains roaring, &c. The words themselves are, admittedly, sound. But the words are not meant for the ear but for the brain, as on the films. They ought not perhaps to be as important as they are. The present talkies are more agreeable than the old silent films. But not because of the words as sounds—listen to them!—only because the brain has things made easier for it by explanations in simple words. So generally on the stage. The dialogue is usually explanation. More than explanation would mean style, and except for a few comic epigrams and a few chance successes, style is not there, meaning by style memorable language. Memorable language is addressed to the ear as well as to the brain. And language that is not memorable is addressed only to the brain and is no more than explanation to make our amusements easier. De Quincey put it rather heavily when he talked of books of instruction and books of power, but he was not far wrong. One of the great questions today is whether we can retain power in words.

My friend had mentioned music—or, at least, song. Well, music. Music, with exceptions, is not representational—a detestable word; say, music does not represent events. It does not, at its best, represent emotions. No art ever can. It may excite emotions; that is, it may arouse in us emotions of which we recognize our ordinary or extraordinary emotions to be impure copies. This may have been what the educational Aristotle was talking about—it cleanses the soul by pity and terror, by true pity and true terror, of which our personal feelings are pretty poor imitations. True terror is not terror that is provoked by what may happen to you; nor true pity nor true laughter. The man who can consciously laugh at himself is, no doubt, better than the man who cannot. But the man who can laugh at the laughable anywhere is better still. Art then provokes true emotions, and consequently does not represent them—which is where all theories of deliberate communication in art break down.

Talking of music, however, brings us to the question of musical criticism. I am not sure that this has not been a doubly bad influence. It accustoms us to believing that we can adequately discuss one art in the technique of another. Can one? Can one criticize music in anything but music? Or if one can, ought one not to regard verbal criticism as a poor substitute for the real thing? Verbal criticism in literature is in the same medium, and I quite see that in some arts the medium is too difficult; architecture, for instance. It would probably be hopeless to try and comment on a new town hall by erecting a bitter tower of toy bricks in the market-place. But why is there not more critical music? How rarely have I heard anything like a *Suite in Discussion of Beethoven* or *Comment on the Overtones of Mussorgsky* (a charming little thing recalling many delights in its original). It is astonishing that musicians should so lightly have abandoned their own power. Imagine a musical war deliberately conducted in its own terms—with Elizabethan titles: *Symphony on Hindemith for the Quacks of Queen's*; *A Few Bars Against the*

Buffoons of Berlioz—and so on. There might be riots in Regent Street as the militant orchestrations of the schools went on. Will not the musicians turn their flutes into javelins and their pianos into bludgeons?

It is possible that the recent reintroduction of the chorus into drama may have some effect—not on music but on song, and not so much on song directly as in the discovery of a dramatic equivalent. We have had to be content with songs because we have had nothing else, but it has been pointed out that the setting of words to music has this disadvantage; you pin them down to a particular set of stressed values, whereas the stresses in reading often vary, slightly, perhaps, on each occasion. It would be pleasant to retain this freedom, while capturing at least something of the extra value of song. It should be possible in drama to ascend and descend the scale of speech, so that a conversation might pass from colloquial talk to a kind of intense singing (only not singing) and back again. The chorus probably is not the place to begin. What the chorus has done so far has been to reproduce something amorphous on the stage, to bring us back to rather than to solve certain problems. It is still a background—however important; it is a mass. But the real interest is what we can do to vary, excite, and emphasize this mass. Variation of speech may help. But there again we shall need a great deal of attention to sound.

Especially in view of the enemies of permissible variation. I had not supposed that these existed until I was involved, unintentionally and unworthily, in the great rhinoceros controversy of a week or so ago. Pedantry, one knew, existed, but it had not seemed likely that anyone was forced to be a pedant. Alas, I now know that the mass—not to say the mob—wishes for pedantry in order that they may reject it. I had supposed that the more words one could have the better, especially taking the needs of poetry into account. It is not so—even among a people so rich in alternatives as, by their whole tradition, the English. What happened was this.

I was called one afternoon to the telephone (not knowing anything about the controversy) to talk with a representative of one of our most distinguished morning papers, the face of whose editor confronts us in the Tube, listening, also telephonically, to distant Chancelleries. The Voice said: 'What do you use as a plural for Rhinoceros?' 'Rhinoceroses,' said I, 'almost the only remaining beauty I was taught in childhood.' 'You don't say Rhinos?' asked the Voice. 'Only in Limericks', said I. 'The feet of your favourite Rhino Are apt to leave marks on the lino, But if you—.' 'You think', the Voice interrupted, 'that yours is the *right* plural?' 'Certainly not,' said I, 'the Oxford Dictionary gives six or seven—rhinoceron among others, a charming word.' 'Yes, we have those,' the Voice said warmly, 'but which of them is *right*?' 'All,' I answered tenderly, 'it is why they are there.' 'But', the Voice went on, or words to this effect, 'there needs must be some one Best way of worship. One nobler than the rest. Which is *right*? Rhinoceroses takes so *long*.' My mind reverted to English verse, to the dance of five syllables in the time of two, to all lovely freedom in law, to the joy of six possibilities, to variation, man's continual delight. I said passionately: 'You could say it in almost the same time. Must you dragoon us? Must you forbid the Rhinoceros to broaden slowly down? . . .'

The next morning in the Tube I opened a paper. I read that I had said 'anxiously' (anxiously!) 'Oh no, no, no, not Rhinos, please!' I read that rhinoceron was a 'monstrosity'; we had all better say 'Rhinos'. I thought again of Wordsworth—'the two great ends of liberty and power'. Liberty and power! I looked up; there was the editor at his telephone, listening to Freedom shrieking. And so she very well may and I hope she does.

RELIGIOUS DRAMA

Contributed to the periodical Good Speech, *April 1938*

IT has become the habit to say, justly, that there is no such thing as Religious Drama; there is only drama. I have said it several times myself. Unfortunately, however, a thing said three times becomes less true with every repetition, unless indeed that thing is the formal and conventionalized statement of dogma. Opinion does not bear such repetition. Let us therefore pretend that religious drama exists, and let us pretend that by religion we mean religion, and not humanitarianism or morals or civics or aesthetics or any other illiterate substitute. We mean drama—that is, plays, of whatever kind—concerned with the relations of man with God.

Such drama may be, roughly, divided into two kinds: the first, those which have to do with the relation of the individual soul and God without the introduction of any mass of tradition; the second, those which may or may not involve that definite relationship, but which certainly involve that tradition. The first class do not involve Christian or any other dogma; the second do. Both kinds at the present time tend to have many examples—almost all bad. I shall, however, neglect the first class and confine myself to the second.

The first reason why most religious plays of that kind are bad is simple. Keats in his Letters says: 'We distrust poetry that has a palpable design upon us.' Most religious plays have precisely this palpable design; they exhibit it, they even brag of it. So much, certainly, they might do and yet remain effective. A good deal of the very greatest poetry has a palpable design upon us—Lucretius, for example, and Dante. At the present time a great deal of writing has the palpable design of the noble and passionate ideals of the political Left, and is the better for it. Propaganda does not destroy art; missionary plays (with whatever mission) can yet be well written and effective. But there is a condition, and it is that the design must not be imposed from without. The propaganda must be the inevitable result of the art. Of course acts of devotion, to whatever god or whatever cause, may be cast in dramatic form. But then they must be so regarded. It is hardly fair, as is not infrequently done, to say: 'Well, we call this a play, and we expect you to be interested in it as a play. But if you are bored stiff by it as a play, then remember it is an act of devotion.' That is to use George Herbert unfairly. God may take a text and preach patience; it is no business of ours to forestall Him. Patience is one of the many virtues that only Deity has a right to demand.

Religious drama then must create its excitement from within. In earlier days it might conceivably have relied on the fact that certain reports—of the Nativity, say, or the Resurrection, or even the Judgement—had probably reached most of its hearers. Nowadays, it almost certainly cannot. If they have heard of these reports at all, they have got the facts and ideas wrong. People, otherwise educated, recklessly confuse the Immaculate Conception with the Virgin Birth, are in complete ignorance of the doctrine of the Two Natures, suppose the Fall to have been disproved by Evolution, and (on a lower level) think that the clergy of the Church of England are paid by the State, or that the theory of the Papacy is somehow affected by the conduct of the Popes. This, it is true, is mere foolishness. But it accentuates the importance of religious drama creating its own intellectual content, as well as its artistic content. In art nothing is exciting but art, but sometimes we can rely on a general educated common sense. At present we cannot.

On the other hand, of course, religious drama has a right to as much tolerance as is given to secular. It has a right to *attention*, and attention to what it is actually doing and saying, and not to what some goop thinks his great-grandmother said and did. It is not finally certain that our great-grandmothers' ideas of Christianity were more accurate than those of some of the medieval writers or of the moderns. Propaganda, if any, of the idea must arise from within, and be created by style. But we must not neglect style because we do not wish to listen to propaganda, and we ought to get the propaganda right.

The 'palpable design' which is the danger of religious drama has become more palpable with the decay of the speculative intellect everywhere except in science, and of its confinement there (naturally) to the specialist. The drama of ideas is not, *per se*, religious drama, and religious drama has not of late shown much tendency to become a drama of ideas. This misfortune will probably correct itself in time; modern religious drama is still young, and has about it generally a kind of adolescent—not to say infantile—simplicity. It embarrasses the hearer; he becomes awkward; he blushes, stumbles, and thinks 'This is dreadful; how can I get away?' Perhaps that also is a confession of adolescence—that over-awareness of an emotional solecism. We are not yet civilized. But it is true that we know too well not *what* such drama is going to say, but *how* it is going to say it. The play, as Wordsworth justly remarked, 'remembers how she felt but what she felt Remembers not'—and that, as he added, is generally a rather low and immature state of mind. All goo-goo and ga-ga.

Christian drama then must—and I think will—recover the speculative intellect. It will consider the nature of God. Except within the Christian Church, God is not supposed to have any nature to speak of; He is left to be universal love, and love itself is not very clearly defined. I am speaking, of course, only of intellect. I am not saying that, outside the Church, men cannot love, though I believe it to be true that, apart from the events which the Church exists to proclaim, man would never have been or be capable of love. But I do not wish the plays of religion to be confined to an indeterminate presentation of an undefined love. They might, in fact, take up the business of defining, with intense excitement, the nature, habits, and mode of operation of Almighty Love, infusing into their excitement a proper scepticism as to its existence at all. It is not dogma that creates narrowness; it is the inability to ask an infinite number of questions about dogma. That is where the medievals scored; they were always asking questions. It will be remembered that a Roman legate once wrote from Paris to say that he did not think it was decent that young men should publicly begin their disputations by arguing against the existence of God. Religious drama ought to argue a great deal more strongly than it does against the existence of God. At present it is far too hampered by good intentions.

About its methods I do not know that one can at present say very much. I think it is too limited, but that fault will probably cure itself. It is very desirable that we should expand our imaginations and also our inventions. I saw once a rather good Passion play—quite the best I have seen—in which two rather curious figures in greyish wrappings appeared as, more or less, Readers. After some staring I determined that they were figures from—or in—the grave, dead things, or the souls of the dead. And these macabre effects reciting the awful story seemed to me a very fine invention. Unfortunately it seems they were not; I forget for the moment what they were—something vaguely celestial. But it will be obvious that the emotional stress would have been increased by a more macabre creation. I would not go quite so far as to say that our present business is to invent a 'demnition horrid' outline, and fill it with the grace and beauty of a great style, but that, I feel, is at least a fairly safe intention. As for style—that, in the end, so far as we can see, is, in the most literal sense, past praying for. Religion is, no doubt, more important than art, but it is also not art, and obviously that fact has two sides. If ever Calvinism were permitted it is in matters of style, so long always as we do not easily suppose ourselves among the elect.

As for Choruses, the Chorus is often, it seems, a matter of necessity in which the author has (very willingly) to oblige the producer. At least I know it has been so in my own case. I am far from saying that one is not responsible, even so, for what one makes of the Chorus, but its primary existence is due sometimes to the number of the actors, their sex, or their capacity. The most obvious uses of the Chorus are (i) to represent multitudinous mankind, (ii) to unite the other actors with the audience. The second use ought often to be superfluous. Commentators in a play ought only to be there if there is the very strongest need for them; or, of course—which is the same thing—if the writer has thought of a number of good things he wants to have in and cannot work off on any single characters. The Chorus supplies the need. But commentators are otherwise dangerously weakening; they are turned from the play to the audience. And if, as Monsignor Talbot wrote to Manning, the place of the laity is in their pews, much more is the place of the audience in their chairs. Their part in a work of art is only *attention*. The quality of their attention is not at present what it might be, but we can hardly expect it to improve until we give them something serious to attend to. In a general way I am rather against Choruses unless the number of people in the society or guild or what not makes it inevitable. But most frequently it will.

An alternative—which I have been trying—is to make the Chorus—after the protagonist—the most important character. This has not often been done, and I think it holds possibilities, both in dramatic opposition (and union) on the stage, and as a method of analysis of the elements of a single 'body', and of synthesis. It is the chief actor confronted not by a mass but by another individual which I have in mind; the second individual being represented by a mass, the Chorus—only not, of course, just like that.

These scattered comments are not offered as patterned criticism. Religious drama is at present almost a new thing. It is the business of those connected with it to see that as it becomes less new it retains that 'continual slight novelty' which, as has been settled for more than two thousand years, is the primary necessity of all art.

BLAKE AND WORDSWORTH

From the Dublin Review, *April 1941*

In the *Vision* W. B. Yeats said of those spirits which he ascribed to the sixteenth phase of the Moon (called the Positive Man), among whom he included Blake, that 'There is always an element of frenzy, and almost always a delight, in certain glowing or shining images of concentrated force; in the heart; in the human form in its most vigorous development; in the solar disc; in some symbolic representation of the sexual organs; for the being must brag of its triumph over its own incoherence'. The last clause, in its relation to Blake, is a comment of genius; it is a description of the *Prophetic Books*. There is a certain likeness to some aspects of our modern world about it, and that both on the totalitarian and the democratic sides; there is certainly an expression of a temptation common to all of us, though all of us have not so high an energy as Blake, certainly not a poetic energy. To brag of a triumph over our own incoherence is natural and impossible; incoherence can only be solved by being reduced to co-inherence, and of that, since it is not ours, it is impossible to brag.

But true though the phrase is as a comment, it is but a comment; it is not a final judgement. The whole attraction of the *Prophetic Books* is that there is an element of co-inherence in them as well as of incoherence. For all the labour spent in their analysis we have not perhaps yet discovered the proper way of poetic approach. Most commentators are compelled to approach them by precisely the way which Blake himself seems most strongly to have denounced —the method of detached intellectual analysis, of prolonged explanation. The great figures of the myth do indeed sit about, in those commentaries, chained in a frozen land: Urizen rules over them. Swinburne (were his prose easily readable) was at least trying another way; and Mr. Yeats was, of course, of another kind. But in general it is so; and in general there is every excuse. Blake depended on his myths being exciting; and alas, the sound itself is too monotonous. We are defeated by the sameness of the rhythms, the unintelligibility of the tale.

If we ask, then, by what means we may avoid (if we think it worth while) Blake's brag and reduce the incoherence to coinherence, another method suggests itself. It is a consideration of the other great poetic achievements of the Romantics. This is desirable, so long as our criticism does not dishearten those others instead of heartening Blake's. Wordsworth in the *Prelude* did something of what Blake asserted he was doing. The *Prelude* is as much about man's destiny as the *Prophetic Books*, and its conclusion not so unlike. Blake, for all the rude things he said about Wordsworth (but he was equally silly about Milton), might not have refused to be called a 'Prophet of Nature'—meaning by Nature what Wordsworth meant, and not buttercups and sunsets ('the secondary grace'). He himself never exalted the Imagination higher than did Wordsworth. 'All things are comprehended in these Eternal Forms in the Divine Body of the Saviour, the True Vine of Eternity, the Human Imagination, who appeared to me as coming to judgement among His Saints and throwing off the Temporal that the Eternal might be established.' So Blake; and Wordsworth:

> This spiritual love acts not, nor can exist
> Without Imagination; which, in truth,
> Is but another name for absolute power
> And clearest insight, amplitude of mind,
> And Reason in its most exalted mood.

The last line marks the distinction between the true Romantic and the pseudo-Romantic. The true Romantic, maintaining the importance of what Blake calls 'the visionary Fancy or Imagination', admits and believes that the holy intellect is part of it. Nor, whatever in his haste he sometimes implied, did Blake ever refuse this test; the *Prophetic Books* themselves break out continually into epigrams of philosophy which pass it triumphantly. The myth may be dim to us; the morals are not. But in Wordsworth the fragmentary morals of the myth have been too often exalted at the expense of the myth (so to call it). Both of those noble poets have been said to repudiate 'the meddling intellect'; in so far as they did, it was precisely the *meddling* intellect which they discarded. The power which they felt and believed was defined by Wordsworth in the grand climax of the *Prelude*—'the *feeling* intellect'. That climax has been a little neglected precisely because it does not 'brag of its triumph over its own incoherence'; on the contrary, it is neither incoherent nor boastful. But it arrives, quietly and passionately, at its end; and its end is the end at which Blake's verse, after another manner, aimed.

The *Prelude* is alive with many themes—among them the themes of Power and of Solitude. The *Prophetic Books* are alive with the same themes, again among others. But where Solitude is, on the whole, unanalysed in Wordsworth, the purpose of the *Prophetic Books* is precisely to analyse it. Their difficulty—that is, their poetic difficulty—is that the analysis is into terms of what in our modern critical slang is called 'private' meanings. It is almost impossible to be poetically excited by being told that

> Skofield vegetated by Reuben's gate
> In every Nation of the Earth.

Yet we know something of 'Skofield'; we know he was the soldier who once intruded into Blake's garden, and thereby unknowingly immortalized himself for ever as an image of supernatural darkness. But when 'In stern defiance came from Albion's bosom Hand, Hyle, Koban, Gwantok, Peachy, Brertun, Slaid, Hulton, Skofield, Kock, Kotope, Bowen, Albion's sons', interest ceases if those names are not, by the story, brought into the story. They are not even allegory otherwise.

The word 'Albion', however, is of another kind. In the Index to Messrs. Wallis and Sloss's edition, Albion is said to be the symbol 'of the true relation of Time and Space with Eternity'; he is also 'the Eternal Man', 'the Giant Man'; he is fallen from the original unity—'the perturbed Man turns away down the Valleys dark'. The very title of the last of the *Prophetic Books* is *Jerusalem the Emanation of the Giant Albion*, and the poem opens with Albion's rejection of this Emanation, which he hides

> Upon the Thames and Medway, rivers of Beulah, dissembling
> His jealousy before the throne divine, darkening, cold.

But the word 'Albion' does not, to the general reader, first of all convey the idea of Universal Man; it means Britain, even perhaps England—'an ancient poetical name for England' say the concordances. And this Messrs. Wallis and Sloss allow, for they point it out, with the references to Albion's 'White Cliffs' and even to the fogs:

> Behold the foggy mornings of the Dead on Albion's cliffs.

Which may possibly have come from Caesar, where other poets have found the same idea of the Dead being related to Britain.

The *Prophetic Books* are strewn with a kind of mystical geography of Britain; some of their best passages are catalogues of Cities.

In the fallen state of Albion these cities are also fallen, images of the Emanation Jerusalem: London is a stone of her ruins. Oxford is the dust of her walls. It is the union of the strange mythical figures with the familiar mythical names which forms part of the fascination of the *Books*, as when Los

came down from Highgate thro' Hackney and Holloway towards London,
Till he came to old Stratford, and thence to Stepney and the Isle of Leutha's
Dogs; thence through the narrows of the River's side
And saw every minute particular, the jewels of Albion, running down
The kennels of the streets and lanes as if they were abhorred.

This kind of union is a thing habitual to English verse; it is in the Walsinghame poem and it is not far (though no names are mentioned) from the *Ancient Mariner*. Perhaps the nearest thing to Blake is the manuscript of Christopher Smart which was edited in 1939 by Mr. W. Force Stead under the title *Rejoice in the Lamb*. That very remarkable sequence of verses had a great likeness to Blake's way of writing, both in its wildnesses and in its thrilling successes. The line

For the Antarctick Pole is not yet but shall answer in the Consummation

has the effect of one of Blake's dark and threatening prophecies; more to the point is

I bless the Lord Jesus upon Ramsgate Pier—the Lord forward the building of harbours;

or:

For I pray for Chichester to give the glory to God and to keep the Adversary at bay.

But it is in the *Prelude* that we have the sense of an 'Albion' almost like Blake's. I think (though I cannot at the moment confirm) that the actual word was used in the 1805 text. Certainly the earlier part of the poem is concerned with the particular nature of 'Albion' —the hills, the dales, the wide spaces, the storms are all part of it; so is Cambridge; so is London. It is there that Solitude appears, or rather the images which are declared to be the embodiments of 'that great Power'. It is also there that that other Power is felt which Wordsworth calls 'the weight of ages', 'weight and power', 'power growing under weight'. That sudden experience struck him as he was entering London, and it was in London that he became aware of the Beggar with the label, when again his mind turned round 'as with the might of waters', the correspondence there of the other Solitaries seen in other parts of Albion.

The manner of Wordsworth and the manner of Blake were different enough. But if the *Prophetic Books* are concerned with some great and awful division by which (at least in *Jerusalem*) Albion is separated from his tender and lovely Emanation, so the *Prelude* is concerned with the division between the forms of England and France. Blake had begun to deal with the French Revolution in his own style, though he abandoned it; and Wordsworth did deal with it in his. But it is no more by the mere nomenclature of geography in him than in Blake. His whole experience of exterior Nature in England—all the earlier books of the *Prelude*—has created a Form; his experience of the opening of the Revolution in France has created another. It is the division between those Forms which brought his own agony on him. He is separate; he is a man betrayed.

> With open war
> Britain opposed the liberties of France.
> This threw me first out of the pale of love;
> Soured and corrupted, upwards to the source,
> My sentiments.

And (following on this, and on the change in the Revolutionary Government of France) Wordsworth continues to fall back into the frozen world of abstract thought divorced from its emanations of life and power. He actually uses the word when, speaking of 'ancient Institutions', he refers bitterly to the 'moral sentiments' which had become 'the props Or *emanations* of those institutes'. Where Blake speaks of Albion as having betrayed and persecuted his emanation Jerusalem, Wordsworth speaks of the ancient institutions of Albion—or of the Form that, in his verse, is Albion—as being disgraced by the emanation of moral sentiments instead of 'varieties of human love'. It might be worth considering, though here there is no space, how far Dorothy was to Wordsworth precisely an image of that true Emanation. In Blake the Emanation Jerusalem is feminine. She is redeemed by the repentance of Albion. Wordsworth was speaking only of the personal history of a child of Albion; but in that it is Dorothy who, like Jerusalem hovering among the 'dark Satanic mills', preserves for him 'a saving intercourse With my true self'.

The Fall of Albion and his Redemption, then, may be held to be presented, one way or another, in both poems. In both poems Albion is related to England: in *Jerusalem*, by the continual use of English geographical names; in the *Prelude*, by the creation of a Form from the vision of mountains, vales, moors, roads, and cities—named or unnamed. This sensation of Albion or England as enduring its sin and passion is a necessary theme of both poems; I do not say the chief theme—that is in one case a supernatural existence and in the other Wordsworth. But one theme it certainly is, and among the more passionate. Patriotism is not always a direct emotion, nor an obviously indirect. The fields and streets of England do not exist only by direct invocation of verse, nor by oblique allusions to cricket-fields or mining-villages.

It is impossible here to discuss the whole scheme of Blake's majestic tale of Redemption. Wordsworth never really told us his in full. But two points may be noted; one from each poet—from Wordsworth, the discovery of 'the feeling intellect'; from Blake, the matter of Forgiveness. In the end perhaps these are not so distant, but they must wait for a poet as great as either before they can be considered in a proper poetic mode.

The Wordsworthian dissolution of false bonds and resolution of perplexities occurs at the end of the *Prelude*. In that climax—a climax no less effective because the sound is subdued—the two themes of power and solitude are brought together, in the removed and interior state of the soul.

> Here must thou be, O Man,
> Power to thyself; no Helper hast thou here . . .
> The prime and vital principle is there
> In the recesses of thy nature, far
> From any reach of outward fellowship,
> Else is not thine at all. But joy to him,
> O joy to him who here hath sown, hath laid
> Here the foundation of his future years
> . . . and he whose soul hath risen
> Up to the height of feeling intellect
> Shall want no humbler tenderness.

It is this which is meant by the Nature of which Wordsworth claimed to be a 'prophet', for it is the mind of man ('A thousand times more beautiful than the earth On which he dwells') in which he is to instruct others. It is a state of unity, in which the intellect no longer 'meddles' but knows and feels at once in rational proportion. The great work having been achieved within, power issues from it outward; the solitude of the spirit in its prime and vital principle issues into communion. It is this which is to aid in the deliverance not only of individuals but of nations, even those that have sunk to servitude, ignominy, and shame. Not only Albion, but all like Powers, are to rise in this experience against their old idolatry. But it can only be achieved by the intense and individual working.

I have said that Wordsworth did not perhaps altogether exhibit the manner of that working, and having said so I repent. So high a poet needs to be submitted to much more closely; we have to exercise towards him precisely 'the feeling intellect'. The words 'power' and 'glory' which he stamps on the *Prelude* everywhere have to become intense with life as we read him. But we may be helped in that by what we learn from other poets, since they,

even as prophets, each with each,
Connected in a mighty scheme of truth,
Have each his own peculiar faculty.

And it is here that Blake's theme of Forgiveness may be introduced.

It is, certainly, the climax of *Jerusalem*, and there are two chief places where the idea is set forward in Images; it is supported in other places and is repeated in the *Ghost of Abel*, the latest of Blake's works. The first of these two places is in Chapter III, in the dialogue between [the Divine Voice and] Jerusalem herself, the lovely and persecuted Emanation of Albion. She is in despair and darkness, except that she sees the 'Divine Lamb' standing by her.[1] The Lamb, who is also the 'Human Imagination' and the 'Divine Body', comforts her with hope of the resurrection of Albion from spiritual death, and shows her 'in the visions of Elohim Jehovah' Joseph and Mary in Nazareth: what follows is wrought up from the phrase in St. Matthew—*voluit occulte dimittere eam*. The grand quarrel between the moral law and the sinning and loving spirit is here concentrated into the two semi-mystical figures. Joseph denounces Mary, who answers with an exquisite appeal not to self-justification but to 'the forgiveness of sins'. Joseph answers that appeal with tears, embraces, and a declaration of the nature of pardon. It is not, and cannot be, conditional; it must be absolute, and at the same time continuous; it is, in fact, the very nature of life. 'The Gods, the Moral Virtues of the Heathen' forgive on condition that the offence shall not be repeated.

But Jehovah's Salvation
Is without Money and without Price, in the Continual Forgiveness of Sins,
In the Perpetual Mutual Sacrifice in Great Eternity.

The condition of non-repetition is a negation of pardon. It is not possible to man nor permitted by God. But pardon without such condition is a name for the direct operation of love. It involves 'sacrifice'; 'every sacrifice for others is a little death'; and the exchange of pardon between all men and women is the nature of the co-inherence which is eternal life. Life as we know it does not exist in spite of injury and forgiveness, but because of and through them, and that not in remote general principles but in actualities. 'General Forms have their vitality in Particulars.' It is the profound grasp of this, emotionally and intellectually at once, which Blake ascribes to the holy Imagination, and this is not far from 'the feeling intellect' which Wordsworth saw as generative of all tenderness, of humble cares and gentlest sympathies. 'All the tortures of repentance', runs the opening, 'To the Christians', of the fourth chapter of *Jerusalem*,

[1] It need not be stressed that Blake's use of such images is not, without consideration, to be identified with the Christian.

'are tortures of self-reproach on account of our leaving the Divine Harvest to the Enemy, the struggles of entanglement with incoherent roots.' It is at this point that he ceases 'to brag of his triumph over his own incoherence'; he has extricated himself from it, and his own Emanation restores him to the lucid charity of the Divine Kingdom as Dorothy restored Wordsworth to the powers and solitudes and glories of his own 'universe of life'.

But even the perpetual Mutual Sacrifice is not the final nature: there is a further union. Albion is to live.

> Jesus replied: 'I am the Resurrection and the Life.
> I die and pass the limit of possibility as it appears
> To individual perception.'

This was in the vision of Jerusalem. But in the fourth and last chapter of the book, after (it may be admitted) a good deal more incoherence, the wilder and more terrible raising of Albion takes place, and here in some odd and obscure way the poem means certainly to become 'patriotic', that is, to be concerned with the *patria*. In Albion's cold trance of death,

> England, a female shadow, as deadly damps
> Of the Mines of Cornwall and Derbyshire, lays upon his bosom heavy.

It is she who first wakes and cries out under the Divine Breath.

> Her voice pierced Albion's clay cold ear; he moved upon the Rock.
> The Breath Divine went forth upon the morning hills. Albion mov'd
> Upon the Rock: he open'd his eyelids in pain; in pain he mov'd
> His stony members: he saw England. Ah! shall the Dead live again? . . .
> As the Sun and Moon lead forward the Visions of Heaven and Earth,
> England, who is Brittannia, enterèd Albion's bosom rejoicing . . .
> Then Jesus appeared, standing by Albion . . .

We must not take this Jesus as necessarily equivalent to the Jesus of history and the Church. But we may realize that the intellectual passion of Blake saw here something that is of that Nature.

From this point the theme of the Forgiveness of Sins advances, a vision of Heaven and Earth. It is the great fundamental covenant not only between man and man but between man and God. It is the operation of 'offering oneself for another', and in this sense it is clear that Blake is right, for there can be only two attitudes towards the sin of another towards oneself; one is to entertain a grudge, the other is not to entertain a grudge. To entertain it is precisely to prefer the selfhood to that other, that is precisely not to offer oneself; and in consequence (what is certainly as important), to prevent one properly apprehending how another is offered instead of oneself. It is as necessary to accept this sacrifice as to make it, and as necessary to live from it.

> Thus do Men in eternity,
> One for another to put off by forgiveness every sin.

Anything else would be the destruction of the 'feeling intellect' and its tendernesses; 'the Human Body' becomes sterile. But in this Covenant, what both poets demanded and declared, is declared in its full 'glory'; the universe

> which moves with light and life informed.
> Actual, divine, and true. . . .
> By love subsists
> All lasting grandeur, by pervading love.

And so in Blake it is this in which exist the divine wonders

> throughout all the Three Regions immense
> Of Childhood, Manhood, and Old Age: and the all-tremendous Non Ens
> Of Death was seen in regeneration terrific or complacent.

All the Forms in this covenant, and only so, have their identities maintained; 'I heard the Name of their Emanations; they are namèd Jerusalem.'

The *Prelude* and *Jerusalem* are poetry and not theology. But to read either—much more to read both—is to become aware in each poem according to its proper mode of a great Form with which in one sense or another England is identified; this Form errs or sins or is deceived; it loses, in itself or in its children, the Emanation or Vision which is its life and becomes lost in a cold world of moral chatter and careful grudge; yet it is, or is to be, restored. Its children are to be the Prophets of that Nature, and declare it. In both poets other nations are to live again through this—'their deliverance', says Wordsworth, 'surely yet to come'; 'O lovely Emanation of Albion', says Blake,

> Awake, and overspread all Nations as in ancient Time.

No doubt both poets were thinking of much more than England, but no doubt (by their own words) both were thinking of England.

II · THE INCARNATION

SENSUALITY AND SUBSTANCE

From Theology, *May 1939*

'For I saw full assuredly', wrote the Lady Julian, 'that our Substance is in God, and also I saw that in our sensualite God is; for in the self point that our Soul is made sensual, in the self point is the City of God ordained to Him from without beginning; into which seat He cometh and never shall remove it . . . and as anent our substance and sensualite it may rightly be cleped our soul: and that is because of the oneing that they have in God. The worshipful City that our Lord Jesus sitteth in is our sensualite, in which He is enclosed: and our kindly Substance is enclosed in Jesus with the blessed Soul of Christ sitting in rest in the Godhead.'

Whatever the Lady Julian meant by 'sensualite', she certainly meant nothing less material or less vital than the whole physical nature; she was not weakening or refining it away. She followed the Church, which, ever since it had rejected the Nestorian idea of a merely moral union of the two natures in Christ, had been committed to a realistic sense of the importance of matter: 'our soul with our body, and our body with our soul, either of them taking help of other', which is not Browning but the Lady Julian again. The operations of matter are a means of the operation of Christ, and the body has not, in fact, as some pious people suggest, fallen a good deal farther than the soul.

This is all elementary enough; it is implicit or explicit in all the rites and all the rituals. It remains, however, that the help which the body gives to the soul has been far less seriously examined than the help which the soul gives to the body. The dichotomy which orthodoxy turned out of its official dogma has continually returned in its unofficial language; the result was epigrammatized in the question of Patmore's daughter: 'Father, isn't marriage rather a wicked sacrament?' The Way of the Rejection of Images has been far more considered throughout Christendom than the Way of the Affirmation of Images—unless, indeed, those images were of the accepted religious kind. Yet the two ways have the same maxim and the same aim—'to love everything because God loves it'. This is their union, and, this laid down, one way is not superior to the other, nor perhaps more difficult.

The result of our unofficial Manicheism has been that when the official representatives of the Church have talked about such things as sexual love (to take one example), they may have said the right things, but they have said very few of them and they have generally said them in the wrong style. The great world and energy of the body have been either deprecated or devotionalized; and by devotionalized I mean turned into a pale imitation of 'substance', of spirit; thus losing their own powers and privileges without, in general, gaining any others. There has been a wide feeling that the more like an indeterminate soul the body can be made the better. But the *Anthropos* in Christ was not 'like' the *Theos*: it was like nothing but itself. So the body is not 'like' the soul; it is like nothing but itself. The principle of our sensuality is unique and divine. It is, no doubt, rooted in substance. 'Soul is form and doth the body make' is a fine Platonist line. But soul ought not to be allowed to reduce the body to its own shadow—at any rate, in the Christian Church.

The result of this shy spiritualism has been, of course, to leave the Church particularly open to attack, or rather to leave its general public particularly open to attack. The Church owes more to heretics than she is ever likely (on this earth) to admit; her gratitude is always slightly patronizing. There existed, in the early part of the twentieth century, a convinced and rhetorical heretic named David Herbert Lawrence. Of what exactly he was convinced it is not always easy to be sure, except on the very broadest lines. He thought that sex was important; he thought physical nature significant; he thought modern industrialism disgusting; he thought men needed leaders—or a leader; he thought also that each man must find out his own foundations, leader or no leader. His style as a leader was much more like Luther or Wesley than Calvin or Aquinas. But on quite a number of occasions he knew how to use words, and he produced for some time a very great effect on sections of the general public. This was accentuated by the suppression of some of his books and pictures by the State, which excited a number of the young to something like a sexual frenzy on Lawrence's behalf, and also cordially interested on his behalf a number of the more mature.

When Lawrence died, at the age of forty-five, in 1930, a number of books were written about him by his friends. This fortune, good or bad, he shared with others. Men and women who had known him wrote about him and about themselves; quite properly, for the only way in which they could explain his effect on them was by writing about themselves. But his capacity and effect as a writer were there subordinated to his personality. That some of the books which appeared should seem to deal too much with the difficulties and disputes between his friends was inevitable; a little spite could not be kept out and a little superiority was eagerly invited in. These things fade; the really interesting question is whether and to what extent Lawrence will fade. Even now, that seems almost impossible to anyone who remembers the thunder of the captains and the shouting; the first reading of the full version of *Lady Chatterley's Lover*, its moving beauty, its increasing repetitions; or the half-jest, half-assent with which one heard of the 'dark gods'—dimly recollecting at the same time the fiery darkness of Boehme or the monstrous fables of the alchemical design.

He convinced only partly by his own language, and partly by his readers' memories—by that and by the sense of the blood, by that and by the sense of poetry. He could not be regarded as a serious poet, though he wrote some good poems. But he had a power to arouse, without any specially memorable phrase, a chaotic sense of poetic images. These certainly could not be even partially analysed; they were of the same kind as those in Blake's Prophetic Books—gigantic and cloudy, unlike the mighty but lucid powers of Milton. And this was accentuated by the tendency of his confused mind to denounce, on behalf of the blood, the graces of intelligence, the holy intellect itself. It is not surprising that he should dislike all that he could understand of Jane Austen, but that he should prefer the 'blood-stream' in Defoe or Fielding, because there was more 'character' in them and less 'personality'—this is a little odd. He thought, no doubt, he was protesting again, in literature, against the weakening of the style, but it was not so; only the richness of Jane Austen did not have to shout its sensuality aloud.

He was greatly moved also by the notion of authority. It seems sometimes that he was chiefly moved by the notion that he was himself authority—and yet he fled from that as much as he turned to it. To judge by his Letters, it was the war of 1914–18 which drove him into an antagonism to his kind, and provoked (as it very naturally might) a sense of separation and therefore—in him—of superiority. Against that sense of superiority, nevertheless, he was always reacting, partly from fear, partly from intelligence, partly from (what is the same thing) humility. He knew that authority comes into action only by 'a dark unfathomable free submission'. Of that kind of submission he saw no sign in the world around him—neither in the mining-village of his birth, nor in the scholastic world of his teaching days, nor in the intellectual circles of his later life. 'Grace does not come through liberty, but liberty through grace', Calvin quoted from Augustine, and Lawrence might have quoted it from either, had he been fortunate enough to know either. He felt that great truth by nature, but he could not find its vocabulary. He felt desperately the cheapening all round him of words, of sex, of life. And he conceived (like the Church) that the redemption lay in something other than morals—however important morals might be, and he was not one to cheapen them. At the end of *Aaron's Rod*, after pages of discussion, he wrote a few sentences which achieve their effect partly by being *there*—at the end:

> There was a long pause. Then Aaron looked up into Lilly's face. It was dark and remote-seeming. It was like a Byzantine eikon at the moment.
>
> 'And whom shall I submit to?' he said.
>
> 'Your soul will tell you', replied the other.

He stopped—most fortunately—there. He could not always stop; he was unlike a Byzantine eikon in that. An insensitiveness to his medium sometimes accompanied his ill-defined gospel; the two inadequacies are related. He would—and did—break off the story of a perfectly good dinner-party to go off, like Thackeray, into a long disquisition. But unlike Thackeray, he has not both his methods on one level, so that the reader is made almost physically ill by the jerk. It is not altogether a matter of his too-often irritated language, for his irritation produced at times the most healthy comments. Few sentences can be more urgently recommended to many Christian writers than: 'You want to whoosh off in a nice little love-whoosh and lose yourself.' God, it has been said, loves Himself as the Good and not as Himself, and love must in general be an act of the will. But Lawrence was aware, in those around him, of love as a poor emotionalism, and of the will as a dry sectarian thing. He fled from such sterilities and liquidities to the power from which they seemed to have been abstracted, to the depths of 'sensualite' and the æonian process of the blood.

Mr. Hugh Kingsmill's study[1] of him is a biography, and carefully not much more than a biography. It ought to serve that purpose for some years, for it must be practically the only book on Lawrence uncoloured by personal acquaintance or intellectual approval or disapproval of its subject's varied views. Mr. Kingsmill has his views, of course, but he tries not to press them unduly and he subdues the natural amusement or unhappiness which some of Lawrence's relations with his acquaintances provoke. 'They filch my life for a sensation to themselves', he said in one of his letters, and it was not altogether untrue; their books show it. But it may

[1] *D. H. Lawrence*, by Hugh Kingsmill.

be added on their side that it was precisely sensation which he offered them and which he professed to be valid. 'The phallic consciousness', he wrote, 'is not the cerebral sex-consciousness, but something really deeper, and the root of poetry, lived or sung.' Certainly a cerebral sex-consciousness is not likely to be the root of much poetry, but then neither is the phallic consciousness unless some kind of cerebralism assists it. Dante asserts that when he first saw Beatrice the spirits of his sensations, of his emotions, and of his intellect were all stirred at once. The first exclaimed: 'Ah wretch! how often I shall be hampered henceforth!'; the second: 'Behold a god mightier than I who is come to rule over me!'; the third: 'Now your beatitude has appeared.' Dante spent a good deal of the rest of his life finding out what exactly they meant. But much as Dante may rebuke Lawrence, he is no less of a rebuke to those who attempt to annex poetry ('lived or sung'—whatever that means) to a spiritualism of sensibility. Poetry is sensual and intellectual—like sex. Both have, as Wordsworth said, 'a strength of usurpation', and Wordsworth went on to say that in that usurpation

> When the light of sense
> Goes out, but with a flash that has revealed
> The invisible world, doth greatness make abode,
> There harbours.

It is the vast union of visible and invisible, tangible and intangible, which is the real business of exploration—anyhow for Christians. The Christians of Lawrence's day did not care for the exploration of the body; he reacted against them with a natural but undesirable violence. Mr. Ford Madox Ford has said: 'Lawrence had the misfortune to become conscious of life in London and in a class in London that by a sort of inverted Puritanism insisted that a sort of nebulous glooming about sex was a moral duty and a sort of heroism.' But the Christians had driven them to it by a kind of nebulous gilding of sex and the body; they had refined the body into an unreal phantom of dim light and called it the Resurrection. Their morals aimed at a docetic Christ, and the awful creeds recalled them in vain.

Mr. Kingsmill's enjoyable book should be accompanied by Mr. Aldous Huxley's Introduction to the Letters, for that presents convincingly the effect of Lawrence's personality on his friends—in a way that others (say Mabel Dodge's *Lorenzo in Taos*) do not. Mr. Huxley quotes Vernon Lee as saying: 'He sees more than a human being ought to see', and he adds, 'To be with him was to find oneself transported to one of the frontiers of human consciousness.' He goes on to say: 'He could cook, he could sew, he could darn a stocking and milk a cow, he was an efficient wood-cutter and a good hand at embroidery, fires always burned when he laid them and a floor, after Lawrence had scrubbed it, was thoroughly clean.' Mr. Kingsmill tells the story of his crying out, in a car which had broken down, and of the mechanics of which he knew nothing: 'I am a failure! I am a failure as a man in a world of men!' Obviously, it was not true. He was a man, he was a writer, he might have been a leader—had he had any idea of precisely where to lead or exactly how, had he heard of the way of Affirmation of Images.

Of that way he was inevitably ignorant. Nor, it seems, did he find any satisfactory other. As a prophet, therefore, he was something of a failure, but, to do him justice, it was a role which he never desired. Unfortunately, the imposed vocation interfered with another authority which he did half-acknowledge, the authority of the English language. He could do things with it, he did them too rarely. He did create a few human emotions; he occasionally achieved something almost non-human. The end of *The Woman who Rode Away* invokes a strange unworldly landscape and action —except for the last sentence or two when some merely silly remark walks solemnly in. He did it in *Kangaroo* and *The Plumed Serpent*—the edge of an inhuman greatness rises on the horizon, and he attempts violently to invoke it, or he reproves us for not knowing it—and it is gone at once. The short stories have sometimes a human, sometimes an inhuman, effect. He tried occasionally the modern style of having no particular effect at all—a thing which lesser people did better.

The same difficulty, the same uncertainty, hover over his efforts at more familiar things. He knew about the world of *Sons and Lovers*, but neither he nor his readers know about the monotonously boring world of 'passion' (passion!) in *The Trespassers*. But perhaps he never came nearer to the actuality of what he thought he was writing about and wanted to write about than in a sentence in *The White Peacock*: 'The soft outstretching of her hand was like the whispering of strange words into the blood, and as she fingered a book the heart watched silently for the meaning.' The wonder, the intense awareness of *meaning*, in such a hand, or in any other such member of the physical body, the moment of great expectation of great wisdom, was the moment he greatly desired to explore. He believed that there was meaning, and his sincerity was in that unresting desire. He wandered round the world seeking it; he blamed Europe, and Asia, and America, for not giving it to him. 'Yet I don't believe in Buddha—hate him in fact—his rat-hole temples and his rat-hole religion. Better Jesus.' The phrase was more accurate than he, ignorant of Christianity, knew. But for reasons the disciples of Jesus whom he did know were incapable of explaining. They had not attended to the Athanasian Creed. Yet that great Ode contains in itself much that Lawrence might have recognized. It does not insist, as he sometimes did, that one must be *oneself*, that one must be *alone*. With probably a greater justice than his, it may be supposed to assume that most people, somehow or other, discover that they are alone all too painfully, and as for being oneself . . . . But it does insist precisely on what he was always emphasizing: that the life of 'sensuality' and the life of 'substance' cannot be separated and must not be confused.

For as the reasonable soul and flesh is one man; so God and Man is one Christ.

One, not by conversion of the Godhead into flesh, but by taking of the manhood into God.

One altogether, not by confusion of substance, but by unity of Person.

If this is so, we may have to recover for all that creation the Way of the Affirmation of its Images. We shall take no harm from it; we need not be morally nervous; its difficulties are no more, though certainly no less, than the difficulties of the Way of the Rejection of Images which, on the whole, the Christian notabilities have so far preferred. The movements for housing and social reform, the consciousness of the dispossessed masses, have already prepared the way as an accident of their own preoccupation. There is no likelihood that we shall become more amorously promiscuous because the other preoccupation is heartened by the physical intellect, because we have more meaning to brood over. The great identity of the *Anthropos* will be preserved the better in the categories of substance and sensuality the more we attend to those categories as such. The *New Life* of Dante does not begin to talk *only* of the spirit; no, that young and great doctor faints at the sight of his beloved; he cries when she cuts him; he is like any hysterical adolescent—that is, like anyone much in love. And the great surge of passion that immortally follows is precisely not a passion in which sensuality is refined away; at the close of the *Purgatory* she says to him: 'You should have been faithful to my buried flesh', *mia carne sepolta*, and in her actual eyes he sees reflected the two-natured Gryphon of Christ. There is no intenser image of the whole business of Romantic Theology—if it may so be called, meaning by the words that kind of theology which devotes itself to the serious study of the great romantic movement such as Dante and Wordsworth knew (in their separate kinds). It is Dante's image of 'the self point of union' where is the City; it is the flash of the sudden usurpation of flesh which reveals the greatness of the invisible City.

The wonder, the thrill, of a shoulder or a hand awaits its proper exploration. At present we have simply nothing to say to anyone in a state of exaltation, watching for 'meaning', except something which sounds very much like: 'Well, don't look too intently.' The hungry sheep look up for metaphysics, the profound metaphysics of the awful and redeeming body, and are given morals. Yet they are encouraged to receive the Blessed Sacrament which is defined to be for the body and the soul. Lawrence was a heretic—good; but he was concerned with a Christian orthodoxy—the orthodoxy of the blood of Man.

How to discover that? God knows; it cannot be done in study circles. We might certainly consider what has been done—there is the Lady Julian, there is Dante, there are Donne and Patmore. There is Lawrence. It is urgent that we should do it; it is even more urgent that we should not be ingenious and that we should take care of our style. Lawrence asserted that 'we shall never free the phallic reality from its "uplift" taint till we give it its own phallic language and use the obscene words.' He was certainly wrong, but he was no more wrong than those who habitually use a vocabulary which completely consists of uplift. For the result of that kind of evasion of 'sensuality' is the destruction of 'substance'. The only 'uplift' permissible is that of the Ascension, and it was a real body (the very root of all sensuality) which there withdrew through all the dimensions. 'Handle me and see—.' Repulsive materialism! But that was how the Divine Word talked.

NATURAL GOODNESS

From Theology, *October 1941*

It is a little unfortunate that in ordinary English talk the words 'natural' and 'supernatural' have come to be considered as opposed rather than as complementary. Something like it has happened with those other words 'nature' and 'grace', but less frequently, since the second two are more often used by trained theologians. But certainly the common use of the first two words implies rather a division between their meanings than a union.

This would be more comprehensible if we meant by 'supernatural' only the world of angels and of God. It is true that God is so wholly 'other' that only in the broadest sense can anything we mean by 'supernatural' be applied to Him any more than 'natural'. But of the two terms we must use one rather than the other. And the forces of the world of angels are certainly different from our own 'natural' forces. It is also true that the Christian religion has asserted that those 'natural' forces are but elements, and even infinitesimal elements, in the whole range of creation. But they are so far harmonious with it that they appear contrary only because of that element in man which we call sin, and they are not insignificant or negligible. The 'supernatural' must therefore in some sense include the 'natural'. 'A new earth' was promised as well as 'a new heaven'. Whatever the promise means, that earth is presumably in some relation to this earth.

Matter, certainly, is by definition the opposite of spirit. It is apparently as far the opposite of God (leaving will and morals out of the question) as God chose to create. But it did not therefore become less significant of Him than that less technical opposite which is called spirit. We have, in fact, only lost proper comprehension of matter by an apostasy in spirit. Matter and 'nature' have not, in themselves, sinned; what has sinned is spirit, if spirit and matter are to be regarded as divided. That they so easily can be is due perhaps to that lack of intellectual clarity produced by the Fall.

There is, I understand, an opinion permissible to the faithful which may be discussed here. I am told that it is related to the great name of Duns Scotus,[1] and no doubt it is, if permissible, familiar to readers of *Theology*. But it is illuminating on this subject and illustrates the problem of natural goodness.

It is, briefly, that the Incarnation is the point of creation, and the divine 'reason' for it. It pleased God in His self-willed activity to be incarnate. But obviously this union of Himself with matter in flesh did not necessarily involve the creation of other flesh. It would have been sufficient to Himself to be Himself united with matter, and that 'united with' means a union very much beyond our powers to conceive; more than a union, a unity. Even now, in spite of the Athanasian Creed, the single existence of the Incarnate Word is too often almost Gnostically contemplated as an inhabitation of the flesh by the Word. But it is not so; what He is, He is wholly and absolutely, and even in His death and in the separation of body and soul He remains wholly and absolutely one. His act could have been to Himself alone. He decreed that it should not be; He determined creation; He determined not only to be incarnate, but to be incarnate by means of a mother. He proposed to Himself to be born into a world.

This decree upon Himself was the decree that brought mankind into being. It was His will to make creatures of such a kind that they should share in that particular joy of His existence in flesh. He bade for Himself a mother and all her companions; perhaps the mystery of the mortal maternity of God was greater even than that, but at least it was that. It was the great and single act of active love,

[1] See note 2, p. xxxviii. A. R.

consonant with nothing but His nature, compared to which the Redemption (if indeed He were infinitely to maintain all souls alive) was but a sheer act of justice. Our flesh was to hold, to its degree, the secrets of His own.

Nothing has ever altered, nothing could ever alter, that decree. I do not, of course, mean even to seem to separate it from His other acts; only one must speak in terms of time. Certainly He acted altogether, He created and redeemed and judged and executed judgement all at once. But it seems that, as far as we are concerned, He also in that act created process and therefore time, time being in this sense the mere measurement of process. Indeed, so determining to be incarnate by a mother, it might perhaps be said that He determined process for Himself also, and even that, for pure increase of joy, He determined that the process should depend on the free-will of His mother and of men. He designed exchange of joy; He gave us the final privilege of owing everything to ourselves as well as to Him. This moment was our primal nature, and nothing has ever altered that fact—not though we may wish it had.

There followed, as we know, the chosen catastrophe which we call the Fall. Whether in that state in which mankind was, the Fall was a single act of a single soul, or the simultaneous act of all souls, this is not the place to discuss. It is, I suppose, possible (since it is to be believed that every human creature sins) that in some way every human nature sinned at once; that the whole web was at once and everywhere ruined. That is irrelevant to the fact that, however it happened, it certainly happened. The will of man sinned. But the will of man was a spiritual quality; it was in his soul. It was that power in him which we call the soul that sinned. It was not the power which we call the flesh. It was therefore the 'supernatural' which sinned. The 'natural', as we now call it, did not. They cannot, of course, be separated. But if, in terminology, they can be, then it is the matter of our substance which has remained faithful, and the immaterial which has not.

The definition of the Fall is that man determined to know good as evil. Whether (as may be) it was indeed an affair of the fruit of a tree or whether that is symbolical does not matter. But if the good, which was whole, was to be known as evil, then process must be known as evil; that is, the process must be to a living death. The end would be hell. But all the qualities and all the glories of that human creation were not in one moment changed to a state of hell. So much the decree of process itself forbade. The end might be inevitable, but it had to be gradual.

His nature, as it were, was still implanted in His creatures; it was, indeed, human for divine, their nature. Nor has that foundation ever failed. They devoted it to everlasting death. But the genius of it, so to speak, was of eternal life. He who had desired His creatures to accept His choice now accepted the terms of His creation; He accepted the choice of His creatures. The Incarnation became also the Redemption. He became the new thing. But that did not prevent Him from being the foundation of the old thing. He was, is, and is to be, the light that lighteneth every man.

The Apostolic and Catholic Faith declared the Redemption of fallen nature, but that Redemption was on the principles and to the principles of our first unfallen nature. Man could not longer be innocent; he was corrupt, and his best efforts were, but for the new grace, doomed to death. But his best efforts were, and are, of no other kind than had been decreed. His blood might be tainted, but the source from which it sprang was still the same. His natural life was still, and is now, a disordered pattern of the only pattern, a confused type of the one original; it is full still of glory and of peace, as well as of bloodshed and despair. It contends within itself. The most extreme goodness may be found in it and asserted of it—so long as the absolute invalidity of it apart from the new life is also declared. The most absolute domination of the new life may be asserted, so long as the accidental goodness of the old is never denied.

It is no doubt true that the operations of the Christian Church for two thousand years—sacramental, doctrinal, and moral—have had a greater effect than we generally realize. When all allowances, however, have been made for this, and for the various legal and social systems which, touched by Christianity as well as by civic security, have faintly aimed at goodness, it remains true that the goodness in the 'natural' order often seems to rival and equal the goodness of the 'supernatural'. Something very much like heroic sanctity exists everywhere. This heroic sanctity outside the Christian Church is a thing for which Christians are always 'making allowances'. I use the silly phrase because it is the only one that fits. They do not, perhaps, mean it to sound so; the effect is due to the use of a great vocabulary by inadequate voices. It is also due to the unintentionally insincere claims made by foolish Christians on behalf of their Christian experience. Vigil, heroism, martyrdom, vicarious life, are common to man. In so far as they are possible outside the Church, they are elements of man's original nature operative within him in spite of, but under conditions of, the catastrophe of the Fall. In so far as they are impossible inside the Church, they are the change in man's fallen nature which even grace has not yet renewed. Nature and grace are categories of one Identity.

What, then, are we to hold is the value of the Christian religion?

It is applicable far beyond itself, in the sense that what it says is the only final validity of those other great acts of goodness. Union with our sacred Lord is obtained by acts. Belief is, no doubt, an act; proper motive is an act; but also an act is an act. The great doctrines are the only explanation and the only hope. But even the great doctrines are only the statement of something as wide as the universe and as deep as the human heart. They do not deny as Creator that which they adore as Saviour, though the Creator had to become a Saviour lest His creation should be wholly lost. It is to be believed that, except by the Cross and Resurrection, no act is valid; and that by that Cross and Resurrection the proper validity of every act is determined. The Christian Church has been charged with the great secrets which are the only facts of existence. But the visible and vocal Church will have to practise much humility, in itself as well as in its separate members, before it can find itself capable of speaking on equal terms with that nature which it has to regenerate with universal blessing.

The Incarnation of the Son of God led to the Cross because it summed up and prevented the otherwise inevitable end of human process both individual and general. But it is at least a question whether the Incarnation only existed to lead to the Cross or whether it was in fact the original act. The Church is the means of penitence and faith. But the lack of penitence and faith cannot altogether destroy the value of what remains of natural goodness. The transformation of natural goodness into eternal goodness demands all stress on both the Incarnation and the Crucifixion. Our great difficulty is that it is much easier to transform eternal goodness, or what should be eternal goodness, into natural goodness. 'When religion is in the hands of the natural man', wrote William Law, 'he is always the worse for it; it adds a bad heat to his own dark fire and helps to inflame his four elements of selfishness, envy, pride and wrath.' But it was the same William Law who wrote:

> Natural religion, if you understand it rightly, is a most excellent thing, it is a right sentiment of heart, it is so much goodness in the heart, it is its sensibility both of its separation from and its relation to God; and therefore it shows itself in nothing but in a penitential sentiment of the weight of its sins, and in an humble recourse by faith to the mercy of God. Call but this the religion of nature and then the more you esteem it, the better; for you cannot wish well to it without bringing it to the Gospel state of perfection. For the religion of the Gospel is this religion of penitence and faith in the mercy of God, brought forth into its full perfection. For the Gospel calls you to nothing but to know and understand and practise a full and real penitence, and to know by faith such heights and depths of the divine mercy towards you, as the religion of nature had only some little uncertain glimmerings of.

Remove the word 'God' from that description of natural religion, remove the word 'religion', and the principles still hold. Those principles are in our nature because of His, and the Word (and we by the Word) are other than all the vocabularies.

THE INDEX OF THE BODY

From the Dublin Review,[1] *July 1942*

In the *Prelude* (book viii, ll. 279–81) Wordsworth wrote:

> the human form
> To me became an index of delight,
> Of grace and honour, power and worthiness.

The most important word there is *index*. There are moments in all poetry when the reader has to ask himself whether a word used by the poet is accurate not only for the poet's universe but for the reader's own. It is a secondary decision, since the first must be only of the poetic value, but it is sometimes important. That is so here; the word *index*, pressed to its literal meaning, is a word which demands attention, and afterwards assent or dissent.

It is true that Wordsworth himself did not develop the idea; he is speaking generally, and in other passages his genius suggests that the index is to a volume written in a strange language. This is no weakness in Wordsworth; it was, on one side, his particular business. Thus the image of the Leech-Gatherer in *Resolution and Independence* is drawn at least as inhuman as human; so is the Soldier in Book IV of the *Prelude* who is the cause of such terror, and the other wanderers; the woman with the pitcher, and even Lucy Gray, are of the same kind. They are on the borders of two worlds, which almost pass and repass into each other. Wordsworth, of all the Romantics, came nearest to defining and mapping that border-land.

There are, of course, also his more exclusively human figures—

[1] For this essay I have been able to compare a manuscript and uncorrected typescript with the text as printed; for 'The Redeemed City' in the next section, an uncorrected typescript. The differences between script and text in that essay are negligible, but in this one, the Roman Catholic editorial censorship (evidently) had removed three passages and a sentence. To mark them seems to give them a fortuitous importance, so I have merely replaced them. It was not possible to follow any script consistently, however, as the author had made a few additions which are only to be found in the magazine. As to punctuation, I have been obliged to use my own discretion in choosing between the texts, though in some instances—as when the *D.R.* compositor had repunctuated Hopkins's poem—the choice was easy. A. R.

Michael, for instance, in the poem of that name. Here the human form suggests to him the grandeur of the moral virtues; it is the suffering and labouring spirit of man which he sees. That may have been what he had chiefly in mind in the passage I have quoted: man as 'a solitary object and sublime', but man also 'with the most common; husband, father', who

> suffered with the rest
> From vice and folly, wretchedness and fear.

But the passage is capable of another reading, and one which proposes to us a real, if less usual, sequence. It is that reading which I wish now to discuss, and the word *index* is the beginning. The question proposed is whether we shall take that word seriously as a statement of the relation of the human form to 'grace and honour, power and worthiness'. The human form meant, to Wordsworth, the shape of the shepherd seen among the hills. There it was high and distant. It was a whole being significant of a greater whole—which is, in some sense, the definition of objects seen romantically. But the lines might be applied to the same shape, seen near at hand and analytically. They might refer to the body itself; it is that which can be considered as an index.

What then would be meant by the word? Nothing but itself. An index is a list of various subjects, with reference to those places where, in the text of the volume, they are treated at greater length. But, at least, the words naming the subjects are the same; and a really good index will give some idea of the particular kind of treatment offered on the separate pages. Some such idea, Wordsworth's lines suggest, the body and even the members of the body may give of the delight, grace, honour, power, and worthiness of man's structure. The structure of the body is an index to the structure of a greater whole.

I am anxious not to use words which seem too much to separate the physical structure from the whole. The fact of death, and the ensuing separation of 'body' and 'soul', lead us to consider them too much as separate identities conjoined. But I hope it is not unorthodox to say that body and soul are one identity, and that all our inevitable but unfortunate verbal distinctions are therefore something less than true. Death has been regarded by the Christian Church as an outrage—a necessary outrage, perhaps, but still an outrage. It has been held to be an improper and grotesque schism in a single identity—to which submission, but not consent, is to be offered; a thing, like sin, that ought not to be and yet is. The distress of our Lord in His Passion may perhaps not improperly be supposed to be due to His contemplation of this all but inconceivable schism in His own sacred and single identity. If our manhoods were from the first meant indivisibly, how much more His!

It is one of the intellectual results of the Fall that our language has always to speak in terms of the Fall; and that we cannot help our language does not make it any more true. The epigrams of saints, doctors, and poets, are the nearest we can go to the recovery of that ancient validity, our unfallen speech. To treat the body as an index is to assume that, as in an index the verbal element—the *word* given—is the same as in the whole text, so in the physical structure of the greater index the element—the *quality* given—is the same as in the whole structure. Another poet, Patmore, put the thing in a similar light when he wrote that

> from the graced decorum of the hair,
> Ev'n to the tingling sweet
> Soles of the simple earth-confiding feet
> And from the inmost heart
> Outwards unto the thin
> Silk curtains of the skin,
> Every least part
> Astonish'd hears
> And sweet replies to some like region of the spheres.

'The spheres' there are likely to mean, first, the outer heavens. This idea is practically that of the microcosm and the macrocosm: the idea that a man is a small replica of the universe. Man was 'the workshop of all things', 'a little world', *mundus minor exemplum majoris mundi ordine, filius totius mundi*. It is a very ancient idea; it was held before Christianity and has been held during Christianity; it was common to Christians, Jews, and Mohammedans; and, for all I know, the scientific hypothesis of evolution bears a relation to the union of the two. Into that, however, I am not learned enough to go. The idea went through many changes, but its general principle remained constant: that man was the rational epitome of the universe. It led, of course, to many absurdities, and (if you choose—like any other idea) to some evils. Some writers catalogued painstakingly the more obvious fantasies: hair was the grass or the forests; bones were mountains; the sun was the eyes, and so on. Astrology, if not based on it, at least found the idea convenient; however we may reject that ancient study, it had at least this philosophic principle mixed up with it—that each man, being unique, was a unique image of the universe, that the spatially greater affected the spatially lesser, and the calculable influences of the stars were only calculable because each man represented and reproduced the whole. Astrology then was a high and learned science; it was forbidden for good reasons, but it was not fatalistic. It did not say 'this will certainly happen'; it said: 'Given these stellar and individual relations, this result is likely.' But the will of God and the wills of men were allowed much freedom to interfere with the result. *Sapiens dominabitur astris.* The paragraphs in our papers today bear as much resemblance to the science as texts lifted up on boards outside churches do to the whole dogmas of the Church. The paragraphs are, I allow, more likely to harm; the texts, on the whole, are innocuous.

Beside, or rather along with, this study went the patterns of other occult schools. The word 'occult' has come into general use, and is convenient, if no moral sense is given it simply as itself. It deals with hidden things, and their investigation. But in this case we are concerned not so much with the pretended operations of those occult schools as with a certain imagination of relation in the universe, and that only to pass beyond it. The signs of the Zodiac were, according to some students, related to the parts of the physical body. The particular attributions varied, and all were in many respects arbitrary. But some of them were extremely suggestive; they may be allowed at least a kind of authentic poetic vision. Thus, in one pattern, the house of the Water-carrier was referred to the eyes; the house of the Twins to the arms and hands; the house of the Scorpion to the privy parts and the sexual organs; and the house of the Balances to the buttocks.

It will be clear that these four attributions at least had a great significance. It will be clear also that in such a poetic (so to call it) imagination, we are dealing with a kind of macrocosmic–microcosmic union of a more serious and more profitable kind than the mere exposition by a debased astrology of chances in a man's personal life. It may be invention, but if so, it is great invention; the houses of the Zodiac, with their special influences ruling in special divisions of the spatial universe, may be but the fables of astronomy; it must be admitted that few certain facts support them. But they are not unworthy fables. They direct attention to the principles at work both in the spatial heavens and in the structure of man's body. Aquarius is for water, clarity, vision; Gemini are for a plural motion, activity, and achievement; Libra is for that true strength of balance on which the structure of man depends.

With this suggestion, we are on the point of deserting the spatial heavens for something else. The like regions of the spheres, of which Patmore spoke, here begin to be transferred to the spiritual heavens. 'As above, so below' ran the old maxim, but even that dichotomy is doubtful. The houses of the Zodiac, in this, do but confuse the issue, except in so far as they, like the whole universe, exhibit the mystery by which spirit becomes flesh, without losing spirit. Perhaps the best verbal example is in the common use of the word 'heart'. Even in our common speech the word is ambiguous. To call Hitler heartless means that he seems to be without the common principle of compassion. It is said that Tertullian (but I have not found the reference) said that 'the supreme principle of intelligence and vitality', 'the sovereign faculty' of man, resided 'where the Egyptians taught—*Namque homini sanguis circumcordialis est sensus*, the sense of man is in the blood around the heart'. At least the pulsating organ presents, for man, his proper physical rhythm in the whole—*mundus minor exemplum majoris mundi ordine*. As our meaning—physical life or compassionate life—so the word *heart*. Compassion is the union of man with his fellows, as is the blood. The permitted devotion to the Sacred Heart is to the source of both. The physical heart is, in this sense, an 'index' to both. Gerard Hopkins wrote, of the Blessed Virgin:

> If I have understood
> She holds high motherhood
> Towards all our ghostly good
> And plays in grace her part
> About man's beating heart,
> Laying, like air's fine flood,
> The deathdance in his blood;
> Yet no part but what will
> Be Christ our Saviour still.

The visionary forms of the occult schools are but dreams of the Divine Body.

All these brief allusions show that there have been some traditions of significance—poetic, occult, religious. Christians, however, may be permitted to press the significance more closely; they may be allowed to ask whether the body is not indeed a living epigram of virtue. There have been doctors who held that Christ would not have become incarnate if man had not sinned; there have been doctors who held that He would. Either way, it is clear that the Sacred Body was itself virtue. The same qualities that made His adorable soul made His adorable flesh. If the devotion to the Sacred Heart does not, in itself, imply something of the sort, I do not know what it does imply. The virtues are both spiritual and physical—or rather they are expressed in those two categories. This is recognized in what are regarded as the more 'noble' members in the body—the heart, the eyes. But it is not so often recognized as a truth underlying all the members—the stomach, the buttocks. That is partly because we have too long equated the body as such with the 'flesh' of St. Paul. But 'flesh' is no more that than (as Mgr. Knox pointed out recently in the *Tablet*) it is 'sex'. The body was holily created, is holily redeemed, and is to be holily raised from the dead. It is, in fact, for all our difficulties with it, less fallen, merely in itself, than the soul in which the quality of the will is held to reside; for it was a sin of the will which degraded us. 'The evidence of things not seen' is in the body seen as this epigram; nay, in some sense, even 'the substance of things hoped for', for what part it has in that substance remains to it unspoiled.

It is in this sense then that the body is indeed an 'index' to delight, power, and the rest. 'Who conceives', wrote Prior,

> 'Who conceives, what bards devise,
> That heaven is placed in Celia's eyes?'

Well, no; not so simply as that. But Celia's eyes are a part of the body which (said Patmore, who was orthodox enough)

> Astonish'd hears
> And sweet replies to some like region of the spheres.

And those spheres are not merely the old spatial macrocosmic heavens, but the deep heaven of our inner being. The discernment of pure goodwill, of (let it be said for a moment) pure love in Celia's eyes, at some high moment of radiant interchange or indeed at any other moment, is no less part of the heavenly vision (so tiny and remote as it may be) because it is a physical as well as a spiritual vision. The word 'sacramental' has perhaps here served us a little less than well; it has, in popular usage, suggested rather the spiritual *using* the physical than a common—say, a single—operation.

Eyes then are compacted power; they are an index of vision; they see and refer us to greater seeing. Nor has the stomach a less noble office. It digests food; that is, in its own particular method, it deals with the nourishment offered by the universe. It is a physical formula of that health which destroys certain elements—the bacteria which harmfully approach us. By it we learn to consume; by it therefore to be, in turn, consumed. So even with those poor despised things, the buttocks. There is no seated figure, no image of any seated figure, which does not rely on them for its strength and balance. They are at the bottom of the sober dignity of judges; the grace of a throned woman; the hierarchical session of the Pope himself reposes on them: into even greater images and phrases we need not now go.

It will be thought I labour the obvious; and I will not go through the physical structure suggesting and propounding identities. The point will have been sufficiently made if the sense of that structure being heavenly not by a mere likeness but in its own proper nature is achieved. It is a point not so much of doctrine as of imagination. That imagination is at once individual and social. The temples of the

Holy Ghost are constructed all on one plan: and our duties to our material fellows are duties to structures of beatitude. The relation of the Incarnation to our own mode of generation is blessedly veiled. But its relation to those other identities of power is not at all doubtful. It is not only physical structures we neglect or damage by our social evils; it is living indexes of life. The Virtues exist in all of them materially, but it is the Virtues which so exist. Christ, in some sense, derived His flesh from them, for He derived it from His Mother, and she from her ancestors, and they from all mankind.

The Sacred Body is the plan upon which physical human creation was built, for it is the centre of physical human creation. The great dreams of the human form as including the whole universe are in this less than the truth. As His, so ours; the body, in this sense of an index, is also a pattern. We carry about with us an operative synthesis of the Virtues; and it may be held that when we fall in love (for example), we fall in love precisely with the operative synthesis.

> Grace was in all her steps, heaven in her eye;
> In every gesture dignity and love;

is much more a definite statement of fact than we had supposed; footsteps are astonishing movements of grace. That we cannot properly direct and control our sensations and emotions is not surprising; but the greatness of man is written even in his incapacity, and when he sins he sins because of a vision which, even though clouded, is great and ultimate. As every heresy is a truth pushed disproportionately, so with every sin; at least, with every physical sin. But, however in those states of 'falling in love' the vision of a patterned universe is revealed to us, the revelation vanishes, and we are left to study it slowly, heavily, and painfully. All that the present essay attempts to do is to present a point of view which has behind it, one way and another, a great tradition—a tradition which, for Christians, directs particular attention to the Sacred Body as the Archtype of all bodies. In this sense the Eucharist exposes also its value. The 'index' of our bodies, the incarnate qualities of the moral universe, receive the Archtype of all moralities truly incarnated; and not only the pattern in the soul and will but the pattern in the body is renewed. Or, better, in that unity which we, under the influence of our Greek culture, divide into soul and body. 'Socrates', Dr. William Ellis writes, 'invented the concept which permeates every part of modern thinking, the concept of the twofold nature of man, of man as a union of the active, or spiritual, with the inactive, or corporeal; the concept, in short, of the organism as a dead carcass activated by a living ghost. Even if we repudiate this idea, we are still half-dominated by it, so deeply does it underlie our pattern of culture.'[1] I am far from suggesting that this is the proper Christian view. But there is, I think, no doubt that it is not far from the popular Christian view. The fuss that has been made about Browning's line (not that that was Browning's fault)—'nor soul helps flesh more now than flesh helps soul'—shows that. It was repeated almost as a new revelation, though indeed the Lady Julian had said almost the same thing centuries before. We have to overcome that lazy habit of the imagination—the outrage of death notwithstanding. We experience, physically, in its proper mode, the Kingdom of God: the imperial structure of the body carries its own high doctrines—of vision, of digestion of mysteries, of balance, of movement, of operation. 'That soul', said Dante in the *Convivio*, 'which embraces all these powers [the rational, the sensitive, and the vegetative] is the most perfect of all the rest.' The rational, or self-conscious, power is indeed the noblest, but we must ask from it a complete self-consciousness, and not a self-consciousness in schism.

It was suggested that the stress of this imagination may be an incentive to our social revolution. For if the body of our neighbour is compact of these heavenly qualities, incarnated influences, then we are indeed neglecting the actual Kingdom of God in neglecting it. It is the living type of the Arch-typal. We have not merely to obey a remote moral law in feeding and succouring and sheltering it. It is the 'index' of power; tear away the index, and we are left without the power; tear away the index, and we are left without the delight. Let the whole to which that index witnesses be as immense as any volume of truth may be, and still the value of that small substance remains. Every student of a learned work uses the index attentively. A good index can indeed be studied in itself. To study the body so is to increase our preparation for the whole great text.

ST. JOHN

Time and Tide *review of* Christianity According to St. John *by W. F. Howard, and* The Christian Failure *by Charles Singer, 1943*

THE Gospel of St. John was for long a refuge for the 'spiritualizers' and a resort for the pseudo-mystics. It seemed to contain little about baptism and little about the Eucharist, and nothing either way that could not be interpreted out of a literal into an allegorical meaning. It could always be used as a blanket through which the heavenly

[1] *The Idea of the Soul in Western Philosophy and Science.*

John cried to the not-nearly-so-heavenly Paul, busily engaged on his work of complicating the simple spiritual Gospel, 'Hold! Hold!' Not that Paul did.

There was, of course, some excuse for this. It is true that the Fourth Gospel is peculiarly the Gospel of the Holy Spirit, and that it particularly stresses the fact that all the events in the life of our Lord, as well as happening in Judæa, happen in the soul; whereas the Synoptics made it crashingly clear that all events that happen in the soul happened in Judæa. Why this second fact should be thought a rather low business is always surprising. But so it was. That God should be born in the spirit was permissible—not that He should be born in the flesh; the new birth by inward fire—yes, the new birth by outward water—no; the mystical union—yes, the physical resurrection—no. And so on. All this the Divine John was supposed, in essence, to support—truth, but not dogma. (Though the picture of Truth tolerantly refusing to be dogmatic—!)

It becomes more and more clear that this division cannot be made. St. John was as much one of the household of faith as St. Matthew or St. Paul; there is in him no escape from it into some little esoteric garden. The esotericism is there, but it is in the facts of earth as much as of heaven—say rather, it is in their being one. The Church? 'Jesus answered them, Did I not choose you the Twelve?' The Eucharist? It is St. John who describes the departure of those—no doubt, all of them mystics—who were shocked by its materialism. The priesthood? It is St. John who records the commission—'whose soever sins ye remit, they are remitted; whose ye retain, they are retained'. The awful subordination of heaven to earth, with every responsibility that it involves, is made more, not less, complex by the Fourth Gospel.

Dr. Howard's learned but never pedantic book is obviously the cause of this meditation. It is, one might say, a study in the words used, as all proper criticism must be. Dr. Howard has wonderfully avoided filling his pages with personal exhortations and semi-pious reverie. In consequence he remains fresh and interesting—especially perhaps in the chapter called 'Eschatology and Mysticism'. All St. John's sublime mystical doctrine does not prevent his belief in a future Parousia. The real distinction in all the Gospels is identical; it is only, when the Voice (within or without; say, within and without, one Voice, one actual Voice) cries 'Lo, I come quickly', between those who say simply 'Come' and those who say 'Come—but not *too* quickly'.

It is convenient (for us who belong to the last group) to mention here Dr. Singer's little book on *The Christian Failure*. Dr. Singer is so passionately sincere, and his historical accusations are so justified by hideous facts, that it is not quite becoming to find fault with a book which all instructed Christians would find it wholesome to read. But on his view the scientific discoveries of the Renaissance make nonsense of St. John. When the universe was understood to be 'infinite', it could no longer be supposed to be 'created'. 'Creation is fundamental to Christianity.' To St. John indeed, as Dr. Howard shows, the characteristic of the whole universe, especially of man, is 'creatureliness'. If man is not a creature, Christianity is untrue. Dr. Singer expects a complete breakdown of the Church. He believes that Christians have 'minimized or slurred' the evils in the history of the Church. I do not know that the Inquisition, Alexander VI, and Calvin (whom he gives as examples) have been much minimized. Finally, he accuses us of having betrayed the Jews to the Germans, in the sense that we did not, before the war, as Christians, denounce the persecution. It is a fervid, and perhaps just, rebuke. Yet acknowledging Dr. Singer's accusations, it is still to be noted that a doctrinal abyss remains. The most fundamental Christian doctrine, Dr. Singer says, 'anticipating even the Incarnation, is that there is a dignity and worth of the individual soul, for without that the Incarnation itself would be meaningless'. It is very doubtful if this is the doctrine of St. John. There it is the undignified and worthless who are to be redeemed; their only value is that they can be made something other. 'The greatest concession to the dignity and worth of the individual is that he shall worship God as he believes God desires. That concession has never been made by Christianity.' Nor by the Prophets of Israel; see the terrible description of idolatry in Ezekiel. Freedom of adoration (within limits, I gather, that exclude the Thug) is a necessity. But the union of that necessity and the Christian necessity is one of the deepest and darkest of all unions. The light that shines in that darkness is not easily seen by easily-tolerant eyes.

AUGUSTINE AND ATHANASIUS

From a Time and Tide *review of F. J. Sheed's translation of the* Confessions, *and of 'A new translation by a Religious' of St. Athanasius's* The Incarnation of the Word of God, *1944*

St. Augustine has, on the whole, suffered more than St. Athanasius from the sympathy of the 'human-hearted' among his readers. The *Confessions* have become 'one of the great autobiographies of the world'. One might almost as well call the four Gospels 'the four best short biographies in the world'. The *Confessions* are continually luring us to 'fiddle harmonics on the strings of sensualism', or of sensibility, for it is not only carnality that is in question. Nowadays we read Shakespeare to discover that he suffered from insomnia; we read the *Cloud of Unknowing* to discover that its author was 'a lovable man'; we remark with appreciative sympathy Augustine praying: 'Give me chastity, but not yet.' We are not, however, nearly so appreciative of the chastity which he undoubtedly got. Yet this is the dramatic climax of the story; to miss it is to miss Hamlet killing the King and only to be interested while the Prince wanders through the corridors of Elsinore. After the famous 'Tolle: lege!' our interest begins to flag. But for Augustine himself it was only then that the serious interest began—when 'our soul by living well begins to be a living soul'.

No doubt the difficulty about chastity was one—only one—of Augustine's personal difficulties. But the climax of the book—the mere literary climax as a book—is only by accident in the personal Augustine at all, even the chaste Augustine. It was certainly not by accident that he made his own story end with the tenth book of the *Confessions* and that the last three books deal with the account of the creation of the world, in Genesis. This was the full and great conclusion. Augustine was issuing into a true and significant world of which Genesis gave a mystical account. That is the whole point, and not to feel it so is to be a bad literary critic. To disagree with him is another matter, but not to see what he is doing is to betray that very literature we claim to admire and safeguard.

Some of his interpretations will seem strange and strained, as do some of the arguments of Athanasius; just as some of Shakespeare's jokes seem dull, and some of Milton's lines flat. But what both these writers were talking about is quite clear: it was 'a new heaven and a new earth', not in the future but all about them. Our Lord had promised them this world back 'a hundred fold', as well as eternal life, and to their own intense and joyous surprise they found they had got it. They were in this new genesis—*tam antiqua, tam nova*—and they wrote about it. It renewed their intelligence as well as their virtue. The *Confessions* devote more space to philosophy than to chastity, and the sense of enlargement is very marked. Speaking of that anthropomorphism of which Christians were, then as now, accused, Augustine, when he discovered what they really believed, burst out: 'I rejoiced, O my God, that Your Church . . . had no taste for such puerile nonsense.' A sentence less quoted than the famous 'but not yet' passage is that in which he mocks at himself for having 'gone on spouting forth so many uncertainties as confidently as if I had known them for sure'. But then the admission of a fornication or two is much more to our taste than the acknowledgement that we solemnly talked twaddle for years. The humility which Augustine found—say rather, that blossoming humility which in that new world *was* Augustine—enabled him to make both admissions in passing. This was what living in 'the reasonable and intellectual mind of Your pure City' permitted.

The treatise of St. Athanasius is one of the Christian classics. It is much to be desired that we may have more of such books, if they can be as clearly done. Athanasius begins with the same fact with which Augustine ends: 'The first fact that you must grasp is this: the renewal of creation has been wrought by the Self-same Word Who made it in the beginning.' He is, of course, arguing and not telling a story, but he is arguing about the same subject—this renewal of the corrupt into incorruption. 'All things', says Fox, 'gave up a new smell unto me.' 'Herein', wrote Law, 'appears the high dignity and never-ceasing perpetuity of our nature.' It is not merely a personal salvation, though naturally this great and universal thing can only be known through personal salvation; you can only live in England by being in England and only in 'the pure city' by being in the pure City. That is what salvation is. The knowledge of it is close enough—entirely human and utterly different, unbearably intimate and unbearably distant. 'All this fantasy', says Athanasius, of oracles and magic and inspirations, 'has ceased', and it is that phrase which permeates all these great writers. They say, as it were, 'I do not mean to sound arrogant; I do not want to seem rude; it is not I who say so; but all this fantasy of yours has ceased. Incorruption exists; this is it. Smell, look, taste, handle: this is creation made new.' 'I heard,' wrote Augustine, 'I understood.'

III · THE CITY

THE IMAGE OF THE CITY IN ENGLISH VERSE

From the Dublin Review, *July 1940*

THERE are in English verse a certain number of recurrent images. One of these is the image of the City; it is built up by many descriptions, similes, metaphors, and maxims. These images, making altogether one greater image, show the City both ideally and actually (and even historically), in schism and in concord, as in heaven and as on earth. I do not propose here to define that image further than to say that it is the sense of many relationships between men and women woven into a unity; and it is the poetic hints of that unity which make the image to be discussed. The best single image of the heavenly City is perhaps in the prose sentence from the Apocalypse: 'I saw the Holy City, the New Jerusalem, descending out of heaven from God.' I remember nothing in verse quite equivalent to that, although Milton at one point runs it close:

> About Him all the sanctities of heaven
> Stood thick as stars, and from his sight received
> Beatitude past utterance.

On the other hand the best line describing an ideal earthly city, the perfection of earthly labour, is to be found in Shakespeare's *Henry V*, in the Archbishop's speech on the similitude of the bees:

> The singing masons building roofs of gold.

It is this line, to be varied, amplified, exchanged, or contradicted, which will serve as the beginning of the discussion.

The main difference between the idea of the City and the idea of the Nation is that the first can involve the thought of choice. There is something fatal about the Nation, something in the blood. It is true that, historically, the City has often been as much a matter of birth as has the Nation. But the sense of deliberate action remains in our imagination; the speech of Pericles determined that, and the movement of Aeneas away from Dido to Italy. Bestowal of citizenship is not quite the same thing as the issue of naturalization papers. We can deliberately found the City; the nation can, at best, only appear. And even in patriotic national poetry it is often particular places which are named.

Of all English poems that which most holds, under those conditions, the growing development of the image of the City is the *Prelude*. That poem is stated to be the story of the development of 'a poet's mind', and the development of every poet's mind consists largely in the adequate growth and analysed growth of the particular images he tends to use. Some may be lost or others adopted, but on the whole there is, in most poets, a retention of the most significant images. This Wordsworth himself declared:

> And O, ye Fountains, Meadows, Hills, and Groves,
> Forebode not any severing of our loves....
> I only have relinquished one delight
> To live beneath your more habitual sway.

But that 'habitual sway' was exercised in those later days because of 'the human heart by which we live'. Every young Romantic poet (of whatever kind his Romanticism may be—amorous, political, religious) has to face the same challenge: can that Romanticism endure belief and intellectual inquiry, can it even endure contradiction, and can it thrive afterwards in a greater, more explicit, poetry, inclusive of that earlier ardour? Dante, the greatest of all Romantics, showed us this in full, but the *Prelude* showed us a great part of it. To say that the later Wordsworth lost his genius is only partly true, but even with that loss he is loftier than all but the very few. He left a few of his own greater images unanalysed, but he showed us how to read poetry, he taught us the place of images.

The process of the development of the City-image in the *Prelude* begins, as all of Wordsworth does, in the great passage concerning the mountain that seemed to stride after him as a boy.

> My brain
> Worked with a dim and undetermined sense
> Of unknown modes of being.

It was a great deal more than Nature that was in those unknown modes; men were there, and man, and the City. The hints of the modes to be known were shown to him at moments—a shepherd, the dead body dragged from a pool, the dream of the Arab. Presently the universities come, and the silent face of Newton, voyaging through strange seas of thought; and then London and France and Paris. The vision of 'the singing masons' rises in the Revolution; the movement towards 'the two great ends of liberty and power'. The word 'power' is all about the *Prelude*. I think there has been so far no sufficient meditation on what Wordsworth meant by it. Nature and the Revolution are almost united in that 'power' within him which is the Imagination ('so called By sad incompetence of human speech'), and there follows that strange moment of exaltation and terror in the room in Paris in which he remembers the September massacres. It is almost the point at which the poem turns on itself: 'all things have second birth'.

At that moment in the poem, when it seems as if the image of the City of man is about to appear fully, as if its 'unknown mode of being' was to be analysed, the catastrophe falls. The British Government declares war on France. The second birth was, for Wordsworth then, a birth into death, or something worse than death. The contradiction of the singing masons is in those other lines describing his nightmares:

> long orations which I strove to plead
> Before unjust tribunals—with a voice
> Labouring, a brain confounded, and a sense,
> Death-like, of treacherous desertion, felt
> In the last place of refuge—my own soul.

These phrases mean very much more to us today than they have done, but that is only to say that we have not attended properly to Wordsworth. We may understand better than we did what he suffered when he found himself excluded by his heart's anguish from what had seemed to him precisely one of the best places of the community (of the City therefore)—the congregation in the village church. They were praying for victory:

> I only, like an uninvited guest,
> Whom no one owned, sat silent: shall I add,
> Fed on the day of vengeance yet to come?

It is inconceivable today. But it had been precisely inconceivable to Wordsworth then. Only it had happened. We may think that he was, then, justified. But that made no difference to his emotions—'a conflict of sensations without name!' His passion had rebelled against his own native home.

It is by such moments of poetic intensity that the *Prelude* labours towards its resolution, the fidelity to that great Nature (which does not here mean daffodils and thunderstorms) of which the proper community of men, the City, is a part. It is as a 'prophet' of that Nature that he, with Coleridge, is to work against servitude and ignominy and shame; it is so that he sees the union of

> the generations of mankind
> Spread over time, past, present, and to come.

'Such minds', he said of those who conversed with that Nature, 'are truly from the Deity, For they are Powers.'

There is another phrase in the *Prelude* which is worth recalling, but it will be more convenient to touch on one or two other poets first.

Both directly and indirectly this image of the City recurs constantly in Shakespeare, especially from *Henry IV* onwards. The direct image is presented only occasionally, as in the speech from *Henry V* from which the 'singing masons' line has been already quoted, or in the fantasy of Gonzalo in the *Tempest*—but that is the old perfectibility dream. A more definite personal symbol of it is in the figure of Caesar in *Antony and Cleopatra*. It is no detriment to the great figures of the lovers and all they stand for to say that there is, among their conceptions, nothing of the particular quality of Caesar's lines:

> The time of universal peace is near.
> Prove this a prosperous day, the three-nooked world
> Shall wear the olive freely.

Cleopatra may imply something different from, and perhaps something better than, this in her strange phrase which is also dependent on the word 'world'—

> O infinite virtue! com'st thou smiling from
> The world's great snare uncaught?—

but this she does not imply. Caesar must be given his own—though no more than his own—virtue. It is the peace and union of men which he represents and sustains.

But it is in other plays that the principles of the City—as maxims or as problems—are involved. I will here name only three—*Henry IV*, *Measure for Measure*, and *Coriolanus*. The problem of *Henry IV* is, of course, the problem of Falstaff, his apparent absolute value and yet the impossibility of including that value in any civic value. Shakespeare seems to have been as aware of this as we are; the figure of the Prince is there partly to save Falstaff from too much continued actuality. He, for example, prevents the robbery being too serious by contriving the restoration of the gold. He defines Falstaff precisely—'the unyoked humours of your idleness'. The Prince is, so to speak, a 'buffer' between this idleness and the actual world. He is, throughout, of the City, and all the relationships of the City in a sense in which neither the Falstaff-idleness nor the Hotspur-ambition can be, and that is perhaps one reason why he, and neither Falstaff nor Hotspur, can be poetically further developed. There is a sense in which something of Falstaff is recovered in the young lovers of the last plays, those figures of youth uttering wisdom and of living beauty being, as it were, eternal in its own nature: 'What do you, sweet, I'd have you do it ever . . .'

> So singular in each particular
> That all your acts are queens.

But so high a nature is impossible for Falstaff, great as he is. Our imaginations approve him precisely and only as the Prince approves him; they *are*, in fact, the Prince, and that is why they can follow the Prince when in *Henry V* he can 'love his present pains' and with an 'eased spirit' move 'with casted slough and fresh legerity'. They can even follow him to the speech before Agincourt which is so much more than patriotic in its emphasis on the happiness of the few who are, there, the City: 'we few, we *happy* few, we band of brothers'. Falstaff has not, and could not have, *brothers*: the King is universal.

But if the temptation of the Falstaff-idleness is something outside the City, the problem of *Measure for Measure* is something much more within the City itself, at least any temporal City. The scenes in that play are, as a whole, mostly outside the brothel or inside the prison, and though it is the brothel which has been most insisted on, it is the prison which is here important. The brothel is the appetite, and the prison is the result of virtue striking at the appetite—an extreme virtue in Angelo, but human. It is precisely because it is human that the problem arises. Claudio has been plucked out of the mass to be an example, and he is to die by the law. But both Escalus and Isabella are morally uneasy about his death. They both raise the question whether a judge may in fact sentence a man for an act to which the judge is himself inclined and which he may indeed himself have committed. How far, in this order which holds and is a necessity of the City in this world, are the executants of that order prevented by their own faults from judging or compelled by their own faults to show mercy? Angelo, in answer, takes the strictest view. We must carry out the law, he says to Escalus; the guilt of the judge has nothing to do with it; if that is ever discovered, then let him also die. When, however, he says something of the same sort to Isabella, she makes a reply which is one of the most familiar speeches in Shakespeare and has, by being dragged out of its context so often, half lost its terrible force. 'If we lose this justice', Angelo says, 'the form of the State will break down.' Isabella, exclaiming on 'man, proud man, Drest in a little brief authority', makes justice almost unjust; at least she makes it ridiculous. It becomes one of the fantastic tricks played before high heaven. She does not deny its validity; she merely makes nonsense of it. Justice must be: and what is justice? This—the angels weeping.

The real solution seems perhaps to lie at the end of the play when punishment is desired by the offender and mercy by the offended. 'Spirits are not finely touched But to fine issues', and this, in its degree, is the finest issue. The issue to which the play is touched is the reconciliation within the City of the justice which both must and must not be. Chastity invoking a mercy beyond that justice has become itself a temptation and a danger to the all but chaste, the all but just, soul. May the possibly guilty condemn the guilty?—all secular government asserts it. Ought we to excuse it because the sin is natural and we may commit it or have (in intention, at least) committed it?—all secular government denies it. The temporal City would fall; 'it must not be'. But in that single speech Isabella manages to suggest that the other way is equally fatal, as fatal as it is fantastic. The fall of Angelo, a much better man than most, is the example of it. Who *dare* judge?—only he, and he breaks as he judges. The possible moment of passion and pardon in the last act is perhaps the solution as it is certainly the play's resolution. But, humanly speaking, is not this solution unreliable?—it will not, in the ordinary sense, *work*? Indeed, even in the play it only works at that last moment of an intolerable necessity, made awful to us in the appeals of Mariana to Isabella.

The third play which I mentioned—*Coriolanus*—is also a play of an intolerable necessity, and of the City. It is reckoned among the tragedies because of the death of Coriolanus; perhaps it should be there also because of the failure of the City. The problem is in terms of the social difficulty; but that is a means just as the terms of the sensual difficulty in *Measure for Measure* are. The one necessary thing—the living together in the City—is found unbearable *in peace*. It can be done in war; Coriolanus can live and fight with his soldiers, but not with those soldiers when they are citizens. But then in war they can live together precisely because they are in a state of necessity, and (death being involved) at the risk any moment of a literally intolerable necessity. But in peace everything changes. The nobles cannot bear to treat the populace properly; the populace cannot bear to live in their poverty; Coriolanus will not allow of freedom, and the Tribunes will not allow of obedience. It is not easily possible to find words for these opposed persons outside the words of the play; they are made up of details; they are all of them right and yet wrong in their rightness. Up to the middle of the play this schism in the City continues; each is caught in a trap, and each one supposes that his own trap is the City. The only way out would be for someone to accept the apparently impossible.

No one will do so, and at the end of the third act, the situation changes. Shakespeare did not choose in this play, as he did in some, to give us a great analytical speech or scene of the alteration in Coriolanus's own mind. He says only, to Aufidius:

> In mere spite,
> To be full quit of those my banishers,
> Stand I before thee here.

He means, that is, to do precisely what the Tribunes and the populace have done, to destroy the intolerable thing with which, as he sees it, there can be no living. As a result of this general determination to destroy the intolerable thing, everyone is left with the inevitable thing—with all that is, and is meant by, the destruction of Rome itself. Choice has almost disappeared, and they are left with Fate.

The approach of the indignant rebel to the shape of the City in which he and his fellow-citizens had found it impossible to live at peace and love together is marked by three stages. Coriolanus had always had a personal tenderness for his friends and his family, for an obedience within his understanding, a *pietas*, and it is this which attempts to reconcile him. The three figures in which it appears are Cominius, his comrade in war, Menenius, his friend in peace, and Volumnia, his mother. All these three are, in a sense, one; they are the City. He rejects the first two; he all but rejects the third. It is only when the phrases become full of the destruction of the image of the City that he breaks.

> Come, let us go.
> This fellow had a Volscian to his mother;
> His wife is in Corioli, and his child
> Like him by chance. Yet give us our despatch:
> I am hushed until our City be a-fire,
> And then I'll speak a little.

The assent of Coriolanus to this plea is the assent to his own death; by that the City is materially saved, but it is also the end of one theme of the play. The return of the ladies to Rome is a silence, and the return of Coriolanus to Corioli is his death. The intolerable having been refused, the inevitable accomplishes itself. Something monstrous has entered in. Coriolanus himself, at the very moment of reconciliation with Volumnia, of submission to her desires who is more an incarnation of Rome than any other woman, says:

> O mother, mother,
> What have you done? Behold, the heavens do ope,
> The gods look down, and this unnatural scene
> They laugh at.

The word 'unnatural' there might, I suppose, refer to the Volscian armies, led by Coriolanus, surrounding Rome. But it seems more likely that it is the actual reconciliation which is, then and there, 'unnatural', so much a portent of his destruction has it become.

There is much else in Shakespeare, but these three plays will serve to indicate the mode of consideration. The City is as much his subject as any of his others, and though poetry is not primarily meant for morals or sociology, yet the intimate consideration of his poetry from this point of view might clarify our emotions and our minds. The Falstaff-idleness is perhaps half a jest, but the stews of Verona are not a jest, and yet the justice of the City becomes a different thing after reading *Measure for Measure*. In *Coriolanus* the City does not want to be the City; Romans do not want to be Rome.

Milton has been already quoted, and apart from incidental felicities of that kind there is not in him so definite an image of the City. It was in the nature of his genius to stress the hierarchic rather than the republican element in the heavenly state, and the invention and construction of *Paradise Lost* excluded from it any help to be gained from presentations of actual cities. The two human figures, Adam and Eve, are compelled to contain in themselves all human relationship. On the other hand, what Milton could and did contribute was the grandest single presentation in English verse of a figure destructive to the City, hierarchic or republican. It has long been supposed that Milton was proud; it has not so long been recollected that Milton equally—and perhaps more intensely—supposed that it was wrong to be proud and even silly to be proud, and that he saw with extreme lucidity the results of being proud. The great rebel against that heavenly state of the 'thick sanctities' is not primarily moved by ambition. He is not even discontented *until* something new and unexpected happens. He is content to be what he is until he finds that a new and interfering Love has disturbed (as he thinks) his own status. It is then that he thinks himself 'impaired',

> Deep malice thence conceiving and disdain.

He believes himself to have lost his just rights. He develops a sense 'of injured merit', and it is from that again that there develops the 'high disdain'.

It is this sense of impairment and of supposed merit injured which is the central cause of Satan's actions. It leaves his actual virtues at first untouched. They are thrown into high relief at the beginning of the poem, but then we must also add that so is the fault. Beyond this rebellious figure expands the vision of an ordered and hierarchical universe, the greatness of God, the tenderness of Adam and Eve. Perhaps the nearest thing to the 'civic' relationship is the courtesy which the figures of the poem display towards each other; a kind of divine charity moves in them and they speak to each other, not only as superiors or inferiors but as separately created. It is never forgotten that if a man is not an angel, neither is an angel a man. Even the hosts of hell speak nobly to each other, and the mutual passion of Adam and Eve is sustained by courtesy. It is Satan's mental discourtesy towards God and the Divine Son which starts him on his diabolic career. He interprets the best as the worst, because he interprets it in relation to his own immediate state. It is this which is opposed as much to the republican as to the hierarchical view of the City: the lack of consideration of humility.

Neither of these views was ostentatious in the verse of the Augustan age (however hierarchical the order of actual society happened to be). That age is in some danger now of having its virtues disregarded owing to religious preferences as it had some time ago owing to poetic fashion. It deliberately limited its diction and its rhythms, nor did it choose to hunt in the wilder parts of the heart. But it knew about them, and it felt indeed that it was fighting against the barbarian tendencies of the heart. The poets of the early eighteenth century, at least, had a sense of danger, and the danger which they envisaged to their intellect and to their civilization presents to us the courage which all culture needs in order intellectually to defend itself. The great example of this defiance is in the close of the *Dunciad*. It is true that we should disagree with Pope upon the character of the enemy there in certain details. Things which he would have included in dullness and stupidity we should believe to be of another nature. But the City, if it is to continue to exist temporally, must defy dullness and stupidity.

> She comes, she comes! the sable throne behold
> Of Night primeval and of Chaos old.

It was against that that the eighteenth century fought.

It would serve no useful purpose to attempt to rush hastily through a number more poets. All that this paper has attempted to do has been to indicate a few points in the mass of English poetry where there have appeared hints of that great and very moving image of the City. It is not a thing that can be easily defined, for its nature is that of poetry, and poetry cannot be turned into anything but itself. Nor can its images accommodate themselves to any principles but their own. Long discussions whether (for example) Milton was an Arian or Wordsworth a Pantheist (not that they were) distract our minds. And the less even that we attend to the Catholicism of a Catholic poet, except perhaps in necessary theological footnotes, the more likely we are to understand his poetry, the more likely to listen to his words rather than our own. Poetry is not a state where we ought to recognize our own words; it is not a conversation.

There are, however, two points which may be finally touched on. The first is Mr. Eliot's *The Family Reunion*; the second is Wordsworth's phrase 'the feeling intellect'. Modern poetry has, certainly, dealt a good deal with the image of the City—inadequately perhaps, but sincerely and seriously. That, however, would need a separate paper. Why I wish to mention *The Family Reunion* is because it carries within it the poetic hints of the civil union of the living and the dead. It might have as a motto: 'the sins of the fathers are visited upon the children': not meaning by that only a physical or mental result—gout or syphilis or imbecility—but a much more obscure spiritual relation. The burden of the guilt of a murder conceived in one generation is carried in another: 'bear ye one another's burdens' is given here a terrible interpretation. I retain a private conviction that Harry in that play is neither quite so exceptional nor quite so superior as he occasionally thinks he is, but I allow that he may be excused for his feelings—given the situation, and I naturally do not accuse Mr. Eliot of agreeing with him. But I do not recollect any other modern work which throws so strange a light on the true relationship of the generations, and therefore on the great principles of the City. Mr. Eliot said some time ago that 'propinquity is not enough', though he put it better. The whole effort of imagining the City, or rather of studying in the poets their imagination of the City—and it was Wordsworth who told us that Imagination 'was but another name for absolute power'—is the use of propinquity as a means to neighbourliness, and so to the continual interchange of courtesies of the spirit. It is that interchange of which the theme of *The Family Reunion* is, between the dead and the living, a sign. And the title itself has, in that sense, a profound meaning.

In that work of transmutation and union, as expressed in English verse, a phrase of Wordsworth's is of peculiar value. In the last book of the *Prelude* he speaks of 'the feeling intellect'. He has been saying that the work of the Imagination is a solitary work; it is the work of 'intellectual love'. It would be rash to assume that Wordsworth did not know what he meant by the words. He proceeds:

he whose soul has risen
Up to the height of feeling intellect
Shall want no other tenderness.

It is the expression of the state of mind which, at the end of the *Prelude*, he saw as the best nature of men. It is also the best maxim of the desired City. The accidents of propinquity can only become the web of the City by the achievement of an intellect so swiftly capable of ordering its emotions that it may itself be said to 'feel'. It knows, and feels as it knows. This activity of the intellectual love includes in itself all other lesser tendernesses. 'All that friendship, all that love, can do' are to be there to complete the man. It is from that point that he too becomes a 'prophet of Nature'. The unknown modes of being are now known: the early Romanticism has worked into the full pattern. 'I saw the Holy City . . . descending out of heaven. . . .'

THE REDEEMED CITY

From the Dublin Review, *October 1941*

THE differences between us and our enemy are many, and there are many different ways of summing them up. One of the more useful is perhaps that implied in the difference between the Race and the City. Whether the doctrine of Race be true need not much concern Christians; since they are not allowed to accept it as a definition of the final state of man, it can be, like any other scientific question, but a matter of minor if notable interest. There is no final idea for us but the glory of God in the redeemed and universal union—call it Man or the Church or the City. It is true that in the present crisis we are not disabled from gratefully accepting the aid of those great allies who, on human grounds, accept the same idea of the City in a more limited sense. The noble republicans of earth, the great humanitarian champions, are to be welcomed with respect and admiration. The lack in their vision of union is that they cannot include the dead; the past, for them, is indeed past, and its agonies remain for ever unatoned. But they have done much, and we owe them all but that which God alone could do. The words of Burke to Wilberforce can be used to them: 'the House, the nation, and Europe', he said, 'are under great and serious obligations to the honourable gentleman'—on that May night when the motion against the slave trade was put forward. Wilberforce was a Christian, but Voltaire was no Christian, and St. Francis was a more orthodox Christian; and yet all of them were striking at one evil, at 'the grand Infamy'—the horror of human tyranny, cold and cruel. That Infamy has been found both within and without the Church; it is always the enemy of the Church, and betrays it where it does not deny.

It is not, however, those noble allies with whom we are now directly concerned. It is our advantage—wholly undeserved—that their heroism is not incompatible with our belief, though they may suppose (largely because of the operation of the Infamy in the past) that our beliefs are incompatible with their desires. The Infamy is one and the same everywhere. The opposite of the Infamy is the City. There is, in the end, no compromise between the two; there is only choice. The choice exists everywhere, at every minute, as a fundamental, though that fundamental may have been accepted, and our business be with the edification of the City upon it. The thing in common between us and our allies, and in dispute between us and our enemies, is the proper freedom of the flesh. No one can, in fact, prevent a man thinking, or interfere with the motions the soul has in itself; what he can do is to prevent utterance. He can prevent the tongue speaking or the ears hearing; the other may or may not follow. All these things are worked out in terms of flesh, and must be; our Lord Himself deigned to work out the conclusion of the whole matter in terms of flesh. It is the outrage upon the physical Image of Christ, the physical vehicle of the Holy Ghost, which is the final impiety here. About the rest we cannot properly judge. The concentration camps and the tortures are the Infamy; the free talk and the nourishment of all bodies (*all* bodies) are the City. There is, in the end, no compromise.

The Holy Ghost moves us to be, by every means to which we are called, the Images of Christ, the types of that Original, in or out of the flesh. It is the intercourse of those free Images which is the union of the City. The name of the City is Union; the operation of the Infamy is by outrage on that union. The process of that union is by the method of free exchange. The methods of that exchange range from childbirth to the Eucharist—the two primal activities of the earth and the Church. There is, in the first case, a mutual willingness between the father and mother which results in the transference of seed. That it is so common does not lessen the trust implied; that one should abandon his seed to another, that one should receive the seed of another, is an exhibition of trust; it is almost the chief natural exhibition of that supernatural quality known as 'faith'—a quality which has one of its own proper exhibitions in the interchange of the Eucharist—'to effect the mystery of unity, we ourselves receive of that which is His what He Himself received of that which is ours'. So the Fourth Council of Lateran, decreeing in the highest things of earth the same doctrine of exchange; but decreeing them also through—I will not say the lowest, for the implication would be, as it has too often been, to reduce the flesh to an abasement unworthy of it. It was, no doubt, we who sinned, and sin, in the flesh; but the flesh itself retains for us many signs of that high calling from which we apostatized. Death itself is an outrage, a necessary outrage, upon a unity. We must accept it, as we must accept, for ourselves or for others, many another outrage. But it has been regarded, from the beginning, as an unnatural thing, a separation in the unseparate.

> Within my soul there doth conduce a fight
> Of this strange nature, that a thing inseparate
> Divides more wider than the sky and earth.

There is, there, no more rule 'in unity itself'.

Except by the restoration of the union. The high doctrine of the physical Resurrection restores to mankind the unity of which it had been deprived. The new union can hardly be scarless; the original Unity, so again unified, must bear the marks of its wounds—as indeed it does: say, to name but one, of the spear-thrust in the side. Yet it is said that this, and the others, are 'glorified'. They wear a double radiance—of the original and of the renovation.

The Holy Ghost, it is declared, drives us towards a union with that Union. What He created, we must choose—accepting in the Re-creation the original creation. That Re-creation was presented to us, in the Apocalypse, under the image of a City. It is precisely the nations, and the races, who are to enter into it. The feast of Christ the King is also the feast of Christ the City. The principle of that City, and the gates of it, are the nature of Christ as the Holy Ghost exhibits it and inducts us into it; it is the doctrine that no man lives to himself or indeed *from* himself. This is the doctrine common to nature and grace.

There is, in those great myths which stand at the beginning of the Bible and hide from us and reveal to us the prolonged catastrophe of our fallen nature, the tale of the first murder. There is in it a very high symbolism. Cain and Abel both made offerings to the Lord. The Divine Glory accepted Abel's and refused Cain's. There are all possibilities of interpretation, but among them is one which suggests that the very purpose of Cain's offering should have been that his brother's should be accepted; that it was in his refusal of this conclusion that Cain sinned. The fire from heaven fell, as is so often its habit, elsewhere than it was implored. The good descended—immediately, in answer to the prayer, as it had been asked, but not where it had been asked. The anger of the one who prayed and offered was aroused by this first of the substitutions; he slew his brother who profited. 'Others have laboured,' said our Lord, laying down the same principle, 'and ye have entered into their labours.' He laid down that principle; He charged the apostles with the knowledge, and sent them to propagate it: this was to be the regeneration of earth, or at least an element in it. He did more; He declared it as

His own. When, after His own substitution of Himself for man, He talked with the disciples at Emmaus, He accused them of blindness to it: 'O fools and slow of heart to believe all that the prophets have spoken, *ought* not Christ to have suffered these things and to enter into His glory?' And afterwards He celebrated for them the great exchange of the Eucharist, and vanished. 'Did not our hearts burn within us by the way?'

It was by an act of substitution that He renewed the City; this He had commanded as the order in both nature and grace. This is (to borrow Gerard Hopkins's word) the 'inscape' of our hearts, and if the Infamy (in us and in others) has ruined that inscape by outrage, as war ruins landscapes and cities, still this is the inscape of the Divine City. It is elementary enough, in our simple natural lives—from childbirth everyone who is not 'a god or a beast' lives by that; there is no other way to live. We are, simply, utterly dependent on others, and it may seem that to stress it so much is to make us over-conscious of a natural inevitability, to make our very breathing unctuous with a revolting piety. So perhaps it would be, if it were not for two things: (i) the universal nature of the application, (ii) the supernatural nature of the principle. These two things, especially the first, the Infamy always denies.

It denies the first, precisely because it contradicts the City. Our Lord expressly reserved to Himself any exclusion from the City. It is certain that He intimated, in the clearest words, the possibility of exclusion from the City; He called that exclusion hell. But He forbade His judgement to be forestalled; if His priests 'retain' sins they do but remit them to Himself. The nearest to adverse judgement that we can go is to pass on to His own judgement; the only judgement we are allowed to pronounce is pardon. Even that is only pronounced in His name; it is not for us to pardon from ourselves. But of that something more may be said presently.

The Infamy then denies inclusion. It denies it first by definition; that is, it makes definition an implicit and immediate exclusion from its own limits. Definition, of course, is necessary. To say 'he is a German' or 'she is a Christian' means that, and only that. It means the absence of certain characteristics and the presence of other characteristics. It may imply human arrangements. But it must not imply outrage. It must not, that is, exclude from the exchanges of nature, or indeed (in whatever sense) from the exchanges of supernature. All it can do is to order those exchanges in one particular way instead of another particular way. It can make, as it were, 'traffic regulations' for the convenience of traffic among men. It can clear our heads but it was never meant to petrify our hearts. Having defined, the Infamy proceeds to exclude, and then, so far as it can, to enslave or to annihilate. It may be observed at work in ourselves every day anywhere; for it is that which rejects in us a universal humility, a courtesy of carriage towards facts other than ourselves, a recognition of the creation even when that creation appears to us displeasing. It hides in the Christian Church as much —or almost as much—as anywhere; the great image of it in literature is in the vision of the Apostasy of the Church at the end of Dante's *Purgatorio*.

But (ii) it denies the supernatural existence of the principle. This, indeed, as has been said, need not of itself be infamous; the republicans of earth may deny it, in denying the supernatural altogether. But it has frequently happened that they have denied the supernatural almost on behalf of its own republican principle; or, if not, then because of what they, with some justification, considered a lack of evidence. The Infamy denies it as part of its habit of exclusion. The evidence for this is again not only in our enemies today; it is in our hearts at all times. Against this denial the habit of the Church in the baptismal Rite has always testified. The new-born child emerges from its natural co-inherence in its mother into a supernatural co-inherence with the saints. It has received the communication of the evil of a fallen world; its blood is tainted from its soul—or from a world of souls—with the Infamy, and it will soon begin disastrously to pay back what it has disastrously received, in the exchanges (unless redeemed) of infernal conflict. At that moment it is caught by others and lifted into an exchange of grace—into others by others, into Another by Another. As the practice of infant baptism became general in the Church, this co-inherence was the more accentuated. The adult might speak for himself; the infant could speak only by others. Repentance and faith, the two first-felt and first-pledged qualities of the new life, had to be on its behalf felt and pledged by others. The inarticulate young creature, as it were, repented before he could sin and believed before he could think. Mystically vicarious, the sponsors were pledged; and their pledge was not released until, duly instructed in the vicarious life of the City, the subject of those pledges himself affirmed his own part in that life, and was permitted himself to approach the vicarious Sacrifice and to feed on the vicarious Nourishment. The operation of the Spirit, who is the Life of the human Image towards its divine Original and had been so invoked in the Baptism, claimed its votary in the Confirmation. That life stretched before him, no more its own than it had been before, but now consciously known not to be its own.

To say so is not in any sense to deny its own responsibility. 'Keep thy conscience with thy brother', said a hermit of the desert, 'and thou shalt find rest.' It is the individual conscience that must be kept so. The commandment to 'bear one another's burdens' is full of great and sacred meanings, but it is, of course, still the individual who must bear; who must choose to bear and have courage to bear, no less than he must choose to relinquish and have courage to relinquish. 'I am no companion for myself,' wrote John Donne, 'I must not be alone with myself. . . . I am the Babylon that I must go out of, or I perish.' The going-out is (to repeat a phrase) into the 'inscape' of the heart, but that inscape can only be faithfully discovered by acts. He from whom the command to carry one another's burdens came promised that the burden should be light, but whether it is light or heavy can only be discovered by carrying it. Nature compels and faith demands such a carrying; to quote Donne again: 'the lights of nature and faith are subordinate John Baptists to Christ'; they are categories of one identity, the principle of the City, the formula of prophecy. It was uttered as a mockery by the incredulous when they saw the City in its agony; they said: 'Others He saved; Himself He could not save.' It was irony, but the Gospel is beyond irony; its affirmations are so literal that they are bound to seem ironical to the foolish, and the ironies of the foolish are discovered to be its own most precise definitions. He who could not save Himself saved others, and required that we should be one with Him in that, as in all. It may be added that He also reserved to Himself the consciousness of that salvation; demanding perfection from us, He exactly forbade us the consciousness of perfection, even if it were achieved. 'When ye have done *all*, say, we are unprofitable servants.' The Glory is always to be observed in others; 'ye are entered into *their* labours'.

The unexclusive life of the City, then, is everywhere vicarious life, up to the level of each capacity. It is as much the instinct of a gentleman as the climax of the saints. The 'bear one another's burdens' runs through all. The Infamy itself will use this, for its own profit, within itself, for the enslavement or destruction of others, as long as it is permitted to last; say, as long as its kingdom stands. Since it is impossible to escape this Life, all that remains to us is to deepen it. In this sense to consider how we live *from* others may be even more profitable at times than to consider how we should live *for* others. Both are necessary to the perfect exchange. The methods of exchange, of carrying burdens and of giving up burdens to be carried; of acting in the strength of others; of making commitments by others; all these may be found to be full of meaning much beyond our ordinary understanding. It is the principle of the priesthood after its kind, and the principle of marriage after its kind. It may be said perhaps of marriage with peculiar propriety that its lights of nature and faith are subordinate John Baptists to bring us to Christ the City. It is affirmed that marriage was instituted in the time of man's innocency, before the City was flawed or the perfect Body wounded. The fidelity which the Church has declared to exist in marriage between Christians, and the finality in it which may be denied but cannot, this side of death, be destroyed, is of this nature, because there the nature of exchange has been accepted both in nature and in grace. The canonical conditions of marriage are rigorous for this reason; it is not proper that there should be any possibility of error. Accepted, they remain rigorous—an example of the truth that the vicarious and exchanged life which the Divine Spirit commands and communicates is not less but more inexorable than the individual and single, and that that also has its hierarchy and order of behaviour. In that life, as it moves in this life, the two shall be one; and the power which either draws on shall be double. This power may be for others besides them, but between them the opportunities of exchange are all to be thrown open. In this degree each may say, when the great experiment is done: 'Myself I could not save; another I saved and another saved me.'

Most clearly perhaps in marriage, but no less definitely in all relationships, the law of bearing one another's burdens exists. It exists necessarily as the active principle of life, and voluntarily as a duty only because our return to all active principles has to be treated as a duty. It is, in that great interior world, as if we had, in the exterior world, to be taught how to breathe. The air of good-will is to be as universal as the actual air; presently we may fortunately be allowed to forget that we are breathing it. Meanwhile there remains to press, as far and as often as we can, in everyday affairs, the principle of vicarious life. The many common exchanges and substitutions of daily existence; the social balance of specialized occupations; the deaths and labours on behalf of others, and the deliberate acceptance of them, which are becoming more and more a part of our life at war; the inter-knit resistance to the enemy; the vigils of holy souls for others; the mystical substitution of the saints; the whole life of prayer and other experience which characterizes the Church; the mystery of the Atonement; the veiled mystery of the Mother and the Son—*figlia del tuo figlio*—which is in some sense the centre of the Universe; and beyond the Universe the co-inherence of the Blessed and Glorious Trinity itself—these are the expositions of the same identity. Reposing in that identity, we may become conscious of it everywhere. More, much more, might be done by the practice of it between ourselves by intellectual and spiritual methods. Mental burdens can be carried as well as physical; and even physical more than we know. The very healing of the flesh might be hastened by it. It is not the reward of sanctity; it is a way of sanctity, but also it is the only way of bearable life. There again, of course, it is improper to be greedy or presumptuous: 'in quietness and confidence shall be your strength'. 'Your life and your death', said St. Anthony, 'are with your neighbour.' 'And who is my neighbour?' The answer has been told us; the only alternative to that answer is to exclude something or someone from neighbourhood. 'I am to love myself', wrote William Law, 'as I love my neighbour or any other created being, that is, only in and for God.'

But, however apt we may be to this new life, it is certain we shall not escape committing or suffering outrage. The Infamy is too much with us for that. This commonalty of evil leads to what is perhaps the deepest understanding of exchange, the exchange of pardon. Pardon in its proper nature is not a single but a mutual thing. There can be few relationships of any depth in which there is not some outrage to forgive; there are perhaps some few. Those who had to do with the saints can have had little to forgive, though the saints probably thought they had; it is what made them saints. To retain or remit a grudge is the choice between the Infamy and the City; it is the choice between the willingness to exclude another and the willingness to include another. Pardon as a disposition of the soul is a necessity—so long as the soul does not make too much of the business of forgiving. Even our Lord did not, when the outrage was worked on Him, seem to forgive of Himself: He referred it to His Father. Forgiveness is always, to the one who forgives, a grave spiritual danger. It should always *have happened*. Examples from literature are Imogen in *Cymbeline* and Miss Bates in *Emma*; both Shakespeare and Jane Austen knew sanctity. Forgiveness then, with every kind of shyness, is a disposition, but to emerge as a perfect act it again needs an act and a mutual act. The two persons concerned must co-inhere in that mutual act, and pardon must be doubly welcome. Like joy (of which, at its best, it is a manifestation) it does not demand forgetfulness but acute knowledge. In our present state it may be wise sometimes to forget; the weight of our memories is too intense a weight of glory for us to bear. But that is an accident of our weak and temporal minds; in eternity it could not be so. 'Every sin', said the Lady Julian of Norwich, 'shall have worship in heaven'; and if this is to be so between the City and its inhabitants, then surely it must be so between the inhabitants themselves. So high a dream cannot be discussed here; only it may be said that this too is a state of exchange and of vicarious life. The offender lives the more intensely in the other's love. But to know it as love he must know it willingly; therefore he must desire it and ask it:

. . . the circumference and form for ever
In Forgiveness of Sins which is Self Annihilation; it is the Covenant of Jehovah.

Such was Blake's definition of the 'Perpetual Mutual Sacrifice in Great Eternity'. The Infamy itself must be welcomed so; but if the Infamy knew it, it would already be one with the City. That is far beyond this discussion. But it may very well be a description of the Judgement which will discover how far we have seriously lived the vicarious life. 'Wherein I find you,' says an Apocryphal record, 'there will I judge you.'

In the last paragraph of the Apostles' Creed the City is defined. 'I believe in the Holy Ghost' is its first clause and primal condition. If it is living, it lives so, and only so, towards Christ; in whom it already lives complete, having (by virtue of His substitution) 'the perfect and simultaneous possession of everlasting life'. Simultaneously all its citizens derive from all. 'The Holy Catholic Church' is its name here, allowing for all proper implications of whatever kind: 'visible—invisible', 'invincible ignorance', and so on. But the other four clauses are, as it were, the four walls of the description in the Apocalypse; or, if the metaphor divides them too much, say they are the four qualities of that life: 'the Communion of Saints, the Forgiveness of Sins, the Resurrection of the Body, and the Life everlasting'. They are the qualities of the renewed perfection of union—interchange, interchange redeeming even the denial of itself, the glory of the holy flesh by which so much was known, the infinite power in all the glory. The glory is the thing happening; it is not, though in our talk we seem to make it so and can only believe in it so, an accident of the thing happening. The glory of God is in facts. The almost incredible nature of things is that there is no fact which is not in His glory. This is the great inclusion which makes the City. If, to use terms of space, we ascend towards it, it is still that which descends out of heaven, and is the cause and course of our ascent. The language of it is in the great interchange of fiery tongues by which the Spirit manifested at the beginning.

ANTHROPOTOKOS

From a Time and Tide *review of* True Humanism, *by Jacques Maritain, and* Solitude and Society, *by Nicolas Berdyaev, 1938*

When Nestorius came to Byzantium, it is said that he found two titles generally attributed to the glorious virgin who was the mother of Messias. One, habitual since then in the Church, was *theotokos*, the mother of God; the other, much less habitual, almost disused, was *anthropotokos*, the mother of Man. Nestorius proposed, as a compromise, *Christotokos*. But the monks, the populace, and Cyril of Alexandria, defeated him, and the supernatural and the natural were defined by the orthodox to exist, with equal perfection, in the single Person.

Such remote Christological quarrels in the slums and boulevards of the Near East are not without interest today. It was the real nature of Perfection as credible and discoverable by men that was then in question, and it is still perfection that we are at. The loss of *anthropotokos* has damaged Christendom; the Middle Ages attempted to recover it by fables, but in general it has been left too much to the revolts against Christendom to demand what should be one of the splendours of Christendom. The coincidence of a book by M. Maritain, and a book by M. Berdyaev, recalls the orthodox doctrine to mind.

. . . Their lines of approach are different. M. Berdyaev is philosophical and interior; M. Maritain historical, political, and (on the whole) exterior. Their stresses are different. Thus, in speaking of the Renaissance, M. Berdyaev says: 'The problem of man's "centrality", of his creative activity, has never been seriously investigated by either Patristic thought or Scholastic philosophy. Renaissance humanism made the first important discoveries in this direction', though he adds it 'was still largely naturalistic in its outlook'. M. Maritain, more sternly, says that 'the spirit of this epoch . . . wished to produce an *anthropocentric rehabilitation* of the creature', and goes on to declare that the protestant conscience, however awfully conscious of its own corruption, yet recovered initiative as against God. 'This irremediably corrupt nature cries out to God, and the initiative, do what one will, is man's by that cry.'

The theme common to both books is the City. The word has already been used by one or two English writers, and M. Maritain also uses it. In discussing 'the historical ideal of a new Christendom', the past statements of future values, he says justly: 'This phrase "the Christian City" must be rightly understood. *In the absolute sense of the words*, the true christian commonweal or city is the Church, and no temporal body.' But even in the absolute sense, we gain by sometimes considering the Church as a City—*anthropotokos* as well as *theotokos*. And in a temporal sense, the image of the City rather than that of race or nation or ideological body is the most useful today. The pages which M. Maritain devotes to the conception of liberty in this imagined City are among the most valuable in his book. He allows that we cannot any more find the principle of unity in a common profession of faith. The 'consecrational concept of Christendom' held in the Middle Ages is no longer possible; the later effort to agree on a philosophic minimum has come to nothing. 'The simple unity of friendship does not suffice to give a form to the social body.' The City must today discover its present form and structure; and by what?

M. Berdyaev, in defining his Existential Philosophy, draws near Society—that is, the City—from the postulated Ego. That postulate must be common, of course, to any approach to the City. M. Berdyaev alters Descartes—'I am not because I think, but I think because I am'; the Ego, for him, exists before consciousness, though, as he adds, 'the birth of consciousness is a very important event in the Ego's destiny'—the little darling! Consciousness, however, has rather misled the Ego, and that is why we are all in the state we are; 'the human consciousness may prove to be an obstacle rather than a means to authentic communion, when it assumes a social form based upon symbolic communication'. Communication and communion are diverse and opposed. The Ego has to achieve personality and communion with other Egos, not by means of that objective exchange which is all it can find in formed communities, but through love, in the spiritual City.

Love, one felt, was bound to come in sooner or later. M. Maritain has it, too, less markedly. He is more concerned with suggestions on how the temporal City may take its structure. But his new Christendom will be distinctively characterized by 'the notion of integral humanism', and this has a relation to M. Berdyaev's: 'At the present time, it is imperative to understand once more that the rediscovery of man will also be the rediscovery of God. That is the essential theme of Christianity.'

One might perhaps press the sentences one stage nearer to each other. What is the characteristic of any City? Exchange between citizens. What is the fact common to both sterile communication and vital communion? A mode of exchange. What is the fundamental fact of men in their natural lives? The necessity of exchange. What is the highest level of Christian dogma? Exchange between men and God, by virtue of the union of Man and God in the single Person, who is, by virtue again of that Manhood, itself the City, the foundation and the enclosure. M. Maritain, in speaking of marriage as it may be in the new Christendom, uses the word 'nourish'—the nourishment which is, this way and that, exchanged between husband and wife. In fact, the affair of procreation and childbirth which is at the root of the continuation of the natural order, of the temporal *anthropos*, is an affair of exchange. This office of substitution did not need Christendom to exhibit it, nor to show of what hostility as well as of what devotion it might be the cause. Christendom declared something more; it declared that this principle of substitution was at the root of the supernatural, of universal life, as well as of natural.

M. Berdyaev says that 'such is the metaphysical mystery inherent in sexuality that . . . a demoniac element of hostility persists between the lovers'. Not only between sexual lovers, if we may for a moment metaphysically assume that there are any others, nor only between lovers. Hostility begins to exist, surely, whenever and wherever we forget that we are nourished by, that we live from—whomever; when we think that we can *choose* by whom we shall be nourished. If *anthropos* has any meaning, if the web of humanity is in any sense one, if the City exists in our blood as well as in our desires, then we precisely must live from, and be nourished by, those whom we most wholly dislike and disapprove. Even the Church, forgetting that sacred title given to Mary, *anthropotokos*, has too often spoken as if it existed by its own separate life. So, no doubt, sacramentally and supernaturally, it does; but so, by the very bones and blood of its natural members, it very much does not. And where the Church has forgotten, other ideologies do not bother to try and remember, and some certainly deny. There is but one dichotomy: that between those who acknowledge that they live from the life of others, including their 'enemies', and those who do not. It is in this sense, indeed, that we must 'forgive' our enemies. And the moment the dichotomy is admitted, it immediately becomes a temptation. Whoever does not admit it is regarded as an 'enemy', and we deny that we can possibly live and be nourished by *him*. *He* at least is alien? No. Terrible humility! we derive from those we denounce; 'though they slay me, yet will I trust in them'.

THE FREE ACT

Time and Tide *review of* The Rights of Man, *by Jacques Maritain, 1945*

WHAT is the opposite to totalitarianism? But what then is totalitarianism? The subjection of all to one authority; the denial of all authorities but one. The opposite therefore is a multiplication of authorities; or at least, say, the giving free play to all authorities. This is the free State—a State which uses its power as much as possible towards the protection and preservation of other powers. It must positively encourage all other honourable authorities continued within it; its business indeed is precisely and only that.

But if this is the nature of the authority of the State, is it also the nature of any authority? Surely, yes; surely this is precisely the very nature and life of authority. Where the family exists, for what else is the parents' authority meant? The child is to grow up to recognize exactly those other persons or things which make a proper demand on him—at school, in business, in love, in logic, in personal and intellectual relationships. 'He made us ready to be free', said the Revolutionaries of Voltaire. But freedom without the opposite of freedom is meaningless; if in freedom there is no suggestion of action, it remains merely a void; if there is such a suggestion, it must either be accepted or refused or modified, and in that sense, freedom is so far lost, or at least is used only to destroy itself along those particular lines. It is so among all proper academic chairs; the student is there encouraged to research, to the discovery of fresh facts; those fresh facts may overthrow the doctrine of his teacher; every right teacher knows it and encourages his pupil none the less for that. But what of those states of being which justly demand exclusion of rivals—say, marriage? Even marriage is not much of an exception. For marriage itself is (among other things) an introduction to loves beyond itself, and if these loves are different in their nature, yet still every marriage has to encourage some sort of apparent rivalry to its uxoriousness if not to its uniqueness, and perhaps thrives the better so.

Something like this seems to me to lie at the root of M. Maritain's theory of the pluralist State; it must certainly be also something of what is meant by 'natural rights', or rights according to natural law. 'Freedom of investigation', he says, 'is a fundamental natural right, for man's very nature is to seek the truth.' He means there, particularly, freedom of speech and expression; but all life is investigation, and the word may properly be allowed to take a wider meaning. 'Society is a whole whose parts are themselves wholes, and it is an organism composed of liberties.' Society always has claimed and always will claim the right to suppress or control those liberties when they seem to be those of 'enemies of the public good'. But once that is said, we are back again in the old problem. If the Germans think the Jews—or if we once thought Thugs—enemies of the public good, must not they or we suppress or banish them? To deny it is to deny the nature of the Republic, the existence of the Public Thing. Persecution, in that sense, always has been and always will be a necessity of the Republic. The prohibition of totalitarian governments in all the liberated states of Europe now is a clear example. 'You may have what government you will, *so long as*—' But without the abolition of that 'so long as' there can be no full freedom.

Yet that licence must be denied in favour of a more fundamental responsibility. The State itself must be willing continuously to die in order to live. The parental idea of the State must conform to the proper parental idea—the child, the citizen, is to be left to the new authorities which it discovers for itself. The refusal of the Allies to permit the existence of totalitarian governments means that they insist that governments must conform to this self-limiting type. The free States are to allow full licence to their nationals to find other authorities. 'The State has a simple function of co-ordination and control.' Not so simple, perhaps, but certainly to co-ordinate these individual freedoms everywhere. Starvation, slavery, even too gross a public opinion—are to be abolished; in order that men may be free.

But free to recognize that opposite of freedom, free to make themselves servants. The only freedom is a freedom to choose obedience. It is true that obedience, in our happiest moments, is a thing so light, so rich, so rewarding, that it is hardly felt as obedience. As when we do not interrupt our friends' part in the conversation. But it is a chosen obedience, an accepted limitation, all the same. M. Maritain speaks, in a noble phrase, of 'the secret of the heart and the free act as such'. Civil life is meant to discover this everywhere.

CHURCH AND STATE

Time and Tide *review of Don Luigi Sturzo's book, 1939*

THE danger of metaphors, and the damage they can do to intelligence, has rarely been better exhibited than by the too familiar comparison of Church and State to soul and body. It is plausible, and untrue. For the Church, by definition, includes the body, and the State, by experience, aims at the soul. It may aim at the wrong kind of soul, just as the Church, at times at least, has seemed to require only a much attenuated body. But normally both are related to both. It is no doubt why the author of the Apocalypse chose to image both by the City in which there was no temple.

Don Sturzo's book is a survey and investigation of the relations of the Church (the Roman Church primarily) and the State; that is, the history of living men in two organizations. They are, of course, the same living men; that is a point which all historians admit and most neglect. Don Sturzo is far too wise and learned (the deserved tribute is double; they are not two words for the same thing) to do so. He begins with the first appearance of the exclusive and intolerant Christian Church, and he ends with the Spanish war. He thinks in terms of freedom in the State and Dogma in the Church. 'The fundamental error', he says, 'is to conceive of Humanism and

Christianity as separate, to keep their values distinct, and often to oppose them, and finally to eliminate one of the two from the redeeming synthesis.' It might be added that this false elimination often arises from a too-hasty reconciliation as well as from a too-rash opposition.

At the present time, for instance, there are many who think that the operations of the Church and the State should be identical; that the State should abandon the use of war in obedience to the Church or the Church proclaim the need of victory in support of the State. It is our modern way of stating the age-old conflict which Don Sturzo has to occupy many lucid pages in describing. The Emperor first *or* the Pope; the king *or* the bishops. He draws special attention to the effort of Paschal II in the twelfth century, who persuaded the Emperor to renounce investiture on condition that the clergy renounced their right to 'regalia', that is, to feudal duties and feudal rights. Neither the most spiritual minds, who objected to the clergy owning property at all, nor the most 'organizational', who objected to the clergy losing 'direction and influence', accepted Paschal's proposals. 'The episode', Don Sturzo says, 'did not have any wide repercussions, either at the time or subsequently.' The great wrangles went on: in any temporal crisis, let both those great Powers act in the same way; let both denounce the enemy. 'Humanism and Christianity,' says Miss Barbara Barclay Carter, summing up the book she has translated with the greatest industry and discretion, 'which form the two-fold basis of our civilization, integrate each other, tending always to a synthesis.'

Yes; but each by its own methods. Setting aside those who by vocation are pacifists at the present time, what is the duty of church-folk as church-folk? Precisely the opposite of their duty as nationals. Their duty as nationals involves separation from and killing of German nationals. Their duty as church-folk involves union with and spiritual dependence on Germans. Both duties must be fulfilled. It is possible and probable that one duty should be fulfilled more particularly by Christian soldiers and one more particularly by Christian priests. But neither can be separated from the other; each exists co-inherently in the other. It is why there are church-parades (to remind the armies of the one) and chaplains (to involve the clergy in the other).

But what then should the Church, as distinguished from the warring State, be doing, and especially those in the Church who have most opportunity? Dare one say—repenting? But repenting what—Versailles or Poland? Versailles, for our own sake; but Poland also because we are all co-heirs in sin. The Church is the knowledge of the mystical substance of man spiritually—in corruption and in redemption, and in neither can men be separated from each other until the heavenly division between tares and wheat, goats and sheep. But the wheat and the sheep were never encouraged by Christ to do the dividing.

In religion then we are all one union in sin. The murders in Poland are, in that sense, our sin. The State (that is, we) must help to put Hitler out of Poland. But the Church must repent because it is not only Hitler but we who are in Poland. It is his moral responsibility to God and the Church. But if it is our moral responsibility to put him out, it is also our religious responsibility to recognize that it is we, in that awful and devastating union, who are in. If we are fighting for freedom, this is the freedom which we must practise in order to fight. To give of our worldly substance to the army or the Treasury is our duty; so is the recognizing of our spiritual substance in the enemy as in his victims. But he will not recognize his? But what has that to do with it? The soldiers are fulfilling one duty; let the priesthood announce the other. This is Christendom at war.

ANTICHRIST AND THE CITY'S LAWS

Notes on the Way

Contributed to Time and Tide, *August 1938*

THE recent *affaire Noyes* and the action of the Holy Office in declaring that the book on Voltaire was 'worthy of condemnation' caused a mild shock to many people and has aroused some talk of issues important to the freedom of literature. I am not, of course, discussing the methods adopted, according to Mr. Noyes, by the Holy Office. The freedom of literature is one of those problems which are generally discussed in the void; that is, without adequate reference to the hypothetical alternative. But the hypothetical alternative is always different according to the actual problem. If the problem is whether the Home Secretary is to decide if *Ulysses* has a harmful effect on the ordinary reader in normal times—that is one problem; if whether I may publish in time of war a brilliant article on the strategic disposition of the fleet, that is another; if whether a still more brilliant—a classic—but offensive description of my actual life may be issued (I living) by a malicious enemy—that is a third. And the present discussion provides a fourth.

The Roman Church holds the view that intellectual freedom to state openly what you believe to be historical truth is a great deal less important than the spiritual salvation of mankind. Any historical view, therefore, even if it is a correct view, ought to be suppressed —temporarily or, I suppose, permanently—if the authorities of the Church in their discretion so decide. All institutions tend to take a similar view in times of crisis. All secular governments certainly do take it, quite properly, in times of crisis. The view of the Roman Church is that we all exist in a very high state of crisis (defined by such words as sin and salvation), and that the prevalence of a wrong view (if wrong) concerning Voltaire is of much less importance than what may be supposed (by its General Staff), on examination, to be the damage done in that crisis by its alteration. Such a view may be wrong, but it is, within itself, valid.

However, as Arnold said, the Holy Roman Church can take very good care of itself, and where Exeter Hall failed, we later disciples of culture are not likely to succeed, precisely because we naturally think the truth about Voltaire more important than salvation. The real interest is the question why the Holy Office found Mr. Noyes's book 'worthy of condemnation'. Mr. Noyes has been a little stern with certain ecclesiastics, but it seems unlikely that the Holy Office can have objected to that. To be severe with an eighteenth-century *curé* is not very bad. Mr. Belloc has been much harsher. Possibly the real trouble is what used to be called the 'debunking' of Voltaire. Or rather, perhaps, the inbunking of Voltaire. In Mr. Noyes's book Voltaire undergoes a change. In one sense it is no new change, for many of us have known him all along as a lover of justice, of intelligence, of honour. Mr. Noyes has gone a little farther; he removes ambiguity. When, close on his death-agony, Voltaire refused Communion: 'Je crache continuellement du sang; il faut bien se donner de garde de mêler celui du bon Dieu avec le mien. . . .' Mr. Noyes makes this (or, rather, a similar phrase) 'fearful and earnest words from the blood-stained lips of a dying man'. As against any suggestion that they were mere 'merriment' and 'persiflage', he is undoubtedly right. But the final line between belief and unbelief in such natures at such times is so faint that they can hardly speak without the phrase partaking of the nature of both sides of the line. The good God has permitted to his creatures a kind of belief that lives by a kind of rejection; a mental attitude not to be sought by man, but where it exists to be admitted. It is perhaps the point when irony has its last fling before it is happily abandoned.

Mr. Noyes has, I think, pulled Voltaire a little far across the line. He has tended (with however many modifications) to substitute a serious Voltaire for a sneering. He has done his best to remove an image of the mocking sceptic. It may be this to which the Holy Office instinctively objects. Voltaire can hardly be turned into a believer, nor has Mr. Noyes tried. But he has on the whole tended to remove his image from the opposite hierarchy. He suggests, for instance, that Voltaire was much more like a Christian than Pascal. It is a question of style. Pascal's famous wager in Voltaire's technique is, certainly, as unworthy as Voltaire thought it. But in Pascal's own style it is quite another thing. There is in Voltaire a suggestion that we cannot wager on truth. There is in Pascal a suggestion that truth is itself to be found only by the most dreadful of wagers. Belief—it is one of our difficulties—is as multifold as believers.

Some good might be done at the present time by an examination of our images, especially images of such states of being as we disapprove; could the examination be trusted. Historically, we are in the midst of a complete change of images, and when I say 'we are in the midst' I mean we do not yet know whether it will succeed. Notorious examples lie in that period so immediately like our own—the Reformation. 'Bloody Mary' was once a popular image (wildly modified in the house where I grew up to 'Sanguinary Polly'); it was not many years ago that I saw a bookshop window alight with titles of 'Bad Queen Bess'. Such alterations soon become merely fashionable. It is this fashion which institutions desire to control. The action of the Holy Office obviously raises the question of whether, in the future, a book 'inbunking' Elizabeth would be 'worthy of condemnation'. It would perhaps be regarded as undesirable that that 'bold bad woman' should be explained away. Are there to be no images of horror and iniquity—of Antichrist?

There have, after all, been very few tolerable images of Antichrist, for there are many difficulties in creating one. Antichrist must not be mad, to begin with. He must not, even, be too romantic. Art cannot bear that. Alexander VI has lost his once high opportunities because of the overwhelming romanticism of his image. Antichrist is bound to be a kind of sterile romantic; there is hardly anything else for him to be—classic he cannot be and realist he will not be, and therefore he must be the one kind of romantic who can become neither—the sterile or pseudo-romantic. Most images of evil are without that sterility. A passion for destructiveness, Black Masses and so on, palpitates with a real (even if disgusting) life. Those images are still fruitful, even if unpleasantly; they are (from some points of view) funny. Antichrist cannot be funny. But neither can he have a serious purpose, except himself. The persecutions and concentration camps of Germany therefore cannot lift Hitler to that image (other things apart). Mere cruelty cannot. Mere power cannot. If I were running a competition column I would offer a prize for the best candidate for an image of Antichrist, with brief reasons. As it is I suggest that we all pause now to make our own selection. (Excluding Mr. A. T. Sheppard, who wrote several novels on the subject.)

My own, until a better is suggested, is Frederick Rolfe, who was called Baron Corvo. Long (how long!) before he became fashionable, I came in dewy youth upon *Hadrian VII* on the shelves of a Free Library—yes—and *Don Tarquinio*. I fell. I made inquiries; I listened. But it was not till I read the *Quest for Corvo* by Mr. A. J. A. Symons that it dawned on me that Corvo was as near an image of Antichrist as one need wish to go. He was, to begin with, a Christian—which is always satisfactory for Antichrist: the separation from the Term in terms of the Term. It is why Alexander VI lasted so long. Indeed, it would be almost possible to conceive Corvo's life as that of a saint, since probably the greatest sanctities are always unknown or misunderstood, and they might easily end in apparent poverty and degradation. But particular details make this difficult to believe—especially Mr. Symons's description of the last letters, as of a pandar, from Venice. Mr. Symons himself leans to an explanation from homosexuality, which indeed may have been the occasion. But it is not only Corvo's anger and bitterness (not unjustifiable) which make of him a candidate for that mythical office. He understood, he desired, love and forgiveness; the conclusion of *Hubert's Arthur*, a very admirable piece of writing, is a noble imagination of a pardon granted by the Saint-King to a crowd of murderers. In *Hadrian VII* the Pope himself is presented as anxious to love, though naturally not succeeding. 'I don't think I know what love is. But I want to—badly.'

Yet the more one considers that image of Hadrian, the more one feels that there is a preliminary to love. One cannot love downwards, *de haut en bas*. That is reserved to God. One cannot love when one thinks oneself superior—even if one is superior. Human love is always between equals, and the most sheikh-like of heroes submits to that eventually, however often he abducts heroines on camels. Hadrian performs acts of violence on his spirit in order to perform acts of goodwill towards those whom he despises. But he consents, it seems, beyond those acts, interior and exterior, to go on despising them. 'He had emphasized his own fastidious aloofness.' While one indulges superiority to—let us go on saying—Hitler, one cannot begin to love Hitler . . . and not for some considerable time even then.[1]

In the account of Corvo, in the books by Corvo, is the same continual lack: a lack of what must be called humility, because there is no other word; the lack of all communication in true democracy,

[1] So the text. But perhaps the meaning is: 'even after superiority has been forgone'. A. R.

in the City. It was not only because he was a genius, as he thought, and as he was, and not only because he was exposed to stupidities and clumsinesses from kindness or anger. He was neither drunken nor lecherous, neither greedy nor malicious: only fastidious. He dreamed of remote and holy Love; he believed in the dogmas of his Church; he pursued God. But he showed no willingness to be the foolish and joyous equal of men and women; if he quarrelled, he demanded repentance from others; he nursed the division which, again because there is no more subtle word, we call pride—though indeed that is subtle enough, rightly taken. He wished to be Christ-like; and so he was, but in that one element in which nothing but Antichrist can be Christlike, in the consciousness of a kind of *otherness* from men.

Compare that image with the image of Coriolanus. In that great tragedy, the tragedy of the refusal of all the characters to choose the inevitable and intolerable thing, Coriolanus himself knows what fellowship is. In battle at least he precisely did not feel superior, though precisely there he was. In the Old Vic production that at least was clear. But Corvo made a virtue out of his superiority; almost out of his virtues. He made a personal virtue out of truth, and so he slipped gradually and steadily out of everything into hell. 'So, strook with dread and anguish, fell the Fiend.' He saw occasionally what was wrong. He must always have the upper seat, the upper hand—in spirit if not in act. It is the definition of the solitude of Antichrist—'deep malice thence conceiving and disdain'. Yet perhaps our vocal contemporary appeals to love suffer from a similar small fault. It is comparatively easy to be kind; unfortunately kindness is not enough. Nothing is enough, which leaves the lover in a condition of conscious superiority over—Hitler.

But it would be fascinating to collect other examples of the image and the myth.

THE LITURGY

Time and Tide *review of* The High Church Tradition,
by G. W. O. Addleshaw, 1941

THIS book is a study of the Liturgy of the Church of England as it was received by the Anglican Divines of the seventeenth century. 'The superficial writer on religious matters would not gain a hearing in the 17th century, unless his superficialities had been purged away by a knowledge of the Fathers. Unless he had read his Chrysostom... his opinions would have been ruled out of court.' These are healthy sentences for present-day writers to consider; those learned clergymen are no longer figures of fun. To dispute with them, as Johnson said of the poets of something the same period, 'it was at least necessary to read and think'. They, as it were, breathed orthodoxy; therefore the liturgy was their natural and holy speech. Mr. Addleshaw quotes from one of them, Thomas Comber, a description of it as 'the life and soul of religion, the *anima mundi*, that universal soul which quickens, unites, and moves the whole Christian world'.

It was not therefore their habit to twiddle and twist the *anima mundi* to the supposed momentary needs of the crowd—or indeed the Court. Edification and order were its secrets; the sacred City could not be built by everyone raising his own little pile of bricks. Men were to be part of it, and so only it of them. The Eucharist, which was the centre and consummation of all the Rites, was the union of the City. 'Sparrow . . . refers his readers to St. Augustine's remark in the *De Civitate Dei* that the Christian sacrifice is the offering of the Church as one body with its Lord.'

The present difficulty is that we have lost the liturgical sense. There are, no doubt, excuses. The liturgy is almost bound to seem to us like one-half of a conversation in which the other speaker is entirely silent. We keep on saying things to God, and God says nothing. Entreaties, adorations, statements, are poured out; they cease; they begin again; but no other voice interrupts our own. We do what we can with Lessons, Psalms, Gospels; we take, in an odd way, both sides, but then we have lost the natural sense of taking both sides; the priest's voice is no longer at times a reverberation of Another's. The sense therefore of a conversation *manqué* is over all.

It may be that this is to some extent at once the cause and the result of so many of our modern prayers and collects.[1] I have sometimes wondered why, when the ecclesiastical authorities need something written, they so rarely turn to anyone whose business is writing. I am not offering myself as a candidate, though since it is to be supposed that a bishop administers his diocese better than I possibly could, there would be no particular egotism in supposing that I might be able to write better than a bishop. But the real trouble lies deeper than the problem of authors; it involves the recovery of adoration, with all its related ideas. The liturgy is much more a thing done than a thing said. Ceremonial is the encouragement of this. Mr. Addleshaw quotes Bishop Andrewes as saying that if our worship is inward only, 'with our hearts and not our hats', something necessary is lacking. The things said are the accompaniments of something done. It is not our business to listen to the other Conversationalist (except as we always should); we do not go to

[1] See Appendix for some collects of Williams's own composition.

church in order 'to get good'. The good will, of course, happen, because the good is always happening; it is its nature.

Mr. Addleshaw discusses the relation of the liturgy to the community, and shows what efforts were made to keep the liturgy both ordered and free. 'It was'—to those theologians—'the prayer of humanity.' It was even more, and more even than the *anima mundi*; it was the voice of Christ in the Church. So, it had in its own especial way a place in the Holy Trinity Itself. It was man in his place there. This is what the respectable ordered service of the Church of England was. People once objected to it for being respectable. Odd! They even objected to putting on their best clothes and saving silver for the offertory. Yet even that was part of the ceremonial, of the thing done, of the order and high sacrifice. Now we have no best clothes we must do without, and I hope the objectors are happy.

VERGIL

Time and Tide *review of* Roman Vergil, *by W. Jackson Knight,*[1] *1944*

THIS is certainly a book which anyone interested in poetry or in our history ought to possess. There are many pages in it of which only the scholar is qualified to judge; there is hardly a page which does not give the amateur help in understanding what scholarship and poetry and Vergil are. The discussion of *sunt lacrimae rerum* is an admirable example, and the way in which Mr. Knight shows 'the main principle of Vergil's expression', which is 'compression into density of meaning'. It is, after all, that kind of thing which is Vergil; the figure of the Roman poet would otherwise be but the vaguest of shades. It was so that Dante knew him, when he first saw the presence in the wood, which might otherwise have seemed a shade: 'Are you that Vergil—and that fountain—which pours out so great a stream of speech?' The image of living and speaking waters is the best.

Must one then, being so indebted to Mr. Knight, take his ruling and write Vergil? I suppose one ought. 'The spelling with an e', he says, 'is certainly right.' He adds, 'but the wrong spelling with an i occurs already at about Vergil's own time.' It might serve as an excuse if 'Virgil' is too deeply rooted in one to be easily pulled up. Besides, the i is more evocative of those other two words to which Mr. Knight alludes: *virgo* and *virga*, maid and rod. Modesty and

[1] The three paragraphs on p. 126 are taken from another review ('Maid and Measure') of the same year, where Williams reverts to the usual spelling of Virgil's name.

measurement are Vergilian qualities, as they are of all great poets. At Athens he was nicknamed Parthenias, or maidenly, as Milton was similarly at Christ's. And for the rod, besides the hexameter (itself a living rod of sound), we all know the medieval dream of the magician; did not 'the wizard Michael Scott' join Vergil's name to those of other enchanters—Simon Magus, Abelard, Solomon? and did not Vergil himself (as they say) write a little book, only as big as his fist, which dealt with all the Seven Arts, and the use of the wand in sorcery? and by such aid make a 'craft' or image of all the regions of the world? But St. Paul converted the king's son who owned the book, and it vanished; and the 'craft' no one has seen since the disappearance of the last of the emperors of the East.

Such measurements of magic are not those about which Mr. Knight is writing, though he briefly touches on them. He studies the measurements of Vergil's own day, and in a sense of ours. If Vergil could be supposed to intrude into the New Testament, he would be that angel who measured the heavenly Jerusalem with a rod—when indeed he was not St. Joseph. Vergil's city was Rome; his rod was (in some sense) *pietas*, *pietas* expressed in his defining lines. In Vergil's day, as in ours, the world-crisis was very sharp. Mr. Knight says of it: 'It was still a problem of the nearly hopeless courage of the nearly helpless individual.... The collapse of civilization was the predominant obsession of Vergil's day.' It is true that we look back at him over the many centuries of Rome, and see him as declaring a thing we know to have existed. Yet Vergil died only eleven years later than Cleopatra, and we know from the *Aeneid* what dangers he saw in her and her 'superfluous kings'. The Fourth Eclogue (Mr. Knight holds) may have been meant for the child of that marriage of Antony and Octavia which had been an attempt to settle the world, and forms the subject of the second act of *Antony and Cleopatra*. Shakespeare, in that play, did not underrate Vergil's theme. It is Caesar who says:

> The time of universal peace is near.
> Prove this a prosperous day, the three-nook'd world
> Shall bear the olive freely.

'The Julian star' in Vergil's day had only just risen above the cloud of Eastern kings. Vergil made of the star a hope, and the hope since then has been joined to other stars. But it was he who defined the hope.

It was not easy. Propaganda had begun, and Mr. Knight points out how shamelessly the Augustan régime lied itself into reputation. Vergil had to support a Government by which he was himself the gainer, and of which he sometimes disapproved. The *Aeneid* has even been held to be 'a disguised attack on Augustus'. Mr. Knight himself says that 'the plan [of supporting the Government] could not easily be carried through with perfect sincerity'. The great poem had to labour with that additional difficulty. But again, as when the gods called Aeneas, there was nothing else to be done. Vergil, as well as his hero, had to find his own sincerity, and in that to found and establish Rome.

The measuring-rod which he used was that *pietas*. Mr. Knight, speaking of the poetry more than of the politics, says: 'Vergil and Horace, in co-operation to some extent, created a new idea and a new pattern of poetry that is classical, in the sense that it must use to the utmost every possibility of perfection.' On the poetic side, this is a definition worthy of serious attention. Classic verse (using the words in their most general sense) aims at gaining 'the highest reaches of our human thought', but it must do so by including all such possibilities, even all such perfections, in an organic whole. The great Vergilian maxim of Roman policy—*parcere subiectis et debellare superbos*—must apply to the imagination; lesser passions must be properly ordered towards greater, and the greater towards the good in and for all things.

This is true also of politics. 'Vergil examined the idea of *pietas*, and found in it, as he learnt to understand it, the central salvation.' The word *pius* has been undervalued. '*Pius Aeneas* is not Aeneas the Pious but Aeneas the True.' He was true to all great duties, to all affections that ought to claim obedience, to the gods and to the earth. The *Georgics* have something of the same—say, decency about them. The delicacy of that honour, that maidenhood of truth, that measurement of action—*virgo* and *virga*—is shown in other Romans. 'Cicero', Mr. Knight writes, 'said that it could be infringed by a mere expression of countenance.' This is high virtue, and it is not so much Vergil's as Vergil. Aeneas was Augustus? say, Aeneas was Augustus in a myth, as Edward King was Lycidas, and Keats Adonais. He was beyond Augustus. Let poetry be as accurate as it can, yet such poetry must be doubly accurate, to the facts known and the structure imagined.

There is a profound sense in which Dante was right to let Vergil lead him through hell. *Tu ne cede malis sed contra audentior ito*—'You, give not way to tribulation, but face it, the more daring for it, and go on.'

> Be you not troubled by the time that drives
> O'er your content these strong necessities.

The firm modesty, the rich measurement, which are Vergil had in their union Vergil's secret of power; and all tenderness went with it. He imagined a moral world.

. . . Virgil died in Brindisi, 19 B.C. There was, away over the Eastern Mediterranean, either soon to be born or perhaps already living, one who was to be the greatest human image of both. Virgil at Athens had been nicknamed 'the Maiden'; he had no child; he left the *Aeneid* behind him. As his executors saved it, there was already perhaps in Galilee the small child who was to be the Maiden of another myth. Could a mortal imagination dare it, one might play a little with time and place—extend Virgil's journeys and anticipate Mary's birth; and pretend that at Tyre or Jaffa the great poet talked with a more sacred creature than even he could dream, the intelligent and innocent God-bearer herself. But what they would have said to each other one cannot imagine. Ordinary things?

Yet indeed the two had much in common. The future voice of Mary was to assert the same maxim of government as Virgil's; '*parcere subiectis*'—'*deposuit potentes . . . exaltavit humiles*.' The hero of the Roman epic was 'Aeneas the True'; the Divine Hero asserted himself to be as true as truth, true to another origin as well as to his earthly *patria*. The *pietas* of Virgil was a part of and an image of a greater. The poem presented a city; the Maid-Mother's son was the foundation of all cities, and especially of his own—*descendentem de coelo a Deo*. Virgil was justice; say, the mortal Joseph of that imagined union. But, of course, the fundamental difference was there.

Virgil's rod, the hexameter, the *virga virginis*, could pierce and measure much, but not the deep apostasy of man's heart, or only with the magical sound of exposition and not with mystical fact. The foundation of his Rome was already split. It was into this split that the son of the other maiden went, not in imagination but in flesh and blood. About his going and his return there accumulated a new poetry. The rhythms of the *Aeneid* changed into marching songs, from many causes, but partly because of the new subject. *Arma virumque*? Centuries answered: *Dulce lignum, dulce clavo, dulce pondus sustinens*. Even Virgil could not give its full sense to 'our Yearning is crucified'; that terror and tenderness was beyond him, but then it was beyond all; it had to be shown. The *sunt lacrimae rerum* is outdone by the phrase Athanasius quoted: 'You shall see your Life hanging before your eyes.'

A DIALOGUE ON HIERARCHY

From Time and Tide, *October 1943*

NICOBAR. Did you by chance read, Eugenio, in recent numbers of the *Spectator* a dispute on equality and degree, where the Hierarchy and the Republic might be said almost to contend? And to which side did you lean in the affray?

EUGENIO. Indeed I was much entertained by the thought of Mr. Addison perusing the colloquy. But you would do as well to ask me if I preferred food or drink, fire or air, sound or sight, man or woman.

NICOBAR. Can we believe both imaginations so necessary?

EUGENIO. We not only can but must. It is true that each of us is likely to prefer to indulge his mind with one rather than the other, as (to dwell a little on my first image) one man most pleases himself with fancying meats and one with considering wines. But the best meals and the greatest nourishments are composed of both.

NICOBAR. Degree is necessary, I concede, in all executives, even if it be elective. But outside them?

EUGENIO. You are to consider that even there it is either of merit or of function, though sometimes (happily) of both. It is often easing to the mind to recognize this distinction, for one may generously yield to function the respect which one would reasonably deny to incapacity. But the principle is wider than that. Even in our present talk there is always a kind of hierarchy present.

NICOBAR. When (these ladies will say) you make obvious to me where I am wrong?

EUGENIO. Or you to me where I. We are not to suppose that the hierarchy of one moment is likely to be that of the next. The ranked degrees of intelligence are continually reordered. Sometimes you, and sometimes (since your modesty permits it) I, and sometimes one of the ladies, shed light on the others; and it is then that you or I or that she is hierarchically ascendant, and at the next moment some other, and so onward.

NICOBAR. This is to consider the amiability of our talk very minutely.

EUGENIO. We are speaking of a sensitiveness which responds best to minutiae. Equality is the name we give to the whole sum of such changes. That, too, must certainly be allowed as a principle, but ask Celia if she thinks of herself as your equal.

CELIA. Either *yes* or *no* seems curiously inadequate.

EUGENIO. And you, Nicobar, do you take her to be so?

NICOBAR. I have never thought her other. But I allow it is not a word that includes everything.

EUGENIO. And what does it not include?

NICOBAR. A glance, a tone, a glow, in either, which the other—must I say *obeys*?

EUGENIO. Why not? On that golden ladder of exchange the angels of joy run ceaselessly up and down; would you deny them any of their heavenly occasions of movement? But it is so that one hierarchy suddenly changes to another.

SOPHONISBA. It is not always easy to recognize the change.

CELIA. I am sure, dear madam, you do not think it so difficult when, by grace, one is free and in love, as (again by grace) all we four are. I know usually when Nicobar will have his way.

NICOBAR. Do I always achieve it?

CELIA. No, dearest; it would not be good for you. And a clear and happy revolt is sometimes permissible—or let us go with Eugenio and call it an alteration in the hierarchies.

NICOBAR. You have now a grand title to justify your obstinacies.

CELIA. It will serve you as well if you ever refuse me your lieutenancy in my own affairs.

SOPHONISBA. These are kind intimacies. But you were talking of society in general, Eugenio, and will you say that that can be based on Celias and Nicobars?

EUGENIO. You and I have known the habit over a longer time and in other relationships, and I think society must apprehend in general what these young ones apprehend in their own particular. There also the degrees continually change. He who is a good master of his craft in music may do ill enough in the theatre, and the Prime Minister must be docile to an expert scullion. Degree is the inbreathing and outbreathing of joy, but with every breath the joy changes. If every living creature is unique, it must necessarily be so.

SOPHONISBA. You would undoubtedly make as poor a hand at my dishes as I at your verse. But are there no stable hierarchies?

EUGENIO. In the organization of society, yes, and I am content to have them. But then they are rather of honourable function than of individual merit. The ancient monarchy of the English is one such. The anointed figure of the King does not 'deserve' to be royal, and this is so clear that it saves us from the claims of merit which oligarchies and aristocracies are apt to set up. It is of a different order. The degrees of merit constantly alter according as we apply our attention to this or that—to dons or doctors, to mimes or mechanics. But the hierarchies of function remain fixed.

CELIA. And the hierarchies of love?

EUGENIO. They are the deepest root of all. They have in them both natural and supernatural functions, and merits attributed if not deserved. There need be no schism there between degree and equality unless egotism sets out to make it. The Mother of God was not an apostle, yet the apostles were—only apostles. Do you suppose she and they wrangled over equality?

SOPHONISBA. Yet you said, Eugenio, that equality was the sum of all the changes.

NICOBAR. And he said rightly. For if each creature is unique, he owes discreet obedience to all others and all others to him; if each is in the base and at the apex, zenith and nadir at once, this great exchange of duty can only be summed so. The classless Republic is a republic of hierarchies, and each hierarchy is the flashing out of ranked equalities. But this equality is known in movement and not in quiescence.

EUGENIO. Celia's smile confirms you—as the shout of the people the undeserving King at the coronation. Shout or smile, you are to consider also that our superiority (whether of merit or function) works best only when it is that with which we are charged by others; our inferiority when it is that with which we intelligently charge ourselves. We were speaking, only the other day, about the dialectical philosophy, but I will venture to use once more a word I do not wish to make tiresome, and say that the important thing about these two principles is their co-inherence. Each exists and is understood in the other, and their fruit in them. The dialectical stress of opposition is hopeful of some new result beyond; but co-inherence means union, and the result here and now. It is said in the Zohar that God may be properly likened to an apple-tree, for the apple-tree composes two colours as God two attributes; and also that the Cup of Blessing is offered with two hands. Let us compare our desired City also to the apple-tree with the colours of equality and hierarchy, and let us take on—O the metaphor fades!—whatever hue is proper. Magnificence and modesty are our maxims.

NICOBAR. Yet magnificence that contemplates its equals as inferiors is in some danger of losing its modesty.

EUGENIO. We must always be in danger of sin, but here perhaps we may 'with a pure blush come off withal'. Each burns strongest and clearest when the other is present. We are unique? let us be modest, for it is true of every creature; but if other creatures will have us play our proper part, let us do it with as much magnificence as may be decently borne. In the very moment of looking down on the ranks below, the whole order is happily changed and one finds oneself looking up at the astonishing blaze of those same ranks now high and high above.

SOPHONISBA. The whole round of creation is understood then in that moment?

EUGENIO. Before Celia and Nicobar—must you leave?—have reached the door. Or I, when we too go, have opened it for you. Good night, and blessings.

IV · PARDON AND JUSTICE

THE CROSS

From a symposium, What the Cross Means to Me, *1943*

ANY personal statement on such a subject as the present is bound to be inaccurate. It is almost impossible to state what one in fact believes, because it is almost impossible to hold a belief and to define it at the same time, especially when that belief refers not to objective fact but to subjective interpretation. A rhetorical adjective will create a false stress; a misplaced adverb confuse an emotion. All that can be hoped is that a not too incorrect approximation may eventually appear. And anything that does appear is, of course, to be read subject to the judgement of the Christian Church, by whom all individual statements must be corrected.

Joseph Conrad, in his *Letters to Madame Paradowska*, says: 'Charity is divine and universal Love, the divine virtue, the sole manifestation of the Almighty which may in some manner justify the act of creation.' The last phrase is not perhaps one which would be used by the normal Christian. But the need for some such credible justification of the act of creation is one of which even the normal Christian may, humanly speaking, be very conscious. Many sermons and pious books are devoted to no other end. Much discussion of 'faith' means nothing else. Nor (still speaking in terms of human feeling) is such a justification unnecessary. The original act of creation can be believed to be good and charitable; it is credible that Almighty God should deign to create beings to share His Joy. It is credible that He should deign to increase their Joy by creating them with the power of free will so that their joy should be voluntary. It is certain that if they have the power of choosing joy in Him they must have the power of choosing the opposite of joy in Him. But it is not credible that a finite choice ought to result in an infinite distress; or rather let it be said that, though credible, it is not tolerable (to us) that the Creator should deliberately maintain and sustain His created universe in a state of infinite distress as a result of the choice. No doubt it is possible to Him.

This would be true, even if it were we ourselves who had made that choice. I am far from saying that we did not. It may be that we were 'in' Adam very much more particularly than is often supposed; it may be indeed that we, in that pre-fallen state, *were* Adam, and that it was we who chose. *Fuimus ille unus*, said Augustine, *quando fuimus in illo uno*; we were the one when we were in the one. But popular doctrine in the Church has rather taken the view that we did not consciously choose that original sin, but are at most its successors and inheritors. The vicarious guilt of it is in us; the derived concupiscence is in us. There remains for us the eternal dying which is its result.

This is the law which His will imposed upon His creation. It need not have been. Aquinas said that God wills His own goodness necessarily, but other things not necessarily. Our distress then is no doubt our gratuitous choice, but it is also His. He could have willed us not to be after the Fall. He did not. Now the distress of the creation is so vehement and prolonged, so tortuous and torturing, that even naturally it is revolting to our sense of justice, much more supernaturally. We are instructed that He contemplates, from His infinite felicity, the agonies of His creation, and deliberately maintains them in it. I do not refer merely to the agonies of the present time; they are more spectacular and more destructive, but not more lasting, nor perhaps very much worse, than the agonies of a more peaceful time. But man has not often known a more peaceful time. And if he had, in the times that he has known, the very burden of daily existence too often seems a curse. The whole creation groaneth and travaileth together.

This then is the creation that 'needs' (let the word be permitted) justifying. The Cross justifies it to this extent at least—that just as He submitted us to His inexorable will, so He submitted Himself to our wills (and therefore to His). He made us; He maintained us in our pain. At least, however, on the Christian showing, He consented to be Himself subject to it. If, obscurely, He would not cease to preserve us in the full horror of existence, at least He shared it. He became as helpless as we under the will which is He. This is the first approach to a sense of justice in the whole situation. Whatever He chose, He chose fully, for Himself as for us. This is, I think, unique in the theistic religions of the world. I do not remember any other in which the Creator so accepted His own terms—at least in the limited sense of existence upon this earth. It is true that His life was short. His pains (humanly speaking) comparatively brief. But at least, alone among the gods, He deigned to endure the justice He decreed.

There is another point of the same kind. It is often said that He was put to death by evil men. Caiaphas and Pilate and Herod are denounced. It is, of course, in some sense true that it was evil which persecuted Him. But I have myself felt that the destructiveness was more common to our experience if we hold, as we very well may, that Caiaphas and Pilate were each of them doing his best in the duty presented to them. The high priest was condemning a blasphemer. The Roman governor was attempting to maintain the peace. At the present time, for example, it is clear that one man must suffer for the people—and many more than one man, whether they consent or not. It is, no doubt, inevitable; it may be right. But we can hardly blame those earlier supporters of the same law. Humanly speaking, they were doing the best they could. They chose the least imperfect good that they could see. And their choice crucified the Good.

It is this agonizing fact which is too often present in our own experience. Certainly our sins and faults destroy the good. But our efforts after the good also destroy it. The very pursuit of goodness becomes a hunt; that which was to be our lord becomes a victim. It is necessary to behave well here? We do. What is the result? The destruction of some equal good. There is no more significant or more terrible tale in the New Testament than that which surrounded the young Incarnacy with the dying Innocents: the chastisement of His peace was upon them. At the end He paid back the debt—to God if not to them; He too perished innocently. With Him also (morally) there was nothing else to be done.

He had put Himself then to His own law, in every sense. Man (perhaps ignorantly, but none the less truly for that) executed justice upon Him. This was the world He maintained in creation? *This* was the world He maintained in creation. This was the best law, the clearest justice, man could find, and He did well to accept it. If they had known it was He, they could have done no less and no better. They crucified Him; let it be said, they did well. But then let it be said also, that the Sublimity itself had done well: adorable He might be by awful definition of His Nature, but at least He had shown Himself honourable in His choice. He accepted Job's challenge of long ago, talked with His enemy in the gate, and outside the gate suffered (as the men He made so often do) from both His friends and His enemies. Which of us has not known and has not been a Judas? He had no where to lay His head? And we? 'Behold my mother and my brethren.'

This then has seemed to me now for long perhaps the most flagrant significance of the Cross; it does enable us to use the word 'justice' without shame—which otherwise we could not. God therefore becomes tolerable as well as credible. Our justice condemned the innocent, but the innocent it condemned was one who was fundamentally responsible for the existence of all injustice—its existence in the mere, but necessary, sense of time, which His will created and prolonged.

This is the more objective side; there is the more subjective. Man chooses, in most of his experiences, between the rack and the Cross, between a prolonged lesser and a shorter but greater pain. I do not wish to seem here to become rhetorical; I do not underrate the great and pure beauties which are presented and revealed to us, the virtue and value of fidelity, the appearance of a new kind of goodness where sometimes the old seems to have been exhausted. Yet it is also true that a kind of death attends us all everywhere. Our best knowledge is dimmed with boredom or darkened by destruction. 'A mist goes up from the ground' or an earthquake shakes it. A languor and a reluctance take us as we endure the undestroyed good, or else the demand for its sacrifice preoccupies us. This occurs so often that we feel it to be in the nature of life; this is what life is. Yes then, certainly, this is what Life is. The Cross is the exhibition of Life being precisely that; more—as knowing itself to be precisely that, as experiencing itself as being precisely that. We are relieved—may one say?—from the burden of being naturally optimistic. 'The whole creation groaneth and travaileth together.' If we are to rejoice always then it must be a joy consonant with that; we need not—infinite relief!—force ourselves to deny the mere burden of breathing. Life (experience suggests) is a good thing, and somehow unendurable; at least the Christian faith has denied neither side of the paradox. Life found itself unendurable. Romantically multiplying each side as our feelings may propose, we cannot go beyond that realism. Life itself consents to shrink from its own terrors; it concedes to us its utterance of our own prayer: 'O not *this*! If it be possible, not *this*!' I am not for a moment equating our sorrows with that; the point is that the sorrow is centrally there. Life itself is acquainted with grief.

And not grief alone. Crucifixion was an obscene thing. It was revolting not merely because of the torture and the degradation, but also because of the disgust; or rather it is revolting to us—I do not know that it was revolting to those who saw it. They were as accustomed to it as our fathers were to burning and castration or we to many years' imprisonment or to the gallows. It was, however, definitely more spectacularly obscene than the gallows; we can hardly, in the nature of things, realize it so, and even our best efforts tend to make it a little respectable. But then again life, as we know it, is obscene; or, to be accurate, it has in it a strong element of obscenity. Again and again we become aware of a sense of outrage in our physical natures. Sometimes this is aroused by the events of which we read in the papers, but as often by the events which happen to us. The Family, for example, is a sacred and noble thing, but the things that happen in the Family are the result of blood antagonistic to itself. 'Love', it is said, 'is very near to hate.' Without discussing the general truth of that, it may be allowed that where it is so, the hate is often of a particularly virulent and vehement kind.

I take these two qualities—the sorrow and the obscenity—as examples of that dreadful contradiction in our experience of life which is flatly exhibited in the living of life by Life. I am not unaware that it will be said that That which dies on the Cross was something a great deal more than Life in any sense in which we understand the word. But I am not now talking of Christian dogma, but of a particular sense of the Cross. 'The feeling intellect' of the Faith is a state of a much more advanced nature than anything I can claim to have known.

I say then that the idea of the Cross does, on the one hand, make the idea of justice in God credible; and on the other certifies to us that we are not fools in being conscious of the twisting of all goodness to ignominy. We may (if it may be put so) approach God with that at least cleared up. We are not being unjust to His creation in the distaste we feel for it, nor even in the regret we feel that He allows it to continue. There would be other things to be said were we now discussing the Incarnation as such, but these are the things to be said peculiarly about the Cross. This is what Almighty God, as well as we, found human life to be. We willed it so, perhaps, but then certainly He willed that we should will.

There is, however, more to it than that. There is Easter. It is not possible to separate the idea of Easter from the Cross. Easter is its consequence. But it is a consequence of which many of us have very little apprehension. There are those who find it easy to look forward to immortality and those who do not. I admit that, for myself, I do not. It is true that the gradual stupefaction of the faculties which normally overcomes a man as he grows older seems to make—if not the idea of immortality more attractive—at least the idea of annihilation less so. Possibly curiosity is the last of one's faculties to be stupefied; possibly the natural egotism which has had a free run in one's life accentuates marvellously the idea of self-preservation as one approaches the apparent end of self-preservation. Possibly one is merely more fussy. Whatever is true, the idea of annihilation is more repellent. But I cannot say I find the idea of immortality, even of a joyous immortality, much more attractive. I admit, of course, that this is a failure of intelligence; if joy is joy, an infinite joy cannot be undesirable. The mere fact that our experience on this earth makes it difficult for us to apprehend a good without a catch in it somewhere, is, by definition, irrelevant. It may, however, make the folly more excusable.

Easter, however, is not only a consequence of the Cross; it is also almost an accident of it. It followed the Cross, but also it began in the Cross. I say 'in' rather than 'on', for by the time it began He had become, as it were, the very profoundest Cross to Himself. That certainly He had always been prophetically, but now the exploration of His prophecies was complete. The Cross was He and He the Cross. His will had maintained, or rather His will in His Father's will had maintained, a state of affairs among men of which physical crucifixion was at once a part and a perfect symbol. This state of things He inexorably proposed to Himself to endure; say, rather, that from the beginning He had been Himself at bottom both the endurance and the thing endured. This had been true everywhere in all men; it was now true of Himself apart from all men; it was local and particular. The physical body which was His own means of union with matter, and was in consequence the very cause, centre, and origin of all human creation, was exposed to the complete contradiction of itself. It would be perhaps too ingenious a fancy, which in these things above all is to be avoided, to say that actual crucifixion is a more exact symbol of His suffering than any other means of death. It is, however, with peculiar explicitness in the physical category what His other agony was in the spiritual (so, for a moment, to differentiate them). He was stretched, He was bled, He was nailed, He was thrust into, but not a bone of Him was broken. The dead wood drenched with the blood, and the dead body shedding blood, have an awful likeness; the frame is doubly saved. It was the Cross which sustained Him, but He also sustained the Cross. He had, through the years, exactly preserved the growth of the thorn and of the wood, and had indued with energy the making of the nails and the sharpening of the spear; say, through the centuries He had maintained vegetable and mineral in the earth for this. His providence overwatched it to no other end, as it overwatches so many instruments and intentions of cruelty then and now. The Cross therefore is the express image of His will; it depends in its visible shape and strength wholly on Him.

In the moment, as it were, of the final so-near-to-identity of Himself and His wooden Image, He spoke. He said: 'It is finished.' It is at that moment that Easter began. It is not yet Easter; the Deposition has not yet taken place. He speaks, while yet He can, while He is not yet as speechless as the wood, and He announces the culmination of that experience. Life has known absolutely all its own contradiction. He survives; He perfectly survives. His—I dare not call it victory—is not afterwards, but then. His actual death becomes almost a part of His Resurrection, almost what Patmore called the death of the Divine Mother, a 'ceremony'. Not so, for the ceremony was itself a work and a discovery, but then proper ceremonies are so; they achieve, as this does. The joy of His self-renewed knowledge perfectly exists, and His Resurrection is (in His Father and Origin) at His own decision and by His own will. It is the will of His unalterable joy which, having absorbed, exists.

This moment of consummation is therefore related to man's inevitable demand that all things should be justified in the moment that they happen. We must perhaps, joyously or reluctantly, consent to leave the knowledge of that justification till afterwards, but we must be willing to believe that it is now. Or better, that the result is neither here nor there, neither now nor then, and yet both here and there, both now and then. There has indeed been much admiration, much gratitude, much love, that God should be made like us, but then there is at least equal satisfaction that it is an unlike us who is so made. It is an alien Power which is caught and suspended in our very midst. 'Blessed be God', said John Donne, 'that He is God only and divinely like Himself.' It is that other kind of existence which here penetrates our hearts, and is at all points credibly justified by our justice. The supreme error of earthly justice was the supreme assertion of the possibility of justice. In His mortal life He never pretended, in making all His impossible and yet natural demands, that He judged as we do. The parable of the labourers, the reply to James and John, are alien from our equality; and so is the incredible comment on Judas—'it were good for that man if he had not been born'. And who caused him to be born? Who maintained his life up to and in that awful less than good? It is in the Gospels that the really terrifying attacks on the Gospel lie.

He was not like us, and yet He became us. What happened there the Church itself has never seen, except that in the last reaches of that living death to which we are exposed He substituted himself for us. He submitted in our stead to the full results of the Law which is He. We may believe He was generous if we know that He was just. By that central substitution, which was the thing added by the Cross to the Incarnation, He became everywhere the centre of, and everywhere He energized and reaffirmed, all our substitutions and exchanges. He took what remained, after the Fall, of the torn web of humanity in all times and places, and not so much by a miracle of healing as by a growth within it made it whole. Supernaturally He renewed our proper nature. By so doing, it is true, He redoubled, at least within the Church, our guilt and our distress. When He had made hope a virtue He had prevented it from being a natural habit. In all failures of love there is left to us only a trust in His work; that is what we call 'faith', a kind of quality of action. It is, however, a trust in what is already done. Not only His act, but all our acts, are finished so. 'Thy will be done on earth as it is in heaven' means precisely that at any moment the holy desire is already accomplished—not perhaps in the sense that we desire it, but in the sense that He wills it. It is finished; we too do but play out the necessary ceremony.

As in bombings from the air, cancer, or starvation, for instance? Yes, I suppose so; if at all, then certainly in those examples. The Church (of which He seems to have had a low opinion) is His choice, but nature was His original choice, and He has a supreme fidelity. It is, in fact, that fidelity which causes Him to maintain His creation and to die for His creation and to renew His creation. It may seem that little has been here said about our salvation through His sacrifice. That would not be quite true, for all that has been said concerns our salvation. Our salvation is precisely our reconciliation, to nature and to the Church—not that they are so separate; our reconciliation both to Him and to our present state, both at once and both in one. We are, by that august sacrifice, compelled to concede to Him the propriety of our creation. I do not know that anything greater could be demanded or done. 'It is He that hath made us, and not we ourselves.' We know that very well. But the General Thanksgiving ('general thanksgiving'—incredible words!) goes farther. 'We bless Thee for our creation, preservation . . . for the means of grace and the hope of glory.' It seems that nothing less will do. We are then required to do it because He does; it is at once a duty and a relief. Let Him do it for us, for at least the Life in Him is not separate from our life: we are allowed to repose in His blessing of Himself, and to confirm ours by virtue of His blessing. The duty and the relief do not remain themselves; they are changed as nature is changed, as the elements in the Eucharist are changed. In the Eucharist He withdraws all into His Resurrection, because the Resurrection is in the sacrifice. This is not the place, however, to discuss the Eucharist. It is sufficient to say that there, as everywhere, to be able to bless is to be in a state of salvation, in a state of goodwill towards Him and all His creation, in a state of love. Only beatitude can properly bless, as only Love can love. In so far as we desire to bless, we are at least believers in a state of salvation now.

Our own guilt, natural or supernatural, is only manifested so. We can hardly be in a state of guilt towards something which is not in bearable relations with us. The Crucifixion, restoring those relations, restores very much more. It permits repentance because it enables us to mean something by sin. Without that act, the infliction on us of something terribly like injustice would have made nonsense of any injustice on our side. He restores Himself to us as God with all the qualities of God merely by being content not to be nothing but God. God can pardon, but pardon is only half pardon unless it is desired; the supreme life of it is precisely in the mutual act. There is no lovingness, mortal or divine, which does not, for its mutual quality, depend on that sacrifice of Himself. 'Others He saved; Himself He cannot save.' If He had saved Himself, it seems, He could not have saved others; He did it by His power affirming, in the Crucifixion, its own lack of power. He maintains us, by His will, in the state of sin in which we are; by His act He makes free to us the knowledge of that state, and of that issuing in Him.

'O fools and slow of heart, *ought* not Christ to have suffered these things, and entered into His glory?' Yes; He ought. He said so: 'The Son of Man *must* . . .' But then also He did. If the glory on which He insists, at such a cost, seems intolerable to us, if the exposition of release from our unhappy state seems as unbearable as the state itself, so that we cannot bear the only alternative to what we already cannot bear, at least that, after all, is the situation; it is He. We may be bold to say that He knows Himself as well as we know Him; after the Cross we can believe that He knows Himself not only as He does, but as we do. In the finishing of that knowledge a little cloud of fresh good arises, the first sense of that cloud into which He was received when He ascended. Whole, He died; whole, He rose; whole, He went up. Not the least gift of the Gospel is that our experiences of good need not be separated from our experiences of evil, need not and must not be. In time they generally are, and even when they are not they are apt to seem unrelated. The authority which the good in our experience seems to have over us, unlike the evil, however much less than the evil it seems to be, is united with that other authority of the God who endured His own. It is the Christian religion that makes the Christian religion possible. Existence itself is Christian; Christianity itself is Christian. The two are one because He is, in every sense, life, and life is He. It is to that, in the Triune Unity, that there is ascribed, beyond all hope, to that only Omnipotence, as is most justly due, all might, majesty, dominion, and power.

THE DOCTRINE OF LARGESSE

Time and Tide *review of* Forgiveness and Reconciliation, *by Vincent Taylor, 1941*

It may be that when the grooms and grocers, the gentlemen and jockeys and (as it were) chauffeurs of Constantinople argued at street-corners about the nomenclature of the Double-Natured One, the effect on the Church was less than good. But we have some reason to think that the opposite state of affairs is no better. Emotionally, if not intellectually, we are still under the impression that the deeper theology goes, the simpler it ought to be. Yet the enjoyments of friendship are more subtle after years; and if our wives or husbands forgive us our debts (as they so often do), it does not follow that we have understood the whole of their complex love in the moment of the first renewed kiss.

'As below, so above.' Even among Christians, the great experiences are often over-simplified, and the words *love* or *forgiveness* are thought to be sufficient. Obscurely resenting the theological disputes of the past, and not at all obscurely evading our moral duties in the future, we ask only that we shall act once and be done with it. The Church was wiser; it provides for a monotony of pardon. It used to be blamed for compelling its members ritually to declare themselves 'miserable sinners' day by day, but it knew very well that if they did not do it ritually they would not do it at all, and it very well knew what in fact they were. It oppressed them with a repentance they had half to feign in order that they should not feign a sufficiency which did not oppress them.

Dr. Taylor's book is an examination of the idea of pardon. It is theological; words which seem to us the dim echoes of evangelical tyrannies mean to him experiences of the soul; and of course he is right. The lack of those experiences in us does not falsify the high diagram. He examines the use of the word in the Gospels, and concludes that it means less than it is usually taken to mean. It is 'the bestowal of mercy and the cancellation of indebtedness'. The restoration of normal relations, which is so often included in it, does not strictly belong to it at all. Before that pure restoration can take place, there must be not only a remission of debt but a communication of validity. Speaking in terms of human relations, it is this which causes the pardoner to recognize an equality in the pardoned; it is curious how apt this stage is to be overlooked, and a faint sense of superiority retained. I am not, of course, comparing the theological and human meanings; I am only illustrating.

This is the prelude to a reconciliation—with God? doubtless, but say also with life, with living itself. Dr. Taylor insists that modern theology is weak here, because, though it makes reconciliation central, it lays too much stress on what the death of Christ shows rather than on what it does. Like all acts, that act (since it was certainly He who permitted Himself to die) exhibited a Nature, but (more than all other acts) it produced, by itself, a result. It is therefore that acts done in union with that act have a unique validity. But that validity operates in the community, in the Church, in the mystical Body which rose, new-blooded, from the shed Blood. 'Only in the community can "the individual" gain his individuality.' 'Sanctification' is that state in which 'reconciliation and fellowship find their goal and consummation'; it is this which is, to raise to its full meaning a term otherwise applied, 'the doctrine of largesse'. 'The language is sacrificial', says Dr. Taylor of other phrases concerned with 'those who are sanctified', and the description is applicable to that phrase also. It was used originally of the Black Prince, who was said also to have a peculiar devotion to the Holy and Undivided Trinity. Whatever one's opinion of the Black Prince may be, the collocation of the two phrases has a great significance. The doctrine of the Trinity is a doctrine of largesse; the doctrine of the Atonement is a doctrine of largesse; the doctrine of the Church is a doctrine of largesse; therefore the doctrine of the individual is a doctrine of largesse.

The operation which begins with the first kiss of pardon is not complete until all fibres of the being, physical and spiritual, are charged with that doctrine; and it is a doctrine of taking as well as of giving. It is easier often to forgive than to be forgiven; yet it is fatal to be willing to be forgiven by God and to be reluctant to be forgiven by men. To forgive and to be forgiven are the two points of holy magnificence and holy modesty; round these two centres the whole doctrine of largesse revolves. This is the pattern of our 'actual situation' in the Church, and 'outside the Church is no salvation'. 'I press on', wrote St. Paul, 'that I may apprehend that for which also I was apprehended by Christ Jesus.' It is this full apprehension with which Dr. Taylor is concerned, and towards which he has provided a pattern of the Way.

JOHN CALVIN

Time and Tide *review of* Calvinism, *by A. Dakin, 1941, omitting the last paragraph*

DR. DAKIN has not perhaps modified Calvinism, but he has at least made it seem credible. Whether any of its early champions would quite recognize it in his arrangement is a matter on which he can speak with more assurance than I, though I can believe that Calvin himself would not much disagree. For Calvin, like other great men, like Augustine and Dante and Kierkegaard, had passion capable of sustaining his thought.

There is nearly always in such men a central energy which our lesser minds dichotomize. What in them is a union, becomes in us a variation and even a contradiction. Thus Dante, in whose vision flesh and spirit were so greatly one, has been turned into a spiritual teacher and even into something like a refined preacher of spirituality as separate from the body. Thus Kierkegaard has turned agnostics into Catholics and Catholics into agnostics. Thus St. Paul himself has been turned into a mystic or an institutionalist. Thus Calvin has been made a predestinarian.

Of course it was so, but it was not only so. 'Man sins necessarily but he also sins voluntarily.' The two adverbs were, in him, infinitely intermingled. The congregations who followed him were less capable; they began to tear them apart, and their opponents enthusiastically assisted the process. They had much justification. His eyes fixed on the necessity of the Divine initiative, Calvin held that, for all men, 'election is not in view of anything they possibly will become any more than in view of anything they actually are. The ultimate is that God has so chosen.' To avoid that terror we have been compelled to dichotomize in our thought, to talk of justice as if it were a quality, separate from God's decree, to which He conformed; otherwise, the terror masters us, as it did Cowper.

Calvin is popularly rejected today. Yet a great number of those who reject him are as likely to be emotional Calvinists as not. The great heresiarchs are in intellectual error perhaps; but the world is less powerful even than that. It is quite common to find someone who says that 'pure Love' is not for him; he is, of course, incapable of it. He accepts perhaps the idea of God: what then? He says, in fact, that God has eternally rejected him; that he is cast out of the only principle; that he is reprobate. Says? he claims it, he takes pleasure in it. Or, in times of despair, he feeds on it, he rests in it; the taste for damnation, the eating of hell, in which at those times we indulge, becomes an appetite and a habit. Without some precious malice life loses all savour. 'Those', Dr. Dakin quotes from Calvin, 'for whom God designs the call to be a savour of death'; it is quite often those that denounce Calvinism who precisely relish 'the savour of death'.

Dr. Dakin mentions the comparison of Calvin with Loyola. One lived from 1509 to 1564; the other from 1491 to 1556; both had the same maxim: 'All to the Glory'; their two great works came out about the same time; through each of them the Glory burned. The passion, as Dr. Dakin shows, has returned today, especially in the shape of Barth. 'The doctrine of predestination will hardly be stated again in so rigorous a fashion as by Calvin.' But orthodoxy has still to combat the emotional predestinationalism of—the rest of us. It may be improper to define the Glory as Calvin did; it is certainly improper to escape from it as millions do. 'The Calvinistic Way of Life' became an unbearable rigidity of will, but the opposite and unbearable fluidity of 'love' today differs from it chiefly in the sense that men are able to delight in that with their predestined escape from Love. Calvin at least knew what he said.

THE IMAGE OF MAN

Time and Tide *review of* The Nature and Destiny of Man
1. Human Nature, *by Reinhold Niebuhr, 1942*

OF all the images which man can carry in his mind, the key image is his own. It is not necessarily the greatest; the unimaged image of Deity lies beyond it. But that greater can often only be seen by the lesser; and our chief argument is whether the image of man which man's mind holds is properly shaped as something which sees not only itself but beyond itself. It is this problem to which Dr. Niebuhr here addresses himself.

We all agree that man justly imagines himself as seeing himself. In this sense he is like the great seraphim who were full of eyes within and without. Or, as Dr. Niebuhr more philosophically says: 'Man's rational capacity involves the ability to make himself his own subject.' He is asserted, in this sense, to stand outside 'nature'; the animals do not do it—or so we suppose; they seem anyhow not to do it rationally. Man therefore is a problem to himself, and perhaps a solution. I say 'perhaps' because Dr. Niebuhr seems to me to omit from his consideration the great agnostics who deny that the infinite problem can be solved, at least by us. Indeed there is nothing to say.

But of most other solutions which those interior eyes have seen, he gives a just account.

The book is not easy reading; Dr. Niebuhr's sentences are apt to run statelily into extremes of length. And the reader must be content to accept his implied definitions. This is particularly so in respect to the word 'Romanticism' which he limits, it seems to me, unfairly. Thus he says: 'Romanticism understands the fact of the goodness of creation in all of its particularity and individuality; but it has no perspective beyond creation.' This is true of certain romantics; it is untrue of others. It might at least as easily be maintained that some romantics have too quickly declared that their perspective stretched beyond creation; they have too easily redressed their world by another, and not only Christian romantics at that. One maxim of the Romantic is: 'This also is Thou; neither is this Thou', and there is his true perspective.

Accepting these limitations for the sake of the book, we may admire Dr. Niebuhr's survey of the varieties of the image of himself which man has found. He recounts the classic and the rationalistic, the romantic and the modern. He devotes the second half of the book to a consideration of the Christian view, and quotes Augustine's epigrammatic definition of the whole problem: 'Therefore is the mind too strait to contain itself.' The answer, one might say, is that though the mind is too strait to contain itself yet it is not too strait to contain God, in whom again itself is contained. The word 'paradox' has become tiresome; it directs our attention too much to the colour and tone of the solution; let us be content with the solution as a fact—at least as an image. Let us have done with irony, even happy irony; it is but adolescent mirth. Things are so; very well, they are so.

God then is held in the mind as in the Virgin's womb; the womb is the more important, for otherwise He could not be in the mind, but we are here considering the lesser. He is, so, conceived—intellectually because carnally first. Within that image of God granted to the human mind is the image of man; say, rather, two images of man—man in perfection and man in revolt against perfection: man as he ought to be and man as he is. These two images exist together; rationalist, romantic, and Christian alike admit them. What the first two are reluctant to admit is defined by Dr. Niebuhr in attacking the moderns: 'Having eliminated the time-eternity dimension in measuring human nature they naturally regard with uncomprehending contempt or fury those aspects of the Biblical view which introduce a further complexity into the time-eternity dimension, the complexity of sin.'

Sin is simple enough in principle. The mind of man holds those two images—of God and of man; like, yet unlike in the sense that one must derive from the other. 'The sin of man is that he seeks to make himself God'; he will be, by himself, the centre of all the derivations. This, it has been said, is the sin of Satan: 'he desired to be', says the *Malleus Maleficarum*, 'to those related to him by a certain dependence, the only source of good'. From some such wish all evils rose, and rise: this is, in man's nature, 'that original sin which it committed of its own free will'. 'Man sins necessarily and yet voluntarily.' Or as Dr. Niebuhr sums it up: 'Man is to be held responsible for actions which are prompted by an ineluctable fate.'

This, in fact, is what we are all up against—the idealist and the romantic as well as the Christian. Dr. Niebuhr applies it to the Nazi self-glorification and cruelty. And we know it is true of any penal code. The solution may be further discussed in Dr. Niebuhr's second volume on human destiny which is to be published later this year. He touches on it here. Man must accept responsibility for the inevitable. 'Man is most free in the discovery that he is not free.' Something like this is the centre of that great purgatorial doctrine by which man is said, being pardoned, to desire the penalty. 'There is no historic structure of justice which can either fulfil the law of love or rest content in its inability to do so.' This is not only true internationally (as it is used in this book) but also nationally—more, between all enemies and lovers. Yet the image of man which is the key-image aspires continually to become such a structure. When the sinner desires vengeance (punishment is too dim a word) on himself, he for a moment approaches it. We have then to set up this transcending structure of the heart; social justice must exist in order that this other may exist; that is, clarity must exist in order that charity may exist. For charity is precisely the accepted image of ineluctable fate.

. . . . .

[I add to this the final paragraph of a review of a symposium on *War and Christian Ethics*, 1940:]

At the end of *Measure for Measure* Shakespeare has a very remarkable scene. He causes Angelo, who has done the injury, to entreat for his punishment, and Isabel, who has suffered it, to entreat for his pardon. I am not sure that this odd climax is irrelevant to the problem. Pardon—that is, the renewal of love—ought, of course, to exist always as a state of soul. But as an operation—it is inevitable that *Messieurs les assassins* should create its opportunity. If they will not—'of other strength Not emulous'—the operation can hardly exist. That such a position entails the most appalling spiritual dangers to the other side will be obvious. That it will be denounced as a compromise is equally obvious. But compromise it is not—it is the effort to mean by love, in the City militant upon earth, something greater and not less than justice.

V · EXCHANGE

THE WAY OF EXCHANGE

A pamphlet in the New Foundations *series, 1941*

It has been of old a general complaint against war that it involves many harmless and unwilling persons belonging to different communities in the conflict between those communities. The general discussion whether we are at war with the German people or not is an example of this. Efforts have been made, and abandoned, to show that the German people are not at one with their leader. What is certain is that at present the vast majority of Europeans greatly dislike the conditions in which the vast majority of Europeans live. Nevertheless they assent, passively or actively, to the action of their governments; they are, so far, compelled to be at one with their governments. 'Like ourselves,' wrote Mr. J. L. Garvin in the *Observer* of 16 June 1940, 'many, many millions of the Italian people abhor this tragedy. They neither hate us nor we them. That can make no difference on their side or our side.'

They and we are, in fact, committed by our governments. Those governments, in the nature of modern society, cannot be checked or much controlled, except at serious risk, by their nationals. We may well believe that the present situation of Europe tends to show that our own Government cannot have deceived us. But then we are still affected by the German Government. We are at war because of Hitler, or because of the general tension between all governments; either way, we are not at war directly because of our own wish, but because of others. We depend upon others. The old cry against governments involving their peoples in war may be inapplicable in this war or not. It was sincere, but (as we now see) useless. We are always in the condition that we are because of others.

This is all so elementary as to sound stupid. Yet to accept this profoundly is difficult. To be in a distressing and painful condition because of others is a thing we all naturally resent. It is often the cause of hatred towards those others, whether in public or private things. Yet until we are willing to accept the mere fact without resentment we can hardly be said to admit that other people exist.

We may reject, we may rebuke, we may contend against their action. But the very first condition of admitting that their existence is as real as our own is to allow that they have, as individuals, as much right to act in the way that they decide as we have. They may be wicked and we good or vice versa; that is a question of moral judgement, and therefore another question. The main fact is that we are compelled to admit their decision, and to admit that our lives, and often our deaths, depend on that.

Such a decision, important as it is in war, is, in fact, no less important in peace. We have, first, to learn that others exist by ceasing to resent their existence. Until we have ceased to resent that existence, merely instinctively, we can hardly be said to admit it. But having admitted it, we have then to decide what we are to do about it; what our attitude is to be towards those other existences, what our relation with them. The great philosophies have given various answers; the great religions, on the whole, the same answer. Out of these the good taste of the West (one can hardly call it more) had, until recently, made a general amalgam which it called, roughly, 'tolerance'.

Tolerance meant, at worst, sullenly putting up with what one could not alter; at best, willingly accepting what one could not alter. It was a little limited by the fact that 'to tolerate' was always considered as an active and hardly ever as a passive verb. One always tolerated and rarely was tolerated. The idea that others had, so to speak, to 'put up with' oneself was rarely practised, deeply and consistently. But, such as it is, toleration was, and remains, a noble virtue—yet a virtue which serves best as a guide to something greater than itself.

The great religions had, on the whole, recommended something more active. Much though they differed in their definitions of God, they did, generally, agree on their definitions of our duty towards our neighbour, even if they did not always agree on the exact definition of our neighbour. The Christian idea was expressed in the phrase 'bear ye one another's burdens'. It encouraged, indeed it demanded, a continual attention to the needs of one's neighbour, to his distresses and his delights. And it defined 'neighbour' as meaning anyone with whom one was, by holy Luck, brought into contact. It required, then, an active 'sympathy', and it spoke of something still higher, of an active and non-selfish love. It went even farther. It declared a union of existences. It proclaimed that our own lives depended on the lives of our neighbours. St. Anthony of Egypt laid down the doctrine in so many words: 'Your life and your death are with your neighbour.'

August as that doctrine may have been, it is clear that it very soon became modified. It is regarded as Christian to live 'for' others; it is not so often regarded as Christian doctrine that we live 'from' others —except certainly in rare experiences. There has been, everywhere, a doctrine of unselfishness, but that the self everywhere lives only within others has been less familiar. The 'bear one another's burdens' became, on the whole, an exterior thing. We sympathized; we assisted. We loved—from ourselves. But there had been more than that in the original thought.

Certainly the great Christian doctrine applied first to the 'household of faith'. Our Lord promised to the members of His Church a particular and intense union with each other through Himself. He defined that union as being of the same nature as that which He had with His Father. The later definitions of the inspired Church went farther; they declared not merely that the Father and the Son existed co-equally, but that they existed co-inherently—that is, that the Son existed *in* the Father and that the Father existed *in* the Son. The exact meaning of the preposition there may be obscure. But no other word could satisfy the intellect of the Church. The same preposition was used to define our Lord's relations with His Church: 'we in him and he in us'. It was in that sense that the Church itself in-lived its children: 'we are members one of another'.

It is not, however, entirely necessary to call the Christian Church in evidence that such is the nature of man. It was as clear to the pagans that in society men depended on each other exteriorly as it is to us. The whole natural and social world depended, then as now, on some process of exchange. Human life, in the Roman Empire, had been specialized; not perhaps so much as ours, but it had been specialized. It depended on an exchange of labours. The medium of that exchange, with us, is money. Money has been called, by the economists, 'the means of exchange'. Our social system exists by an unformed agreement that one person shall do one job while another does another. Money is the means by which those jobs are brought into relation. It is, usually, the medium in which particular contracts are formed. And contract, or agreement, is the social fact of 'living by each other'.

This is the widest sense of social exchange. Within smaller groups —families or friends—the same thing is always taking place, sometimes irritably, sometimes happily. The more intense the element of love between two or more persons, the more clear, generally, that exchange of activities is. There certainly, in such states of natural love, doing it 'for' someone else produces precisely that sense of increased well-being, of increased life, which the great doctrine asserts. The difference, of course, is that, in such cases of love, there have arisen naturally the conditions of goodwill towards the 'neighbour'; where, however, those conditions do not naturally exist, love depends upon the will, and the difficulty of believing that we ourselves live by such acts is correspondingly greater, since the will does not, by itself, create emotion.

There is one great natural fact—a fact at the very root of all human facts—which involves a relation very much of the nature of exchange, or of something more than exchange. It is the fact of childbirth. Before any child can be born, the masculine seed has to be received by the feminine vessel. The man is quite helpless to produce a child unless he surrenders the means to someone else; the woman is as helpless unless she receives the means from someone else. It is a mutual act—but not only in the sense that two people agree to do something together. They do do something together, but they do it by an act (as regards the child) of substitution. It is not two people carrying a burden at the same time; the mother carries, literally, the burden. By the substitution of the woman for the man the seed fructifies. New life (literally) exists. It exists by the common operation of the woman and the man, and that operation involves something of the nature of substitution.

That substitution produces the new life. That new life exists literally within its mother; it inheres in its mother. The value of the sexual act itself is a kind of co-inherence; the two participators intend (violence apart) a renewal of mutual vigour from the most extreme intimacy of physical relationships. With conception comes the physical inherence of the child. And this is renewed through all the generations; each generation has inhered in that before it; in that sense without any doubt at all, we carry, if not another's burdens, at least the burden of others.

Such is the natural fact. At the root of the physical nature of man (so long as free choice exists) lie exchange of liking, substitution, inherence. The nature of man which is so expressed in the physical world is expressed after the same manner, only more fully, in the mental and spiritual.

The formal threefold division is a nuisance, but it may momentarily stand. What unites the three worlds is precisely this business of 'living from others'. In the mental world, for example, we derive nourishment, energy, and it is not perhaps going too far to say 'life', from great art. Appreciation of great poetry, for example, gives us this sense that though we read and remember the lines, yet the lines are greater than we are and contain us—'felt in the blood and felt along the heart'. It is not, however, in art, however great, that the secret lies; that cannot be more than a part of it. If this principle of exchange, substitution, and co-inherence (inhering in each other) is at all true, then it is true of the whole nature of man. If it is true, then we depend on it altogether—not as a lessening of individuality or moral duty but as the very fundamental principle of all individuality and of all moral duty.

In the records of the Thebaid, of the strange ascetic monks of the Egyptian desert, followers of St. Anthony, the thing was put plainly enough.

> A certain old man used to say, 'It is right for a man to take up the burden for those who are akin (or near) to him, whatsoever it may be, and, so to speak, to put his own soul in the place of that of his neighbour, and to become, if it were possible, a double man; and he must suffer, and weep, and mourn with him, and finally the matter must be accounted by him as if he himself had put on the actual body of his neighbour, and as if he had acquired his countenance and soul, and he must suffer for him as he would for himself.'[1]

So great a business of exchange and substitution fills the phrase 'bear ye one another's burdens' with a much fuller meaning than is generally ascribed to it. But that fuller meaning is no less practical than the usual meanings of being sympathetic and doing exterior acts 'of kindness and of love'. It is very proper that they should be done. But that is because we ought to be 'members one of another' —*membra*, limbs, not members of the same society. Christians are not members of a club; they are 'members' of the Church, which is not a club. Men and women are not members of a club; they are 'members' of mankind, which is not a club. From childbirth to those (in Dante's phrase) 'adult in love', there is but one Nature. That Nature is not divided from grace; it is indeed (let it be said with submission to the theologians) the nature of grace. The difference, in that sense, is only a difference of power.

How then is this to be practised? By 'bearing one another's burdens' interiorly as well as exteriorly; by the turning of the general sympathy into something of immediate use; by a compact of substitution. It is the word 'compact' that is to be stressed. I am not ignorant that in many cases such a substitution may take place instinctively, by the operation of an instinctive love; a wife for a husband, a lover for a lover, a friend for a friend. Still less am I ignorant of the great operations of this kind—in prayer and sacrifice —carried out by the religious Orders. But we are not dealing here with the most intense states of natural love or with the most advanced sacrificial victims of religion, but with ourselves and with the ordinary man. It is ordinary life which might be, more than it is, shot with this principle; it requires only, I will not say faith, but the first faint motions of faith.

Compacts can be made for the taking over of the suffering of

[1] *The Paradise of the Fathers*, Sir Wallis Budge.

troubles, and worries, and distresses, as simply and as effectually as an assent is given to the carrying of a parcel. A man can cease to worry about *x* because his friend has agreed to be worried by *x*. No doubt this is only a part of casting all our burdens upon the Lord; the point is that it may well be a part of it. No doubt the first man may still have to deal directly with *x*; the point is that his friend may well relieve him of the extra burden. So also one may bind oneself more surely by promises made by another on one's behalf than by one's own promises; one may practise a virtue on behalf of another more easily than for oneself. The mere attention of the mind to such a life of substitution will itself provide instances and opportunities. What is needed is precisely that attention.

And, of course, common sense. There are as many dangers in that life as in any. We have to avoid portentousness; we have not to promise anything we obviously cannot do. But perhaps there is very little that could not be done. It does not follow that the payment must be made in the same kind as the original need. This is probably peculiarly true of physical needs. It is in small things that the practice could be begun—sleeplessness or anxiety or slight pains. It is between friends and lovers that the practice could be best begun; always remembering that in the end he whom holy Luck throws in our way is our neighbour—as much as (but perhaps not more than) he whom we go out of our way to seek. To begin the way in small things conveniently is better than to dream of the remote splendours of the vicarious life; not that they are likely in any case to seem very splendid when they come. To begin by practising faith where it is easiest is better than to try and practise it where it is hardest. There is always somewhere where it can be done.

The doctrine of the Christian Church has declared that the mystery of the Christian religion is a doctrine of co-inherence and substitution. The Divine Word co-inheres in God the Father (as the Father in Him and the Spirit in Both), but also He has substituted His Manhood for ours in the secrets of the Incarnation and Atonement. The principle of the Passion is that He gave His life 'for'—that is, instead of and on behalf of—ours. In that sense He lives in us and we in Him, He and we co-inhere. 'I live; yet not I but Christ liveth in me' said St. Paul, and defined the web of universal power towards substitution. To love God and to love one's neighbour are but two movements of the same principle, and so are nature and grace; and the principle is the Word by whom all things were made and who gave Himself for the redemption of all things. It was precisely the breach in that original nature which the new Nature entered to fulfil. But either way it is our nature that is concerned. Our natural life begins by being borne in another; our mothers have to carry us. This is not (so far as we know) by our own will. The Christian Church demands that we shall carry out that principle everywhere by our will—with our friends and with our neighbours, whether we like our neighbours or not.

Such a labour has, almost immediately, two results. In the first place, it encourages a state of mind which may perhaps be called humility—but not so much as a virtue as a mere fact. Humility, said the author of the *Cloud of Unknowing*, consists in seeing things as they are. If our lives are so carried by others and so depend upon others, it becomes impossible to think very highly of them. In the second place there arises within one a first faint sense of what might be called 'loving from within'. One no longer merely loves an object; one has a sense of loving precisely from the great web in which the object and we are both combined. There is, if only transitorily, a flicker of living within the beloved. Such sensations are, or are not; they are, in themselves, of no importance. But they do for a moment encourage us, and they may assist us to consider still more intensely the great co-inherence of all life.

It is said (among other examples of substitution in the Church) that the blessed St. Seraphim of Sarov laid on a certain nun 'the ascetic discipline of death, that she should die instead of her sick brother Michael, whose work was not yet done'.[1] The deaths of those of the English who are being killed every day are, in their manner, 'instead of' us. Between the two the ladder lies by which our capacities run up and down, like angels; and the Joy of the Word which is the ladder because of the Creation and the Incarnation and the Atonement sustains all. From childbirth to the Divine Trinity Itself the single nature thrives; there is here no difference between that natural and that super-natural.

Our chief temptation is to limit its operation. We can believe it happily of ourselves as regards our lovers and our friends; we can accept the idea, at least, as regards strangers; we cannot so easily as regards those of our 'neighbours' who are, individually or nationally, inimical to us. We feel it as an outrage that we should be intimately interrelated, physically and spiritually, to those who have offended our pride or our principles; our very physical bodies revolt against it. It is why one hears of frustrated lovers committing murder; it is why our Lord warned us that murder was in our hearts. We desire to be free from the necessity of contemplating or practising the awful truth. But the doctrine will not let us escape so. It is not for us to make a division; that power our Lord explicitly reserved to Himself. If we insist on it, we can, in His final judgement, *be* separated. That is hell. But only our selves can put us there, and we

[1] *St. Seraphim of Sarov*, A. F. Dobbie-Bateman.

cannot put others there. Virtue, in this as in all things, is merely to understand the republican fact.

It is republican because it exists everywhere and at all times. No civil or international war can alter it. No neglect of social duty can change it; if we are guilty of such a neglect then it will be we ourselves in whom the co-inherent life will tend to perish, and therefore we who will draw nearer to that 'perishing everlastingly' which will one day be hell. The great Rite of this (as of much else) within the Christian Church is the Eucharist, where the co-inherence is fully in action: 'He in us and we in Him.' The prayer after Communion in the ritual of the Church of England expresses it:

> Almighty and everliving God, we most heartily thank thee, for that thou dost vouchsafe to feed us, who have duly received these holy mysteries, with the spiritual food of the most precious Body and Blood of thy Son our Saviour Jesus Christ; and dost assure us thereby of thy favour and goodness towards us; and that *we are very members incorporate in the mystical body of thy Son, which is the blessed company of all faithful people*; and are also heirs through hope of thy everlasting kingdom, by the merits of the most precious death and passion of thy dear Son. And we most humbly beseech thee, O heavenly Father, so to assist us with thy grace, *that we may continue in that holy fellowship, and do all such good works as thou hast prepared for us to walk in*; through Jesus Christ our Lord, to whom, with thee and the Holy Ghost, be all honour and glory, world without end.

The 'good works which thou hast prepared for us to walk in' are those that belong to 'that holy fellowship'; they are therefore those peculiarly of exchange and of substitution. They are prepared and they are there; we have only to walk in them. A little carrying of the burden, a little allowing our burden to be carried; a work as slow, as quiet, even as dull as by agreement to take up or give up a worry or a pain—a compact of substitution between friends—this is the beginning of the practice. The doctrine will grow in us of itself.

THE WAY OF AFFIRMATION

An article called 'The Church Looks Forward', from the St. Martin's Review, *July 1940*

In fact, of course, the Church does not, in her full existence, even on earth, look forward. She looks centrally, she looks at that which is not to be defined in terms of place and time. It is either the nature of God at which she looks or the nature of things as known in God. It is *now* that the Kingdom of Heaven is fulfilled, generally and individually.

Even in less absolute terms, the Church must not look forward too much. Her future is in the movement of the Holy Ghost and the resolution of our temporal knowledge into terms of Christ is the doing of the Holy Ghost. But though this is the nature of her life, she knows it in the mode of our more usual life. She does not, and under present conditions she cannot, fully realize that continuity of glory. There is therefore a double sense in which it may be said that the Church does look forward: it may be said to correspond to the two great virtues of faith and hope—faith in the nature of God, hope in the nature of things in God. These virtues are not mere abstractions; they are the names of substantial life in its different preoccupations. They are even the names of the physical body in its proper reaction to actuality; perhaps they have been too confined to the invisible operations of the soul.

The Church is to be distinguished from the world. But the physical bodies of her members relate her very intensely to the world. The union of the Church and the world is material in the flesh. But the world, taken in this sense, is not the only element in the flesh; the flesh, even apart from matters of Redemption, is not wholly fallen. It has indeed been dragged down with the soul. But the soul is illuminated to know the principles of the unfallen flesh, and in the Redemption to recover them after the new method, to discover the substitution of a new kind of experience for an old. Whether we always recognize the experience for what it is is another matter; our business is to pursue it under authority. There are two main directions. The first is concerned particularly with the nature of things in God; the second with the nature of God. Neither, of course, can exist entirely without the other. It is not possible for the Christian to attend only to men and women (say) and not at all to God in Himself. But neither is it possible for him to attend only to God in Himself and not at all to men and women. The most remote hermit generally has to attend occasionally to his own meal, however frugal. The most overworked doctor has to say the Lord's Prayer with its clauses concerning God in Himself.

We may find the intensity of both these great ways of the soul (and of the Church) revivified. It is possible that there may come to exist a fresh impulse of ascetic life in the Church; and by asceticism I do not mean hardships of the body only but of the mind and of the soul: the hardships and martyrdoms necessary to all those who are called to a life of separation (so far as possible) from all 'creatures'. Such outbreaks of austere vocations have occurred often in the history of the Church. This is a matter which can only be recognized by souls capable of and called to that vocation. It is, certainly, the duty of every member of the Church to examine himself or herself whether he or she is called to such an interior work.

And it is also a duty to give the correct answer without any regret or dissatisfaction. It is a duty if the answer is 'no' quite as much as if it is 'yes'. There is likely to be as much rejection of ourselves on the one way as on the other.

It was once suggested—and the suggestion was made neither profanely nor scandalously—that among all the Orders of the Christian Church there lacked one to our Sacred Lord as 'a gluttonous man and a wine-bibber'. Considering that the very term Christian rose as a term of abuse and was then adopted, these other terms of abuse may not be without their own value and instruction for us. Food and wine are here the definite symbols of the 'creature', more so as a divine Way than the locusts and wild honey of the Precursor. It is the following of our Lord in this knowledge of the creature which has been a part of the work of Christendom and may well be a greater part in the future. The doctrine of our Lord as God with its corollaries took centuries to work out. It is, certainly, now attacked. It is in dispute between Christendom and all that is not Christendom. But it is not in dispute within Christendom; all that has been finished with. The other doctrine of His Manhood, with its corollaries, has still to be worked out and put into action.

Its corollaries have indeed arisen during the last century, even more clearly than ever before. More and more Christians have felt it their absolute religious duty to ensure, as far as possible, the existence of a just State. Mr. Middleton Murry has pointed out that, under present conditions, we only succeed in establishing anything like a just State under immediate pressure of war. Until that pressure exists we are content to leave a heavy proportion of our citizens in a state of direct or indirect despair; in a state, that is to say, in which, humanly speaking, any gospel, even the Christian, is bound to be incapable of reception. It is forbidden to the Christian to entertain despair: how much more to inflict it!

Despair is infectious; a State in which it is unconsciously permitted to exist is lost. We may, however, leave that particular prospect for others: it is sufficient to say that the duty there incumbent on us arises as much from our Lord's physical relation to men and women as from the order of His Deity.

It is something of the same sense that lies at the beginning of another problem to which the members of the Church will have to address themselves—the problem of marriage. Speaking generally, we have up to the present time insisted on the morals of marriage but we have not based them on any doctrine of love. We have rejected divorce but we have done so without any clear idea of the reason; and it is much to be feared that, in rejecting it, we have called in the help of all kinds of fallacies, inaccuracies, and even definite untruths. Natural life produces a vision of beauties, energies, and glories about which the comments of the officers of the supernatural life seem anxiously inadequate. When the same inadequate voices declare that the corollary of those strange benefits must be a lifelong fidelity, they must expect to be asked why. One answer is that it has been proved socially desirable, which seems doubtful and even unlikely. Another is that it is the Will of God, which (if likely) is inexplicable. A labour of intellects is required. There have already appeared recently several books on the subject of marriage. I cannot discuss them for I have not read them. They may remain few, they may be the precursors of many more.

The last sentence brings us to a point of looking forward on which a great deal depends in all the preoccupations of the Church. Her missionary and her contemplative activities depend, it is agreed, on the Holy Ghost. The activities of the Holy Ghost depend on nothing but Itself. But the success of the activities of the Holy Ghost (within the Church) does depend on a something beside Itself—it depends on the honesty of Christians. The honesty of Christians is a very desirable and also a very difficult thing. There can be few Christians alive who have not been aware, in themselves or in each other, of that great temptation—'to lie on the Lord's behalf'. It has in the past done untold harm to the Church, and it will again unless it can be overcome. It takes many shapes. It is apt to *pretend*—to pretend that intellectual arguments are valid when it should be clear that they are fallacious, that moral iniquity exists where there is no proof of it, and so on. An extremely distinguished dignitary of the Church once printed the statement that the proportion of happiness to unhappiness in a man's life was as nine to one—an absolutely unjustified statement. (I do not say it was false: the whole point is that one ought not to make that sort of generalization at all; it is unprovable.) This kind of thing is still too common. Accuracy, accuracy, and again accuracy! accuracy of mind and accuracy of emotion. If the Church is to look forward to a wholesome mental life her members must discipline themselves to honesty. The indulgence of any prejudice must be regarded as sinful, and an intellectual sin is as bad as a physical.

Yet the life of the Church is single and not divided into intellectual and physical, and in her (militant here upon earth) the two affect each other as much as in any of her children. If her honesty can be recovered there might be recovered with it the fullness of her charismatic and prophetic ministry. It is not in any sense to deny the order which has developed in the Church to say that the New Testament seems to contemplate the charismatic ministry as being the common possession of all believers. Whatever texts may be regarded as symbolic and whatever as literal, it is hardly possible to regard as other than literal the promise of a new life which shall be unharmed by earthly accidents, though not perhaps by earthly malignity. The disciples may be put out of the synagogues or even killed by the hatred (the righteous hatred) of those who conceive that they are doing God service so. But the casual 'deadly things'—the serpent or the accidental venom—are to be harmless as far as they are concerned. And if those, then perhaps the accidental diseases and dangers of ordinary human life also—unless indeed those were, in certain cases, deliberately welcomed on behalf of others and in the cause and name of charity.

The rediscovery of such a high power as normal to the operative Christian is far enough away at present, and it is difficult to imagine how it might come. Nor indeed is it altogether desirable to imagine it coming; it is probably true that we shall never reach that state unless and until we are willing to welcome those distresses on behalf of others. We have lost, I think, to a very large extent the idea that we can effectively welcome them; it lingers chiefly in the intuitive natural desire of men and women at rare moments and under rare conditions. But conditions which are comparatively rare in the life of 'the flesh' should be comparatively common in the life of 'the spirit'—not meaning, by those words, the visible and invisible parts of our organism. What is necessary is the life of 'faith', the substantial existence in us which we call faith. It is our business to recover *that*. The Holy Ghost will then do what He will, and it seems possible that we may humbly believe that at the right hour He shall teach us 'what we shall speak'—when to make offers and when to receive offers, when to dismiss 'devils' and when to endure them.

The doctrine of the Christian Church depends on the substitution, in the last experiences, of our sacred Lord for us. The activity of the Christian Church may have to recover, more than is commonly supposed, our substitution, one for another. The most important thing is to get our minds accustomed to the idea of that activity: attention without fever, speed without haste. The Atonement of our Lord restored this power to man; the Holy Ghost now, as originally, confirms, nourishes, and directs it. In the old legend Adam and Eve were, originally, one being. It is a profound symbol. Justice, charity, union; these are the three degrees of the Way of the Affirmation of Images, and all of us are to be the images affirmed.

ONE WAY OF LOVE

Time and Tide *review of* Passion and Society, *by Denis de Rougemont, 1940*

M. DE ROUGEMONT's book is a study of passionate love. By passionate love he means suffering love, and by suffering love a love that delights in its sufferings, a love that looks forward to suffering, a death-desire, 'the active passion of Night'. He chooses the *Tristan* story, especially in Wagner's version, as the most striking example of this. 'I mean by the passion myth that image of the Dying Lovers erected by the disturbing and vampire-like crescendo of Wagner's second act.' It is this passion myth which 'is the great mystery of that religion of which the poets of the nineteenth century were the priests and prophets'. Nine times out of ten it leads to adultery. Statistics, M. de Rougemont says, show this.

But the nineteenth-century poets did not invent passionate love. The fact has existed at all times. At a certain moment in European history it became a myth. 'The earliest passionate lovers whose story has reached us were Abelard and Heloise.' It was in the middle of the twelfth century that passion created an awareness of itself and called itself courtly love—under the influence of the spreading heresies of death, renewed Gnosticism, Catharism, Albigensianism. Thus there began—in this experience of sexual love—'a struggle between two religious traditions', between death and life, which lasts today in the conflict over marriage.

M. de Rougemont warns his readers that anyone who disagrees with his thesis shows thereby that he is a victim of the myth. This would be almost enough to kill comment were it not for that grand doctrine of ambivalence by which the critic may retort on him that anyone so conscious of it as he is must himself be a victim. The myth is presented here with such force that it becomes almost attractive. Of his historical views M. de Rougemont says that even if they 'appear disputable to the stern eyes of the expert, they remain accurate to the precise extent to which they are brought in here—as illustrations and not as demonstrations, as analogies having a spiritual significance and not as scientific discoveries'.

I am not at all sure what this means. The troubadours, it is asserted, were the singers, the evangelists, of the myth, of the pursuit of an infinite dolour. But if M. de Rougemont is not claiming this as historically so, if he uses their sayings only as examples of what *he* means, what becomes of the historical thesis? It does not perhaps much matter, so long as the book is understood to be rather a brilliant presentation of a real danger and a real morality. But it is worth pausing, in considering the metaphysical problem, on the fact that M. de Rougemont hints that Dante was no better intellectually than he should have been; he even quotes Aroux in favour of the Mohammedan derivation of the *Comedy*. He also says, rather darkly, that we do not know whether or not Shakespeare was 'privy to the secret traditions of the troubadours', but that *Romeo and Juliet* is set in Verona, and Verona was a main centre of Catharism in Italy; and he points out that when Romeo finds Juliet dead he makes a magnificent speech saying that he will die too. One might add that Romeo and Juliet both prefer to be together at night rather than separate by day. Which only goes to show what Bogomils and death-desirers and disciples of unhappy love they were.

After this it is not surprising that 'Milton underwent the influence of Cabalistic doctrines', or that he had Robert Fludd for 'a master in occultism'. Milton, it seems, never decided between *L'Allegro* and *Il Penseroso* and their themes. But he too 'is led into inferences similar to those expressed by the Cathars'.

Evidence of this kind is unworthy of M. de Rougemont's serious capacity and sincere intelligence. If he has treated the troubadours in the same way, the poor creatures were innocent enough. Dismissing such points, it remains that M. de Rougemont, in tracing his myth, has exposed to us several valuable lines of thought, and has concluded with a wise discussion of marriage. He defines it as 'the institution in which passion is "contained" not by morals but by love'. He refuses to defend it on any pseudo-rational ground; he bases it, referring frequently to Kierkegaard, on the 'absurd'. On his way to this really fine conclusion, he has dealt with the mystical tradition and with many examples in literature of his main thesis. 'The history of passionate love in all great literature from the fifteenth century down to our own day is the history of the descent of the courtly myth into "profane" life, the account of the more and more desperate attempts of Eros to take the place of mystical transcendence by means of emotional intensity.' It is the spread of this passion from the sex-relationship to the political that has caused our present world—'the stupendous catastrophe of passion become totalitarian'.

It is this side of the book, the comments, the suggestions, the Christian idea, which is valuable, and which Mr. Montgomery Belgion, who has translated it, has expressed in English as epigrammatic as the French. We ought not to ask M. de Rougemont for more than he wished to give. Yet something more ought to be said. There is another state; there is an activity of Light as well as 'an activity of Night'. It is a state of vision rather than passion (in

M. de Rougemont's sense), though it is not less passionate. It desires and demands the full exercise of the intellect for its exploration; it communicates, for a moment, the great virtues which have later to be slowly achieved and are the only means to its blessed fulfilment. I do not say it is universal, though (on the evidence) I believe it to be common. A great deal of literature deals with it; it is indeed in Shakespeare and Milton and many others. When the lover sees the beloved in light, when he or she (in the proper sense) adores, when (is it to say too much?) some sense of the eternal identity of that other is flashed on him or on her—this is the beginning of many an 'ordinary' love-affair. It is very likely to lead to suffering; pride and egotism are not easily annihilated. But it always knows its past.

It would be a thousand pities if M. de Rougemont's passion-myth were identified with this fact of vision by any rash reader. The great tradition of romantic love—renewed like the phoenix in each generation—is quite other than the desire of death. The passion-myth is a heresy of it: at moments a temptation; in moments of agony a very great temptation. The grand pattern of the real glory takes long to explore, and involves many opposite experiences, including boredom. It too, as in Dante, leads to politics and the City. Dante was no Mohammedan: the Divine Child spiritually lives in the two gay lovers. By virtue of the Incarnation Eros and Agape are no longer divided, though they may be again the next moment. 'Ye know not in what hour the Son of Man cometh.' Nor in how many modes.

THE JEWS

From a Time and Tide *review of* Redeeming the Time, *by Jacques Maritain, 1943*

THE subjects treated by M. Maritain in this collection of essays are many. . . . If I choose [for review] the essay on the Mystery of Israel, it is not to underrate the others. But Israel, and our behaviour towards Israel, is one of the most urgent means of redeeming the present time.

M. Maritain insists on its importance. He denounces Anti-Semitism as strongly as Pius XI; he quotes from the Pope the noble phrase: 'Spiritually we are all Semites.' But it is not enough to denounce. The Jewish problem remains. It would be better to call it the Jewish Mystery. 'Israel is a mystery. Of the same order as the mystery of the world or the mystery of the Church.' This is to approach the whole matter theologically; but Christians and orthodox Jews cannot approach it in any other way. It is because Christians have not, in general, so approached it that they have so often failed to manage that extreme courtesy with which they should carry themselves towards Jews, especially towards orthodox Jews. The unorthodox, like unorthodox Christians, are another matter; for both of them it is a matter of merely behaving as decently as possible under the stresses of the world.

But for the orthodox on both sides it is very much more. There is a burden on each. The Jew is confronted with (as it seems to him) a preposterous blasphemy, the most awful of blasphemies; and that, it will be noted, springing fundamentally from his own people, from himself. The Christian is confronted by the rejection of the Faith by that from which the Faith sprang; say, with the denial of himself by the (temporal) source of himself. This is not the same thing as the quarrel with the world. 'If the world hates the Jews, it is because the world is well aware that they will always be *supernaturally* strangers to it', M. Maritain says. 'It is the vocation of Israel which the world execrates.' The Jew cannot 'settle down'; that is what angers the world. If he has forgotten his vocation and does not wish to disturb the world one way, then he is—one could almost say *compelled* to do it another. 'Do what we will—or even do what it will—the people of Israel remains the priestly people. The bad Jew is a kind of bad priest.'

This is all true and wise. But the relation of Israel and the Church—like it or like it not—must be more intense. It is something in our blood which springs; it is a hatred (if it is a hatred) between fathers and children. I think perhaps M. Maritain might have stressed this a little more. There is a Fact between us, and neither side can forget the Fact. Let us talk of art and culture, of government and business as we will, and still when the Sabbath and Sunday come we remember—the Jew the Christian blasphemy, the Christian the Jewish infidelity. The Jew hears the Christian declaring that the High and Holy One took flesh; the Christian sees the Jew crucifying the God-Man. How, at bottom, can there be peace?

It must certainly be a peace theologically experienced; I do not mean merely talked about in theological terms; that is unavoidable. All missions to the Jews do that. But missions to the Jews are very daring things. For the Jew is alone in his conversion (if it should happen) among all the nations of the earth; he, and he alone, is in a special relation to the God-Man. And if and when he is converted (this is what Christians forget) he will remain in that special relation; more, for it will be accentuated by the conversion. 'If one is never so much in the right', M. Maritain very properly writes in his study of Bergson, 'this is nevertheless so great a privilege and so undeserved, that it is always appropriate to apologize for it. It is a courtesy which must be offered to truth.' This can hardly be too much stressed; it should be in our manners whenever we are right. But how much more towards those who, once they are convinced, are right in a way we can never be; for our own rightness comes only through them. 'They shall be our fathers and we shall be their sons.'

St. Paul, as M. Maritain recalls, laboured at this great relationship. He warned his Christians not to boast; they were but grafted on to the tree. 'Thou bearest not the root, but the root thee.' He went farther. He wrote, and hinted a greater mystery of Israel: 'For if the casting away of them be the reconciling of the world, what shall the receiving of them be but life from the dead?' M. Maritain gives: 'If the dispossession of them hath been the reconciliation of the world, what shall the reintegration of them be, but life from the dead?' There is between Israel and the Church a great exchange; we exist in and by means of them and they in and by means of us. There is a sense, nevertheless, in which a Jewish convert must feel himself twice an exile. It is because the Christians generally only succeed in treating him as then not quite a Jew. But he is in fact more a Jew, for he is then doubly of the race 'whence issued his God and the immaculate Mother of his God'; he is closer than any Gentile in his very nature, in his flesh, to the will that not only chose the Jews but chose to be a Jew. If they come to us for a moment to be let in, it is we who shall be for ever let in by them; or Pilate's gibe 'The King of the Jews' would have lost its meaning. In that theological life, the mystery of Israel and the Church is again a mystery of radical exchange, an exchange of ancestral selves. And our theological manners ought to confess it.

THE SOCIETY OF JESUS

Time and Tide *review of* The Origin of the Jesuits,
by James Brodrick, S.J., 1941

It may almost be said that the origin of the Society of Jesus was *Amadis de Gaul*. That, at least, was the first part of the origin, the first volume of a two-volume work of which the second was the *Spiritual Exercises*. Few in this age, perhaps few in any, have read both; and even Fr. Brodrick's sympathy, which is broad, fails from what he calls 'the nonsense of *Amadis de Gaul*'. Yet I seem to remember it was one of the books that Cervantes saved from the bonfire of La Mancha. St. Ignatius would, no doubt, have agreed with Fr. Brodrick, but then he was in the exceptional position of a knight-errant who became a general, and had to turn his romances into manuals of drill. That is what the *Exercises* are.

Ignatius began as a romantic. He was a true romantic; that is, he was a master of prudence, a realist. All true romantics claim to be realists, but most of them are allowed to be realistic and prudent merely about themselves. Ignatius was in that great tradition, and he was more, he was one of the expanders and expounders of it. 'The ambition of his generous heart', in Fr. Brodrick's admirable phrase, dilated. He discovered that Love could be directly loved and that it directly loved. He seems to have been about thirty when the great illumination fell on him near Manresa. 'His mind was suddenly, in an instant, illuminated with so deep an understanding of spiritual things that not all he learned to the end of his life seemed to him its equivalent.' It was the prudence of that understanding which he had to teach.

The communication, by virtue of the sublime *Exercises*, has succeeded in the four centuries since. Fr. Brodrick shows how it first spread. His volume is only the beginning; it is much to be hoped that the others will follow—'progressively more exciting instalments'. It was in September 1540 that the Order began. It has been marked ever since by the prudence of its Founder. Even when it has been vilified or misunderstood, it is the same prudence that has been slandered. The controversy, for example, in the *Provincial Letters* is about that. It might perhaps be held that Pascal failed in his great Apology for the Christian religion precisely because he had insufficient prudence; at least it is impossible to read the *Letters* without realizing that the Jesuits were often right where Pascal was wrong merely because of that prudence. It is not to say that, at that time, the sons of St. Ignatius were better men than Pascal; that, fortunately, no one can tell. But, slandered or sinful, the sins and slanders were of that kind. Their discretion may have been indiscreet, but the indiscretion was, so far forth, Ignatian at source.

That, however, is a century later than Fr. Brodrick goes at present. The chief figure besides Ignatius in the book is not an enemy but a friend, a companion, a son, Francis Xavier, and perhaps the third figure is another Francis—Francis Borgia, Duke of Gandia. It is astonishing how we all think of quite another person when we use that title; so easily is the reputation of Alexander VI preferred to that of his greater kinsman. Swinburne and Michael Field are partly responsible, but even more the pure Fat Boy enjoyment of feeling our flesh creep—innocent, so long only as it does not confuse our historic perspective. Fr. Brodrick not only corrects this, but even makes the correction enjoyable. And he corrects it in another way—he does, subtly and delicately, justify his title in so far as it is the Order itself which here becomes important. In less than six years after the Foundation Xavier was in Amboina, Borgia was building the first Jesuit university at Gandia, and Jesuit theologians were arguing at the Council of Trent. St. Ignatius's directions to these last have about them an intellectual discretion not over-often attributed to him. 'Be slow to speak . . . listen quietly . . . give the reasons on both sides . . . be careful to displease nobody . . . exhort to good habits . . . visit the hospitals . . . shrive and comfort the poor and bring them something whenever you can.' So well did they obey this last charge that they 'were in a short time able to report to Ignatius that they had "provided clothes for seventy-six poor people, giving each a shirt, a smock, leggings and boots"'.

'For eighteen years Ignatius remained tied to his desk in Rome', whence he directed the activities of the thousand members of the Order, moving them continually to labour and to love. He was a very great man; his greatness is known by the quality of his work, such that his Order so greatly survived without him. It was and is a company devoted to the direct rather than the indirect love of God. I do not know what might not be done today by an Order of similar intensity working, if the phrase may be used, along the lines of the indirect love. The priesthood have their vocation, but those who are not of the priesthood have theirs. 'The ambition of generous hearts' might seek to rival, say, the least of the children of Ignatius, along that other way: not that he left it untrod—witness the seventy-six poor people at Trent! There are movements everywhere at the present time, agitations and summonses: let us then keep our Order secret; let it not be organized but by that prudent ambition. It will have as many 'difficult and heroic feats' as Ignatius himself loved; it shall depend on less, as a Company, even than the Jesuits, for they did at least know each other; but we shall not, or only by holy Luck. Its derivation shall be from God through others; its meditation on those indirect derivations; its aim the propaganda everywhere of that sensitive and humble knowledge. It shall not be a social or religious movement but it shall be at the bottom of all in the sense that it is their true and only justification in mere fact.

If it could have any history, it would be necessary to ask Fr. Brodrick, who is obviously the preordained historian of Orders, to write it. But it will not. Secret and certain, its only history will be in the conversation of the Companions and in the slow stilling and deepening of their eyes.

APOLOGUE ON THE PARABLE OF THE WEDDING GARMENT

From Time and Tide, *December 1940*

THE Prince Immanuel gave a ball:
cards, adequately sent to all
who by the smallest kind of claim
were known to royalty by name,
held, red on white, the neat express
instruction printed: *Fancy Dress.*

Within Earth's town there chanced to be
a gentleman of quality,
whose table, delicately decked,
centred at times the Court's elect;
there Under-Secretaries dined,
Gold Sticks in Waiting spoke their mind,
or through the smoke of their cigars
discussed the taxes and the wars,
and ran administrations down,
but always blessed the Triune Crown.

The ball drew near; the evening came.
Our lordling, conscious of his name,
retained particular distaste
for dressing-up, and half-effaced,
by a subjective sleight of eye
objectionable objectivity—
the card's direction. 'I long since
have been familiar with the Prince
at public meetings and bazaars,
and even ridden in his cars,'
he thought; 'his Highness will excuse
a freedom, knowing that I use
always my motto to obey:
Egomet semper: I alway.'

Neatly and shiningly achieved
in evening dress, his car received
his figure, masked but otherwise
completely in his usual guise.
Behold, the Palace; and the guest
approached the Door among the rest.

The Great Hall opened: at his side
a voice breathed: 'Pardon, sir.' He spied,
half turned, a footman. 'Sir, your card—
dare I request? This Door is barred
to all if not in fancy dress.'
'Nonsense.' 'Your card, sir!' 'I confess
I have not strictly . . . an old friend . . .
his Highness . . . come, let me ascend.

My family has always been
in its own exquisite habit seen.
What, argue?' Dropping rays of light
the footman uttered: 'Sir, tonight
is strictly kept as strictly given;
the fair equivalents of heaven
exhibit at our lord's desire
their other selves, and all require
virtues and beauties not their own
ere genuflecting at the Throne.
Sir, by your leave.' 'But—' 'Look and see.'
The footman's blazing livery
in half-withdrawal left the throng
clear to his eyes. He saw along
the Great Hall and the Heavenly Stair
one blaze of glorious changes there.
Cloaks, brooches, decorations, swords,
jewels—every virtue that affords
(by dispensation of the Throne)
beauty to wearers not their own.
This guest his brother's courage wore;
that, his wife's zeal, while, just before,
she in his steady patience shone;
there a young lover had put on
the fine integrity of sense
his mistress used; magnificence
a father borrowed of his son,
who was not there ashamed to don
his father's wise economy.
No he or she was he or she
merely: no single being dared,
except the Angels of the Guard,
come without other kind of dress
than his poor life had to profess,
and yet those very robes were shown,

when from preserval as his own
into another's glory given,
bright ambiguities of heaven.

Below each change was manifest;
above, the Prince received each guest,
smiling. Our lordling gazed; in vain
he at the footman glanced again.
He had his own; his own was all
but that permitted at the Ball.
The darkness creeping down the street
received his virtuous shining feet;
and, courteous as such beings are,
the Angels bowed him to his car.

VI · ON THE ARTHURIAN MYTH

Introductory Note to the Arthurian Essays

To those who, like myself, think the *Taliessin* cycle the finest part of Charles Williams's work, this section will be of particular interest. It provides, with pp. 78–90 in *Arthurian Torso*, his own notes and commentary on his poems. The first piece, which I have called 'Notes on the Arthurian Myth', was written in the late twenties or early thirties as an explanatory introduction to the original cycle. It is taken from a typescript (I do not know whether the manuscript exists), unaltered except for the addition of one or two punctuation marks. The author would not have printed it as it stands, of course, but it contains some valuable clues to his thought: it does, however, refer to some persons who were not included in the later cycle—the Princess of Byzantium, for instance, and Tristram. 'In a sense, Tristan was superfluous', as Williams said in the review here reprinted. Other ideas, such as that of the three bands of knights who were to represent the mineral, vegetable, and animal creation, were not developed, but the events referred to are all to be taken as part of the argument, even though no poem describes them.

After this outline of his themes, I have printed his short article on the making of the poem; then a review which gives his ideas on the subject of Tristram and Tristram's relation to the whole myth; last, the important article called 'Malory and the Grail Legend', which can be read as continuing where the pages of the *Torso* break off. The reader will find some points repeated, but that was inevitable unless the essays were to be mutilated.

The passages which follow here are only for those who are interested in the origins of the *Taliessin* poems. I cannot possibly describe the whole of Williams's mythological scrap-book (*circa* 1912–16, see p. lviii of my Introduction), which indeed contains more diverse material than any poet could have unified, but I will mention a few of the ideas which he developed, and some promising ones which came to nothing.

As to the Grail theme itself, his interpretation was already mature, and there are scattered through the book pieces of the narrative, some of which I draw together here.

[The questing knights lie down to sleep] under a great tree, so huge that it seems as if it might be Igdrasil.[1] Percivale and Bors dream (cf. the dream of the squire in the High History)[2] what actually happens. . . . The knights (in the seeming dream) come (in the ship) to Sarras, are imprisoned (?in Malory for a year—but possibly here for nine months, between the question and the achievement, symbolizing the darkness of the child in the womb . . .); an earthquake opens the doors, they come out into a darkness so that they cannot see the sky or the streets, but it is full of a rain of light (sometimes pure and dazzling white light, sometimes silver or golden, sometimes red flame) sufficient for them to go up to the Chapel. The pang and cry (of their ladies) at the entrance where all lesser loves are torn from them. When Galahad goes to the achievement of the Grail, Bors falls prostrate; Percivale on his knees hears nothing but sees Galahad achieve. Bors hears a choir of voices, terribly clear, direct, remote, and poignant, saying 'Let Us make man'. A darkness falls on both and they are taken from the Chapel.

The question asked . . . is equivalent to the question of the Virgin ('How should these things be?'): it releases the energies frozen by the Fall (cf. the king's incurable wound): Galahad is born and maintained to ask this question. Dubric,[3] earlier in the poem, points indirectly to the resemblance between the Virgin and Sir Galahad.

In some versions of the myth it was Percivale's or Gawaine's failure to ask this question—'What serves the Grail?'—in the presence of the Grail, which was the great disaster. It did not find a place in Williams's later cycle, though it may be that he would eventually have included it: in this connexion it is worth recalling what he wrote in the *Torso* (p. 84):

They [the unasked question and the Dolorous Blow] are, of course, strictly speaking, alternatives. It is certain that we must keep the Dolorous Blow; a loss of that would mean a loss of the Wounded King, which cannot be imagined. The only question is whether we can have the unasked question also.

It would not be impossible, if the whole thing were regarded as a tale of the Fall—individual or universal. The union would be in the fact that the lack of the question would mean the lack of an answer, and hence an ignorance of the true nature of the Invisible Knight.

To return to the journey of the questing knights, *before* the achievement which was described in the earlier paragraph:

From Igdrasil they come to the shore and embark in the vessel with the body of Percivale's sister. (?Blanchefleur: qy. called 'sister' only as a kind of

[1] The mythical world tree, connecting heaven, earth, and hell. I do not know what suggested to Williams the idea of introducing it, unless it was the passage in the *High History of the Holy Graal* where Perceval lands from the magical ship and 'looketh underneath a tree that was tall and broad . . .' where he finds two men, white-haired yet young of face, as Williams's Pope was to be. But see the passage quoted on p. lii from *The Figure of Beatrice* for its connexion with the general image of the Forest.

[2] See p. 5 in the Everyman edition of the *High History*.

[3] Archbishop of Canterbury, who played an important part in the original cycle of poems.

name to describe their virginal love: then Bors's lady (?Helayne) encourages him to go upon the quest . . . Blanchefleur comes dead to Sarras. Thus the corporeal passions are left behind,—the mental come nearer—the spiritual only achieve. But note the importance that this achievement takes place in Helayne's heart also (or could)—she is not on a lower level than the knights and Blanchefleur.)

The ship, in which the Graal moves amidst cloud and mist, moves through the seas to the dark and silent quays of Sarras. On the way Galahad stands at the prow looking out towards the city. Percivale begins to sing the song of parting with Blanchefleur, a song of farewell as the souls draw near the place of ending.

Or ?should this be sung under Igdrasil and before the embarcation.

On the return of Bors and Percivale, note that they pass from the Chapel to the quays, across the seas, and to Igdrasil, in a very little time. 'Only so long did this journey take as for the moon to pass through . . .' (?what divisions of the sky *does* the moon pass through).

The Grail achieved about the same time as Arthur returns to fight Mordred. . . . As the old unity of Logres is breaking up, because the circle is too small, the new and perfect unity is achieved.

Here, set down all those years ago, is the material from which 'The Last Voyage' was made. Although so much was added later, the changes from Malory are already there—the carrying of Blanchefleur's body in the same ship, the song of Percivale, the closing up of the time sequence.

In relation to his time scheme, I bring together fragments from various parts of the book, which show his tentative plans.

?any real objection to time and distance being ignored, and Mohammedan knights introduced. But see dates of Mohammedans in Spain—the Caliphate of Cordova: which would (or might) almost reconcile the two.

Knowledge that Time and Space are only modes of thought. 'is not this the beginning of all magic?' (E. Nesbit.—*Amulet.*)

?Bring Arthur and his surroundings in England, about A.D. 500, forward and parallel to Charlemagne and his surroundings in France, A.D. 800: so as to obtain the full effect of Islam, in Africa, in Spain.

Dubric tells the tale of the Dolorous Stroke. The action proceeds on the one plane until, at the sitting of Galahad in the Perilous Seat, the whole action is assumed on to a higher. Man becomes conscious of the Quest, but this is only after the quest has been begun in him; and the assumption of the chair by Galahad = his conscious acceptance of the quest.

The Dolorous Stroke. If Arthur is a reflection of the Maimed King, this must happen before his birth. [But see Williams's discussion of this point in the 'Notes', p. 175.] ?then Balin at Uther's court. Or, to make everything happen at once (if it were possible in poetry!)

Dante. Note the souls in Purgatory can't, one supposes, fall to hell. The symbolism is in terms of space. The Graal symbolism has to avoid this. The Graal (whose centre is everywhere etc.[1]) is to some a test, to some fruition, to some union, to some torment. [He notes elsewhere the idea that 'having the

[1] . . . and its circumference nowhere.

food they liked best' in the presence of the Graal means that the change was in their minds, not in the actual food.]

Merlin has not yet been connected with Time, but is '?sacramental science' and

natural man ('heathen') conscious of the quest, planning it and working for it, but ignorant of its full meanings.

?Is he the 'natural body' resolved again into its elements. . . .

Merlin the self-consciousness of Arthur. . . .

Nimue ?'holy Nimue' ?beneficent Nature: patroness of Merlin (?sacramental science), foster mother of Lancelot (human passion in the domain of Nature, where it grows into the knowledge of sexual things, whence it may become the father of Galahad = pure passion for God . . .). ?Her enchantment of Merlin = his old age and death—Nature destroying her lover, in ordinary process.

This became (in 'The Departure of Merlin')

She who is Nimue, lady of lakes and seas,
articulation of limbs, accumulation of distance,
brings all natural becoming to her shape of immortal being,
as to a flash of seeing the women in the world's base.

Well has Merlin spoken the last spell,
worked the last image, gone to his own . . . .

Merlin was also to be one of 'The three great men of Arthur's household', the others being Dubric and Taliessin—scientist, priest, and artist. And he was to be

'learned in Virgil. This might help to connect Rome with the supernatural.'

It is to be noticed, too, that the impulse towards inclusiveness, the wish to bring in every part of human nature, is already present, as when he writes:

Against the knights of the Quest to be set another figure—a kind of Thersites—who jeers at them and their desire, and at all good things,—full of filth and ribaldry.

But filth and so forth—their place in the universe? the action of Love in them? Love in the bodily functions?

Of the possibilities set forth in the book which came to nothing, the most interesting is that of a character called Fabio, an Epicurean whose purpose is to give the

evolutionary vision of the world, of its aeons of life and development, wherein the Roman Empire is only a breathing space and Egypt a moment's advance or retrogression. The vision of this hardly to be given to any Christian, because of the comparative unimportance of the individual; nor to any Saracen. . . .

Fabio, 'a noble agnostic', was to have Belisarius's secretary as a friend—this because Belloc had written: 'In the sixth century the secretary of Belisarius writes with a fine pagan contempt of the fables and marvels of the Christians.' Fabio was to possess the manuscript of the last, lost Promethean drama of Aeschylus, where Prometheus is reconciled to Zeus, and to quote it in talk with Dubric.

Fabio refers also to the gods contemplating, even pitying, human suffering, but still untouched by it. Dubric compares them to the angelic powers, who do the same: but presses on to look behind them to the Love which is moved and responsive to human beings.

also

?Fabio read the story of Eros and Psyche, either in full or simply the argument—'Eros, the lovely winged boy', connect with the terrible youth, or (more dreadful) the 'burning babe' of Love in Christian tradition.

Neither Fabio nor Sir Dagonet, who was to have been 'not a fool but the person who asks apparently useless questions—"Why do doors open?" "Why does water flow down-hill?"', found a place in later developments. Sir Dinadan, with his irony, fulfils something of Dagonet's function, and the greater importance of Taliessin probably made it impossible to include any other intelligence detached from the Quest itself. Dubric, too, disappeared as the idea of the Byzantine Emperor was developed: the figure of the Pope had been part of the plan from the beginning, and was retained, but perhaps there would hardly have been room for three centres of spiritual power. In the Notebook there is only one mention of 'the Byzantine Imperator' as that to which Arthur owes allegiance, and the Princess has not yet made her appearance.

Last among the possibilities which remained undeveloped, may be mentioned Morgan Le Fay—who, according to the *Oxford Companion to English Literature*, is the original Lake Lady, from whom Nimue is derived. Williams did not so identify them, but his poem did not find room for them both.

[Morgan] Is she, or could she be, an 'avatar' of a kind of false beauty, as Lilith, or Helen of Troy (if the real Helen was in Egypt). . . .

Helen was at last deified: ?Galahad foresees the agony and salvation of Morgan.

Those last words recall the 'shriek of pain and joy' of the Negress in *Seed of Adam*, as she cries 'and holy is his Name'. Perhaps, after that, Williams had no need to include such a moment in his poem. At any rate, Hell in the poems we have is only rendered powerless: the tentacles of P'o-l'u are gripped for ever on the ocean bottom by the roots of Broceliande, the trees of Nimue.

I add to this brief account of its beginnings, the hints which remain of how Williams intended to continue the cycle. After *Taliessin through Logres*, the collection which followed was to have been called *Jupiter over Carbonek* (see the reference in 'The Prayers of the Pope'), and two lists of projected Contents with that title survive. Probably they were both made before the publication of the *Summer Stars* (the one which I have called 'A' certainly was), for some of the material described was used in that book. But the *Summer Stars* was never meant to be more than Work in Progress. For clarity's sake I give both lists here, though some poems are common to both.

A. Prelude—Nestorius [printed in *S.S.*]

1. The Emperor's design for the union of Logres and Broceliande: the Porphyry Rite [see 'The Calling of Taliessin' in *S.S.*]
2. Merlin calls the lords and Balin and Balan
3. The throne and council of Arthur: judgement against Gawaine—to show mercy
4. The invisible knight
5. The Dolorous Blow (Garlon asks pardon?)
6. Interlude: the Rose Garden [printed in *S.S.*]
6. [*sic*] The Departure of Blanchfleur [Blanchfleur without the e, as Williams often wrote it. Printed in *S.S.* as 'The Departure of Dindrane']
7. The Tournament of Lonazep
8. The Pardon of Palomides [see the second of the notes printed after List B]
9. The Conception of Galahad [see No. 6 in List B]
The Dissolution of the Household
The vision of the Pope [see 'The Prayers of the Pope' for this and the above]
Bors to Elaine [an unpublished fragment exists of this poem]

B. 1. The Emperor and the Zodiac [see 'The Rose Garden' in *S.S.*]
2. Taliessin and the Co-inherence
3. Broceliande and the Images
4. Balin and the Dolorous Blow
5. The Tournament of Lonazep: Palomides and Lancelot
6. Lancelot at Carbonek: Merlin and Brisen
7. Arthur and the Pope [a fragment in terza rima exists, probably a trial for this poem]
8. Mordred [? a fresh poem, or the one printed in *S.S.*]
9. Gawaine
10. The death of Blanchfleur

On the back of List A are the following notes:

Garlon invisible outside Broceliande; within he is seen 'with a black face'; in Sarras—the Holy Spirit? Azrael?
Balin will not 'forgive' the universe, though Merlin and the Church warn him. (Lancelot does besides Palomides (as in Guinevere) hence Galahad.)

Of the Quest

The Burning Sepulchre
The Death of Blanchfleur

NOTES ON THE ARTHURIAN MYTH

WELL then—Logres is the world before it is in order, and Arthur is man coming in it. The establishment of the Kingdom is the establishment of man, and the Table is—or are—the qualities and capacities of man. The Dolorous Blow is that fact—call it the Fall, as I should, or whatever you like—which has set man in a state of contradiction and antagonism with himself and the universe. It is, in the poem, the use by Balin le Sauvage of a sacred Relic or Hallow for his own purpose and protection. In poems, or a poem, not yet done it will be shown how Balin attacks Garlon the Invisible Knight, the son[1] of King Pelleas the Keeper of the Grail, how he is thereon attacked by Pelleas and his men, and how he seizes the Spear and wounds Pelleas with it. This is the use of creation and personality for man's own safety or gain, and confusion ensues. The wound of Pelleas is incurable, until a Redeemer shall come. (The Spear and the Cup are the mystical symbols of personality, created out of the Heart of Deity that it may fall into the Heart of Deity.) But heaven takes action as immediate as the fatal results. The royalty of Pelleas is divided—he is, as it were, himself divided. That of him which is still the Sacred Keeper lies wounded but living in Carbonek; that of him which has to take action is transfused into Arthur, but there it hardly knows itself. I am aware that this is difficult, because of the time-scheme. Balin rides from Arthur's court—from Camelot, and yet Arthur does not begin to be till Pelleas is wounded. But perhaps, if you consider that the Fall (or what not) *was* once, and yet is repeated in each of us, this is not so inappropriate.

But the heavenly rulers—who are neither in Camelot nor Carbonek but in Sarras the divine city—are to direct the coming of the

[1] Probably a slip of the pen for 'brother', as in Malory. These poems, as I have said, were never written. A. R.

redeemer, i.e. Galahad (who is not exactly Christ, but rather man's capacity for Christ, or—to avoid dogma—let us say, for divine things). He must be of the blood of Pelleas, and therefore his mother must be Helayne, Pelleas's daughter. But his father?

One's first thought is Arthur. But the myth never anywhere at any time so far as I know makes Arthur the father of Galahad or the achiever of the Grail, and it would need a degree of courage approaching presumption to alter a great traditional story, coming with the authority of poets and ages, in its main lines. Besides, I think there is a reason against him. The fatality, the curse, the result of the Dolorous Blow, has to work itself out through the King. He and his two sisters—Morgause and Morgan—are man loving himself and hating himself. This—and not mere incest—is the reason that Mordred is born of Arthur and Morgause. And Mordred is entire egotism, Arthur's self-attention carried to the final degree. This is why it is he who wrecks the Table.

The Destined Knight is born of Lancelot who is (*a*) eighth in succession from Christ (8 is the number of the Christhood), and of his blood; (*b*) the strongest and greatest knight alive (person as distinguished from office); (*c*) much more than Arthur concerned with love as a thing of dolour and labour and vision. (Arthur at first just thinks Guinevere would be a convenient adjunct of his royalty.) Lancelot then is to be brought to Helayne. And how? In the parts of Carbonek Nimue begins to work. Nimue is holy undefiled Nature—Creation outside man—and she sends her two servants Briseis and Merlin, the one to Carbonek to attend on the destined Mother, the other to Logres to help establish the Kingdom, build Camelot, and bring Lancelot to Carbonek. Merlin is in some sense Time, and also Wisdom.

The Table is built. The knights are capacities of man and modes of being (but also knights). To name a few:

Tristram is also a great lover, but, unlike Lancelot, he is out for his own hand. He is an individualist as against the State. Even his fidelity to Iseult and his leaving Iseult of the White Hands are largely dictated by his own ideas of what he wishes to be. His story is therefore of tragedy and death.

Gawaine is the kind of man who is very keen on the honour of his house and his own honour and proper dignity. He is a charming creature, so long as everyone looks up to him and gives way to him. Palomides is the knight who begins by believing in good and evil almost (as so many do) as two separate origins and powers. He is, like most of us, a dualist. He then becomes a Mahommedan and believes in one control. He then becomes a Christian and believes in reconciliation, transmutation, and Unity. Also he is especially man combating and overcoming sex (the Blatant Beast). He is in some sense an image and shadow of Galahad, for it is significant that he is baptized (after his conquest) on the day when Galahad comes to the King's hall.

But of all these Lancelot has his heart mostly on pure love. It is he who is mostly concerned with choosing necessity (which is the subject of all great poetry). It is, I think, through his courtesy to Palomides who has insulted and injured him, and whom he rides to assist in his danger, that he comes on the road which by Merlin's enchantments leads to Carbonek. It is through his illumination by Guinevere that he is brought to Helayne. But because his devotion to the Queen could not bear to transfer itself to any other (*could* not—he is in passion, not law), he himself is given magical drink by Briseis, and the Merciful Childe is born of pure passion and pure law. Thus, as always, the purpose of God produces salvation after an unexpected and shattering manner. For when Lancelot knows what has happened he falls into madness until the birth of Galahad.

After this event the story of the Table begins to turn inward as well as to pursue its normal course. Merlin, his work done, is received again into the mystical darkness from which he emerged (as St. Joseph disappears after the birth of Christ). Galahad comes to Camelot, and the Sacred Graal, i.e. the reunion of all things, is seen in a vision. The two other knights who are to achieve are joined to him. They are Percivale and Bors, and these again are at once knights and capacities.

Bors is the ordinary man, married, with children, the King's servant. But he is also the spiritual intellect concerned, as it must be, with earthly things.

Percivale is at once Taliessin in his highest degree, and a virginal lover (because he and Blanchefleur have no time for anything else); but also the spiritual intellect concerned with the significance of things and with the Quest.

But as for the High Prince, I doubt whether he is concerned with even the Quest; he is only aware of the End.

At last, therefore, the three questing knights come again to Carbonek, where the High Prince heals the Wounded King. Personality is restored for its proper end. This is the restoration of man to a proper state of health and peace, and is contemporaneous with the death of Arthur who is reassumed into Pelleas. But there is yet more to follow. There enter into the hall three other bands of three knights (who are, I think, the mineral, vegetable, and animal creation, also restored), and Christ appears out of the Graal, summoning them to a farther End. In Sarras all things are assumed to Galahad and he is assumed to Christ.

But because this is all interior, the other time-scheme of the Table has to run its course. Arthur's fault of self-attention drives him to make war on Lancelot, and (against the warnings of the ghost of Gawaine) to pursue Mordred. In the shape of a little viper, Garlon, the Invisible Knight—who is Satan to us but the Holy Ghost to the supernatural powers—provokes the last battle. The curse of the Dolorous Blow works itself entirely out, for Mordred and Arthur slay each other in some remote place on the borders of creation—or almost. All-but-Desire destroys Entire-Desire, and is saved by Bedivere, and the barge where are the Queens (I think, Morgan, Morgause, and Nimue) which passes out to Avilion, itself the orchards of Carbonek.

Lancelot is left alone—save Taliessin the singer—to say mass for a twelvemonth and a day.

And all this history Taliessin has seen (1) in the cycle of the Table; and (2) in the spiritual life of the Princess of Byzantium, who recurs constantly throughout as the image of all that a mistress is to her lover, and the Blessed Virgin is to the Church, and every elect soul is to the world.

There are, of course, many other implicit suggestions and meanings. But these will be sufficient.

[Here I add, for the sake of clarity and with Professor Lewis's permission, a couple of passages from an exposition of *Taliessin through Logres* which Williams made for him. Professor Lewis had written the relevant parts of these into his own copy of the book, and had destroyed the original. He lamented this, when he came to write his Commentary, not realizing that Williams had kept and distributed some copies of it; but in fact all that is essential is to be found in the Commentary, I merely add Williams's own summary here for the reader's convenience. A. R.]

The Empire then is (*a*) all Creation—with logothetes and what not as angels and such—(*b*) Unfallen Man; (*c*) a proper social order; (*d*) the true physical body. I left it female in appearance because the Emperor must be masculine, but this is accidental. The Empire is the pattern; Logres the experiment. The Emperor is God-in-operation or God-as-known-by-man; (ii) Fate; (iii) operative force—as and according to the person concerned, but mostly here the God relation. Islam is (*a*) Theism; (*b*) Manichaeanism; (*c*) heavy morality; (*d*) Islam. The themes are the divisions of the Empire—Caucasia, Gaul, Logres, &c. Caucasia is the physical fundamental (*a*) the buttocks; (*b*) basic senses; (*c*) direct sex; (*d*) village society. Gaul is 'fruitfulness' (*a*) the breasts; (*b*) traditional organization; (*c*) scholastic debates and doctrines; (*d*) theology. Byzantium is rather the whole concentration of body and soul than any special member. The pirates are barbarous and chaotic instincts and uncivil ideas. The slaves are (I think) the pirates' kindred or captives or captives from the other themes (cf. Circassian girl in the *Arabian Nights*). Taliessin is the poetic imagination in this world and Percivale the imagination of the other and of the universe; he is the brother of Blanchefleur = substitution.

The 'cut' hazel is measurement and power—of any kind, and the 'uncut' and the hazel-nuts are the fruit: it is the measure of doctrine in Lateran and the Church; of morality to the slaves, of 'psychology' to Merlin; it grows everywhere in Logres, and is at once the necessity of abstract statement, commands, and so on, as 'cut', and the actuality of 'natural grace' (so to call it) as uncut.

2. Broceliande is somewhere round Cornwall and Devon, to the west of Logres. It is regarded both as a forest and as a sea—a sea-wood; in this sense it joins the sea of the antipodes which lies among its roots. Carbonek is beyond it: or at least beyond a certain part of it; C. stands between B. and the full open sea, beyond which is Sarras.

Mystically it is the 'making' of things. Nimue is the Nature of Creation as the mother of Merlin (Time) and Brisen (Space): she is the source of movement and of distance. She is almost the same state represented by the Emperor's Court, but more vast, dim, and aboriginal. The huge shapes emerge from B(roceliande), and the whole matter of the form of the Empire, and all this is felt in the beloved.

THE MAKING OF *TALIESSIN*

From the Poetry Review, *April 1941*

WHEN I was asked to write a few notes on the composition of one of my poems I permitted myself to propose the series called *Taliessin* because probably I know more of the way that that was written than I do of any other. The Editor was good enough to accept this suggestion instead of insisting on my composing a special poem for the purpose.

It has sometimes been said that it is necessary to know Malory's *Morte D'Arthur* in order to follow *Taliessin.* I very much hope that this is not so, both because I should think it improper in principle for any poet to require from his readers the knowledge of another work and also because the chance of any interest in *Taliessin* would thereby be considerably decreased. But it is true that *Taliessin* did, in a sense, begin with certain things in Malory. It began also, perhaps even earlier, in a vague disappointment with the way in which Tennyson treated the Hallows of the Grail in

Balin and Balan. I am not attacking Tennyson as a poet; I am only saying that in this particular respect his treatment of the Sacred Lance as a jumping-pole left a good deal to be desired and even to be done. I may perhaps be allowed to say that my readers must be asked to treat such sentences with goodwill. I am not claiming to be better than Tennyson. It was clear that the great and awful myth of the Grail had not been treated adequately in English verse. What then of English prose?

At first, and for a long time, I was inclined to think that Malory had done it. It is true that the main part of his novel was irrelevant to the theme, but the hints in those parts which dealt with the theme were of very high value. It could not, surely, be by accident that the three Lords of the Quest were distinguished as they were along the line of mortal love. The character of the High Prince Galahad, of course, was taken by him direct from his original. I was too young to have been deceived, at that time, by the nonsense talked a little earlier about Galahad being bloodless and so on. Our general culture served me better. Galahad could not be preoccupied with women because he was preoccupied with something much more vital. But next in degree was Percivale, and Percivale was in some undefined love-relation to Blanchefleur who was called his 'sister', and whose dead body was carried to Sarras by him and by the other questing lords on the Ship of King Solomon. And lastly there was Bors, who was, it seemed, married to the Lady Elaine and the father of two children. Here was a significant hierarchy; and yet the hierarchy was one, for all three reached Sarras, and if Galahad alone achieved, yet it might be held that the Galahad-in-Bors achieved as much as did the individual High Prince.

> By three ways of exchange the City sped to the City;
> against the off-shore wind that blew from Sarras
> the ship and the song flew.
>
> Before the helm the ascending-descending sun
> lay in quadrilateral covers of a saffron pall
> over the bier and the pale body of Blanchefleur,
> mother of the nature of lovers, creature of exchange;

I take these images then as examples—the Sacred Spear bleeding with the human blood of Christ (that is also, of Man), the Dolorous Blow, and the three hierarchical lords of the Quest. And from that point the history of Taliessin is a history of two things: (i) of the development of the Images, (ii) of the discovery of the rhythmical technique. I shall not be expected here to give a full account of either; it would be of interest to no one; it would bore me to write; and it would quite certainly be untrue. But I may take a few detached points.

As far as the Images are concerned, I suppose one of the most important is the identification of the Empire of Byzantium (in one significance) with the human organism. I shall maintain against all accusation that this, as they say, *happened*, and was not due to a curious ingenuity on my part. I could not undertake to say in what order that identification proceeded. If one considered at all the general historic period of Arthur, it was clear that the great and outstanding institution (beside the Church) was the Empire, and whether one set the centre of the Empire at Rome or at Byzantium was a matter of choice. That I did choose Byzantium was due, perhaps, to a romantic love of the (then) strange, but it was a little due to the sense that the Byzantine Emperor was a much more complex poetic image than the Roman. Mr. Yeats had not then written his Byzantium poems; or if so, I had not read them. In one or two earlier poems of my own, the Emperor was a kind of sacerdotal royalty. But gradually he became—I would not simply say God but at least God as active, God as known in Church and State, God as ruling men.

> The Acts issue from the Throne.
> Under it, translating the Greek minuscula
> to minds of the tribes, the identities of creation
> phenomenally abating to kinds and kindreds,
> the household inscribes the Acts of the Emperor;
> the logothetes run down the porphyry stair
> bearing the missives through the area of empire.

What else religion is had obviously to be kept for the Quest and the Achievement of the Grail. Byzantium then was the place of the centre, the providence of the actual world.

The use of the word Caucasia is another example of development. The word was originally 'Circassia'; it came, of course, from the harems of the *Arabian Nights*, and I had used it lightly in certain allusions to frank non-significant sex affairs. But presently the use of that word became impossible for several reasons; it refused to bear the weight with which I wished to charge it. Fortunately the other word Caucasia offered itself. It was more historic, it had larger scope, it (like Byzantium) was capable of *meaning* more. That it referred (anatomically) more particularly to the buttocks was a late development. I can never see why the buttocks are funnier than any other part of the body; they support us when we sit, they are balance and (in that sense) justice. They are erotic, it is true, and that was an advantage for the poem; but they are plainly and naturally so; they are not mixed up, as eyes or hands may be, with the active moral question.

Another image which turned out to be capable of more than one significance was the hazel. Merlin had been saved by Swinburne, in the new force with which in *Tristram of Lyonesse* he charged the Merlin–Nimue relationship, from the weakness of the older tales, and when the prophetic wizard of Malory was considered free from this, he took on all the qualities of Time. But he remained a white magician, a theurgic power, and the rod of a magician is not a toy. It is energy and direction. It occurred to me that in the traditions this rod was normally of hazel, and the dictionary confirmed this. But rods are used for more than magic; as 'goads for cattle, disciplines for offences, measuring-rods, &c.'. So the cut rod of hazel became everywhere an instrument of order and measurement. It corresponded to the arm and to prosody, to anatomy and to law, to all roads and rules. The uncut hazel, with its nuts, is in some sense the fruition of this.

> The nuts of the uncut hazel fall
> down the cut hazel's way.

Relating to this 'cut' significance are such references as:

> 'with the hazel of ceremony, fetched to his hand—cut,
> smoothed, balsamed with spells, blessed with incision—
> he struck from the body of air the anatomical
> body of light;'

> 'I have known,'
> she said, with the scintillation of a grave smile,
> 'the hazel's stripes on my shoulders; the blessed luck
> of Logres has a sharp style, since I was caught free
> from the pirate chaos savaging land and sea;'

> 'On the opposite wall, in a laureate ceremony,
> Virgil to Taliessin stretched a shoot
> of hazel—the hexameter, the decasyllabic line—
> fetched from Homer beyond him;'

Such developments of images, as every worker in verse knows, are generally aided, and perhaps even chiefly caused, by the mere work at poems. I should be afraid to say how often the search for a rhyme or even for a longer or shorter word produced a new movement in the Images. The line 'the ejection to the creature of the creature's rejection of salvation' was probably entirely brought about by the rhymes. It is true that such movements must be critically watched; ingenuity and haste are temptations, and pseudo-significances have to be rejected. The whole content of a long series of poems (especially if future poems on the same subject are intended) may not be clear at once, nor indeed can be. But enough is clear to purify the rash tendency to take *anything*; what Mr. John Sinclair has called, in the Introduction to his translation of Dante, 'the quality of relevancy' is of importance; it is necessary to what Shakespeare in the *Dream* referred to as the growth of 'something of great constancy'. I have observed that to be true which I had before suspected—that, in any such series, the Images have continually to be re-imagined; everything is given and yet nothing is permanently given. The poet who, in his own mind, mistakes his own word for the thing imagined is lost.

On the more technical side the only matter of interest is, I think, the use of interior rhymes. It is clear that, if one is using them, there should be some habit, if not law, in their use. It would be dangerous and silly to use them without some sort of norm, even if the abnormal is present almost as often as the normal, or more often. The poet must have an arrangement in his mind, however he may think it necessary to rearrange it. In certain stanzaic poems, for example, the interior rhymes are exactly repeated in each stanza. In other non-stanzaic poems I have had in mind the provision of two rhyme-words to each two lines; but these may be arranged as one wishes, and may indeed sometimes result in multiplying rhymes in one group and leaving another group without any. I do not find I altogether wish to continue using them; the verse of future poems may, I hope, be more sparing, and even here one poem, *The Son of Lancelot*, is very nearly free from them. I must not now say more. No pains are too great for poetry; it is sad that the pains do not always produce the poetry. One can but do what one can, and let the result be, carefully dissociating one's mind from any sense of personal importance in that to which one must give all one's personal energy. The more that dissociation can be managed, the greater the pleasure in the whole arduous business.

THE CHANCES AND CHANGES OF MYTH

Time and Tide *review of* La Grant Ystoire de Monsignor Tristan Li Bret, *edited by F. C. Johnson, 1942*

STRICTLY, this book demands review by a scholar, and it would have to be a scholarly review. It is the first publication, since 1586, of a part of a particular version of the French Prose Romance of Tristan; it contains the early history of Tristan, the drinking of the potion and the beginning of passion—'Li uns regardat l'autre moult attentivement'—the episode of Palomides, and many other of the adventures. It was, I gather, from variants of this source that Malory drew his version.

In a sense, Tristan was superfluous. We had already the great central tale of unfortunate love. We had also the less full-grown story of Sir Lamorack and the Queen Morgause of Orkney. There could, it seems, in those days be hardly a queen of myth who did not 'look outside her wedding-ring'. Yet there was difference as well as likeness; and the difference between the Lancelot story and the Tristan story is remarkable. Malory, so far as one can guess, did not see it, but Malory is full of a high suggestiveness which he never could, or never cared to, develop. There are two of these which are perhaps worth noting.

The first is that one is left with the impression that Tristan is never a lord of the Table. He did not, it is true, quite move in the strict Table country; Cornwall and Brittany were no more than feudal appanages of King Arthur's Logres. But—I admit I have not checked the innumerable tourneys and joustings—also, he seems to be free from any allegiance to the Table. He will fight against it or for it as the whim takes him. In this he is the opposite of Lancelot who followed the rules of tourney, and only ceremonially opposed his peers. Tristan is the great individualist and is always expressing his own personality. The greatness of Lancelot was that he had no ideas of that sort. His sore grief was that he was in a position where he had to behave as if he had.

The second is the love-tale. The distinction between the two is primary; it is the Sangreal; that is, it is Galahad. Because of Galahad, the Tristan story is pagan, the Lancelot Christian. By this I do not mean—what is obviously untrue—that the two began any differently. They began, as tales, exactly where all tales begin, because somebody wished to tell them. It is true those tales may first have been of gods and afterwards of heroes; goddesses were first rapt away, and afterwards queens, and in our day millionaires' daughters. The Tale has been a necessity. I could make out a case for it as the grand beginning of all myth and all religion. 'The tongue is an unruly member', but it has ruled humanity. The necessity of the Tale on the Tongue is the true predestination of man.

We need not wonder then if the tales of Monsignor Tristan and Monsignor Lancelot, and the queens Iseult and Guinevere, were alike in their beginnings. By the time they reached Malory, they were different; by the time they draw to us, very different. On the one side was the potion, which had at first been half negligible, but had been made (I suppose largely by Wagner) important, the grief of King Mark, the vengeance of Iseult of the White Hands, the double death. The tale is of fate and tragic love; there is nothing beside or beyond. But the tale of Lancelot is precisely not tragic; in Christendom there is no final tragedy except in art, which may for a time properly forget its environment. There is obstinate evil, which is not at all the same thing. 'Ah, Lancelot,' said Sir Ector, 'thou were head of all Christian knights.' He was therefore forbidden tragedy; madness and desolation and a torn heart do not mean *that*. The myth gave him instead a great enchantment.

It is to be remarked that Lancelot and Guinevere were not of the kind of Dante and Beatrice. There is no celestial significance about Guinevere, or at least not visibly. It is a direct carnal passion, as we have it to read. 'I take God to record', said Sir Lancelot, 'in you I have had my earthly joy.' There had been a different kind of grief in it than ever even Dante knew. 'Truly,' said Sir Lancelot, 'my sorrow was not, nor is not, for my rejoicing of sin, but my sorrow may never have end.' Nevertheless, too many adulteries have pleased themselves with false images of Lancelot; it was his kiss that betrayed (as Dante justly saw) Paolo and Francesca into hell. Allowing that, we must allow too the mysterious redemption, through the sorrow of loyalty and the loyalty of sorrow, of the flesh of Lancelot and Guinevere, in the begetting of Galahad by the Princess of the Grail. The actual direct carnal passion has this result, but it also agonizes in itself. The Queen said: 'Therefore, Sir Lancelot, I require thee and beseech thee heartily, for all the love that was ever betwixt us, that thou never see me more in the visage.' 'Now, sweet madam,' said Sir Lancelot, '. . . the same destiny that ye have taken you to, I will take me into, for to please Jesu, and ever for you I cast me specially to pray', but in the same speech he names the Sangreal and 'Sir Galahad, my son'.

There was nothing of all this in Tristan, and no such strange filial salute as Galahad sent his father. Dante, Lancelot, Tristan, are three ways of love. The tale of Tristan is the last great pagan myth. Dante put him (but not Lancelot) into hell; it was too severe. Swinburne served him well, and he and Iseult deserved Swinburne—

> But peace they have that none may gain who live
> And rest about them that no love can give,
> And over them, while death and life shall be,
> The light and sound and darkness of the sea.

What that rest does not know—deep let it be!—is the ship that runs over the sea, upon which stands the glowing son of Lancelot, with the salute to his father still singing on his lips, as he draws to the presence of the Sangreal.

MALORY AND THE GRAIL LEGEND

From the Dublin Review, *April 1944*

THE Twelfth Book of Malory's *Morte D'Arthur* ends with the following words: 'And here followeth the noble tale of the Sangreal, that called is the holy vessel: and the signification of the blessed blood of our Lord Jesus Christ, blessed mote it be, the which was brought into this land by Joseph of Aramathie.' The Seventeenth Book ends: 'Thus endeth the story of the Sangreal, that was briefly drawn out of French into English, the which is a story chronicled for one of the truest and the holiest that is in this world.' The five books between are occupied with Galahad and the achievement of the Quest.

It is not my purpose here to discuss the origins of the Grail story —Celtic, Classical, or Christian. Much attention has been given them. The Grail itself has been traced back to 'heirlooms belonging to the house of Atreus' and to 'the wars of the ancient Irish gods'. The first view was put forward by Mr. Charles B. Lewis;[1] the latest discussion of the second is in the recently published *Origin of the Grail Legend* by Professor Arthur Brown. It is, no doubt, true that Chrétien de Troyes, who seems to have begun the Tale, may have been vaguely influenced from both sources. Writers are apt to take over agreeable ideas from any source. Thus Professor Brown discusses the four-sided fairy cup of plenty in Irish mythology, and points out the insistence on the number four in Chrétien's *Percival*. This is exactly the kind of detail which might easily have appealed to and been taken over by a Christian writer; the Evangelists, the four-sided City, &c. On the other hand, when Professor Brown speaks of a castle surrounded by a river which is crossed by a bridge and writes: 'H. R. Patch has argued that the river and the bridge that often accompanies it are oriental material worked over by the Irish', he gives Mr. Patch too much importance. Houses on islands, even if supposed to be in the Other World, must have been too natural to Chrétien for him to need suggestions from the marvels of the Oriental and the Celt. He could do that sort of marvel by merely looking out of his medieval window.

There is perhaps still room for some consideration of the Tale as it has existed in the English imagination. There are a number of texts, even without involving those of the Middle Ages. They occur mostly in the Victorian poets—Hawker, Morris, Tennyson, Swin-

[1] *Classical Mythology and Arthurian Romance*, published for St. Andrews University; Oxford University Press, 1932.

burne—and they are mostly unsatisfactory. There is, however, no need to explain this by dragging in religion; it is much more easily and truly explained by saying that none of these poets had the full capacity of the mythical imagination. If we can read the *Idylls of the King* without remembering what critics have said about them, we shall find a great deal of good stuff. But it is true that Tennyson was really writing (and very properly) a modern moral story, as he said he was. He could not—he did not try to—get the Myth. Thus Balin, in the Grail Castle, instead of wounding the King with the Sacred Lance, uses it as a jumping-pole. This is a serious lapse. Morris arranged a highly decorative and highly delicate pageant of Galahad. The poet who, in an occasional touch, gets nearest to the tone of the Myth is Swinburne. This will seem odd unless we realize that the poetic capacity for Myth is quite different from the human capacity for religion; a fact not without relevance to our general belief in religion as well as to our criticism of verse.

But it is, of course, in prose rather than in verse that the thing has remained for us in English; it is in Malory, and in Sebastian Evans's translation of a part of Chrétien's *Percival* under the title of the *High History of the Holy Graal*. The latter book is a very noble piece of work. But it is, as it were, a detail; the whole grand Myth—or at least much of it—is in Malory. There is, however, even in Malory, a certain suggestiveness which Malory does not seem altogether to have understood. The present article does not intend to discuss how far these significances are in Malory's originals; its writer would be incapable, and the discussion would be irrelevant. The point is not where they came from but what they have become.

One main fact, however, must be mentioned. There are, in the history of the European imagination, a few moments when a superb invention of the very first importance takes place. I doubt whether there has ever been one of more real power than that of the invention of Galahad; not even excluding that of Dante's discovery of Beatrice as the theme of the *Commedia*. That, one really feels, must, sooner or later, have happened; there were so many poets in love. But the invention of Galahad as the son of Lancelot might easily not have happened. Someone—M. Vinaver[1] says a Cistercian—at some time in some place thought of it; it was a moment as near to divine inspiration as any not technically so called can be. It is, of course, necessary to speak cautiously here. M. Vinaver himself opposes the idea, put forward by other writers, that there is any 'mystic affiliation' between Lancelot and Galahad. He properly distinguishes between the Court of Arthur and the Court of Heaven. 'The author

[1] *Malory*, Clarendon Press, 1929.

of the *Queste* [the Galahad romance]', he says, 'was conscious of an acute conflict between the two kinds of chivalry, and never derived the one from the other. Galahad's mysticism can by no means be fathered upon Lancelot.' This is certainly true. But it is equally true that Galahad himself has certainly been fathered upon Lancelot, and that therefore their relation—even in division—is a very particular relation. Their distinction exists in a kind of imaginative union; the greater (however much greater) derives, in that Myth, for ever from the lesser, and something in each of their differing hues illumines the other.

Malory took the tale over. He either took over with it, or else he invented, certain details. It may be objected that my choice of these details is arbitrary, and I entirely agree that there are many insignificant details in Malory. He fills his pages with all sorts of things which may be fascinating but are not (in our sense) mythical. But there are some which are mythical in the sense that they seem to have a profound spiritual relevance. The whole question of Courtly Love may be ruled out at once. Malory was not concerned with that technique, any more than (at least, directly) with the greater passion and truer vision of the Dantean Romantic Love. Lancelot and Guinevere do not develop that. But they are still passionately and permanently in love. It is almost impossible for either of them to alter the exterior situation. A very little extra touch here and there in the *Morte* would have made it quite impossible—a little heightening of the realistic side of the kingdom of Arthur. The chief man in the kingdom after the King cannot throw up his job at once, and the Queen can certainly not throw up hers. The struggle after virtue, the happiness-unhappiness, the mere infinite tiresomeness, and the beauty, are all in the situation.

But there are (and here we begin the Myth as Malory has it) other people about. One of these is the Saracen knight Palomides. Palomides is in love with the Queen Iseult, but she is married to Mark and in love with Tristram. That, however, is not relevant to the Myth, except that the misery of Palomides accentuates his bitterness. He will not be christened, 'howbeit in my heart I believe in Jesu Christ and his mild mother Mary', till he has done certain great deeds, and overcome the questing beast (which is not without a likeness to the inner agony he suffers). At the seven-days' tournament at Lonazep, in that discourtesy to which he is prone, he commits an outrage against the laws of chivalry, and insults and injures Lancelot. Lancelot forgives him—'Sithen my quarrel is not here, ye shall have this day the worship as for me . . . it were no worship for me to put you from it.' But Lancelot carries his courtesy farther, for soon after the tournament is closed he finds Palomides in the hands of those who are about to put him to death, and rescues him from twelve knights; 'and Palomides kneeled down upon his knees and thanked Sir Lancelot'.

Lancelot in fact had a great many activities besides being in love with Guinevere: 'thou were', said Sir Ector of him, 'the courteousest knight that ever bare shield. And thou were the truest friend to thy lover that ever bestrod horse. And thou were the kindest man that ever struck with sword.' It is immediately after his exhibition of courtesy towards someone who has injured him—this is the significant, if accidental, detail—that we find Lancelot riding towards the mysterious castle of King Pelles, who is the Keeper of the Grail; it is shown between the hands

> of a damozel passing fair and young. O Jesu, said Sir Lancelot, what may this mean? This is, said the king, the richest thing that any man hath living. And when this thing goeth about, the Round Table shall be broken; and wit ye well, said the king, this is the holy Sangreal that ye have seen. . . . The king knew well that Sir Lancelot should get a child upon his daughter, the which should be named Sir Galahad, the good knight, by whom all foreign country should be brought out of danger, and by him the Holy Greal should be achieved.

There is about this a known predestination: 'the king knew well that Lancelot should'. Lancelot is here the predetermined father of the great Achievement; he is the noblest lord in the world, the kindest, the bravest, the truest. But he will not have to do with any woman but the Queen: 'when was Lancelot wanderingly lewd?' And Galahad must certainly be the child of the Grail-princess and certainly not of Guinevere. How is it to be done? It is brought about by holy enchantment and an act of substitution. Lancelot is deluded (as it were, by a courtesy of terrible condescension) into riding 'against night' to another castle, where he is received 'worshipfully with such people to his seeming as were about Queen Guinevere secret'. He is given a cup of enchanted wine and taken to the room where the supposed Queen is: 'and all the windows and holes of that chamber were stopped that no manner of day might be seen'.

I am not unaware that the substitution of one woman for another is common enough in the romances; it is the kind of substitution that makes this so thrilling. The vision is of 'the best knight', labouring in that threefold consciousness of God, the King, and Guinevere, received into the outlying castle of the Mysteries, and then by the deliberate action of spiritual powers drawn on into a deeper operation. He dismounts: around him are those who seem to be the Queen's servants, but it is not so; the assumed forms, the awful masks, of this sacred mystery attend him; he is taken to a chamber as dark as the dark night of the soul; and there the child who is to achieve the Grail is begotten.[1]

And the next morning? Here, it must be admitted, Malory fell away from what the Myth demanded. He sends Lancelot back to the Court, sends the Princess after him, describes the anger of Guinevere, enchants Lancelot all over again, causes him to meet the Queen, and then drives him mad because of his disloyalty to her. There is some very good writing, but it will not do. What must obviously happen is that immediately on waking in the Castle of the Substitution, Lancelot realizes the deception; which he does—'anon as he had unshut the window the enchantment was gone; then he knew himself that he had done amiss. Alas, he said, that I have lived so long; now I am shamed.' It is then that his mind should be overthrown; it is very proper that he should leap from that window of awful realization 'into a garden, and there with thorns he was all to scratched in his visage and his body; and so he ran forth he wist not whither, and was wild wood as ever was man; and so he ran two years, and never man might have grace to know him'.

So far as I can see, there is no particular reason for two years; nine months would have been a better time. Presently he comes again to the house of the Grail, and there 'by force Sir Lancelot was laid by that holy vessel; and there came a holy man, and unhylled that vessel, and so by miracle and by virtue of that holy vessel Sir Lancelot was healed and recovered'. He remains for some time in disguise and seclusion, calling himself only 'Le Chevalier Mal Fet, that is to say, the knight that hath trespassed'. The trespass is, no doubt, chiefly his unintentional falsity to Guinevere, but then in Malory truth is part of his passion; Lancelot does not believe that he will become true to the King by being untrue to the Queen. He may fail to manage to be true to both, but this is his intention. He is merely overthrown by that element in him which, because of his love and courtesy, is predetermined 'where Will and Power are one' to make him the father of Galahad. There is no compromise with the sin, but there is every charity towards the virtue.

At last Lancelot meets with Percivale and returns with him to the Court. The name of Percivale brings us to the second part of the Myth. Time has gone by, but time is not in Malory very strictly attended to. Galahad is taken to a Convent of White Nuns, where he is brought up. But the tale passes on from Lancelot's return almost directly to the coming to the Court of the High Prince: not indeed that in Malory 'the High Prince' is Galahad's title at all; it

[1] It is necessary to guard, through the whole Myth, against any identification of Galahad with Christ. Galahad is only that in the human soul which finds Christ.

belongs to Galahault, who is quite a different person, and not of much importance. He had once been; it was he who had brought Lancelot and Guinevere to their first kiss in one of the love-romances where the greater interpretations were not imagined. As a result he had gained a literary immortality, for he had been given a famous line in the *Inferno*: 'Galeotto fu il libro e chi lo scrisse.' It is proper that the title should pass from him; in a myth there ought to be more than charm, sweetness, and physical delight to justify such a phrase.

It is Pentecost; the King holds his court. One rite has already been solemnized. Palomides has been reconciled with Tristram and has been baptized by 'the suffragan of Carlisle'. 'And so the king and all the court were glad that Sir Palomides was christened. And at the same feast in came Galahad and sat in the siege perilous.' The second sentence is premature, but the tale passes on to give a full account. A fair gentlewoman who says she has come on King Pelles' behalf (Pelles is the Grail King) asks for Lancelot and carries him off to a nunnery in a forest. It is a brief episode, but very moving, for there Lancelot unknowingly knights his son—'seemly and demure as a dove, with all manner of good features'. 'On the morn, at the hour of prime, at Galahad's desire, he made him knight and said: God make him a good man, for of beauty faileth you not as any that liveth.' Lancelot's consent goes with Galahad's desire; he does not know what he does, but he does what courtesy and largesse demand; and both he and his son are the more advanced in the Way.

In the tale of Galahad himself at Camelot it might be held that there has been since Malory a certain alteration in values. We are not so much affected by the pulling of swords out of stones floating on rivers (besides, there have been too many of them) as by such other things of possible significance as the coming to every knight at the feast of what food he desired, and of the laying to rest of the High Prince in the King's bed. The first and dominating fact is, of course, the sitting of Galahad in the Siege Perilous. But the meaning of this would require a whole thesis of the meaning of the Siege and of its making by Merlin. The magical foreknowledge of Merlin is certainly not ordinary magic; it is not contrary to grace, though Merlin himself is somehow apart from the whole question of sin and grace. He is rather as if time itself became conscious of the future and prepared for it. The sitting of Galahad in the Siege is the condition precedent to all achievement; and Tennyson's phrase may serve for the moment—that he cried: 'If I lose myself I find myself.' At the supper there is a blast of thunder and a beam of seven-times-clear sunlight; all the lords see their companions fairer than before, and all have the meats and drinks that they love best. I have wondered if this second result would not be more convenient if it were taken to mean that what each had actually before him was precisely to his most satisfaction. It would fit the first better; it is what is there that is fairest. The world is in the Grail, which then appears, but it appears covered and carried invisibly. It must, of course, be so, or there would be no further achievement, and the tale would have to stop. But in every great Myth the technique and the meaning are one; only it does us no harm to realize that the tale, as well as the meaning, has to be kept going. This is the world in the Grail, but it is (also and therefore) at first the world clothing the Grail, so that it cannot be seen in itself. Vows are taken by the lords to seek it out, much to the King's sorrow, for he knows that this will break up the great fellowship. The Queen has a brief interview with Galahad in which she declares him to be Lancelot's son, but 'as to that, he said neither yea or nay'. 'And in the honour of the highness of Galahad he was led into King Arthur's chamber, and there rested in his own bed.'

This is a very great sentence, for it is at once the fulfilment and the frustration of the three lordliest personages, whether they like it or not. There lies in the King's bed that which is the consummation and the destruction of the Table. To Lancelot it is the visible defeat of his treasured fidelity, and the success and defeat of his own life.[1] And to the Queen it is her lover's falsity and her lover's glory. The Queen has some glorious phrases: 'I may well suppose that Sir Lancelot begat him on King Pelles' daughter, by the which he was made to lie by enchantment, and his name is Galahad. I would fain see him, said the queen, for he must needs be a noble man, for so is his father that him begat, I report me unto all the Table Round.'

It is then this living, tragic, and joyous Resolution of all their loves that now enters on its own adventure. They had all talked of love; let them now love this. Its quest begins, and must be passed over here. Towards the conclusion the High Prince reaches Sarras with two companions; they are Percivale and Bors. There seems a significant reason, though Malory does not develop it, why it should be so. Galahad, of course, has no relation with human loves (except Lancelot); his whole function is the Quest. But Percivale finds a lady who declares herself to be his sister. Obviously in the tale this is meant literally, but in the Myth it has not so much the significance of kinship in blood as of kinship in spirit. It is a human relationship, but it is one known only in the companionship of the quest; it is conjoined love, but love conjoined in the Grail. The lady is of a

[1] Williams had a footnote here, which was based on a wrong text, current before Professor Vinaver's edition was available. See *Arthurian Torso*, p. 87, C. S. Lewis's note.

holy temper; on the journey she dies by giving her blood for another lady who is sick. 'She said to the lady, Madam, I am come to the death for to make you whole; for God's love pray for me.' This again is an act of substitution, but clear and without deceit. Her body is found again when the three lords reach Sarras, though indeed it might well have been taken with them in the ship that carries them across the last ocean, and have made a fourth to the living three.

But the third, Bors? Bors, one might say, is the ordinary fellow. Malory (and here he allows the Grail fellowship rather more than he need have done) does not say he was married. But he does say he had a son by another Elayne, 'and save for her, Sir Bors was a clean maiden'. The Princess of the Grail was called Elayne, and though it is an unimportant point it is admirably right that a wife, for there is no need to deny her the marriage which the tale implies in principle, should have the same name. But if we allow Sir Bors his marriage and his work in the world and his honest affections, see how perfect the companionship of the three lords becomes! There is the High Prince, wholly devoted to his end in the Grail; and there is Percivale with his devout and self-less spiritual sister; and there is Bors with his wife and child. These are functions each of the others. The High Prince is at the deep centre, and the others move towards him; but also he operates in them towards the world. These are three degrees of love. Their conclusion is proper to them. Galahad is assumed into the Grail. Percivale after that assumption remains a hermit by the City of Sarras, where that other sacrificed flesh of his sister is buried. Bors returns to Camelot, joins Lancelot, is made a king, goes on a crusade, and in the last sentence of the book dies, with Sir Ector, Sir Blamore, and Sir Bleoberis, fighting against the Turks, 'upon a Good Friday, for God's sake'.

The conclusion of the Quest itself is found in Sarras, which is beyond and across the sea from the house of the Grail. There is a suggestion that though the Grail in Logres is the consummation of the life of Camelot, yet the Grail beyond seas is only the beginning of the life of Sarras. Galahad is the living suggestion of that other life. When he and Percivale and Bors reach Sarras, they are put into prison by 'the king of the city', who is a 'tyrant', but after a year he dies, and Galahad is made king. This might indeed be thought to have a great meaning in religious experience: after the endurance of tyranny comes the time of sovereignty. Another year of this brings them to their end. Joseph of Arimathie says Mass—only he? only he in Malory, but there is a phrase which suggests more: 'a man kneeling on his knees in likeness of a bishop, that had about him a great fellowship of angels *as it had been Jesu Christ himself; and then he arose and began a mass of Our Lady*'. The italics are mine; they will suffice to suggest that at that moment something like the Creation and the Redemption exist at once. Galahad is called; after Communion he parts from his companions; and it is then that one of the greatest phrases in Malory is used. Galahad says to Bors: 'Fair lord, salute me to my lord Sir Lancelot my father, and as soon as ye see him bid him remember of this unstable world.'

If the state of these great mysteries, where one like Christ begins a mass of Our Lady, is recognized, that final salutation has its full value. It is then that the High Prince remembers, recognizes, and salutes his father. The times have been changed since the love of Guinevere and the enchanted darkness of the chamber of Elayne, but Galahad derives from all. 'The unstable world'—yes; but it was thence that he himself came. The rejection of importunate love—yes; Guinevere herself is to say so;[1] but it is through the mystical substitution which lies even there that the High Prince was begotten. Lancelot was a master of courtesy, and it is so that Galahad is fathered on him. He himself never achieves the Grail, but at the point of a greater achievement than any he could have known, his son's greeting (full and ungrudging) reaches him, through another (still and always through another), 'Fair lord, salute me to my lord Sir Lancelot my father.'

[1] 'Therefore, Sir Lancelot, I require thee and beseech thee heartily, for all the love that was betwixt us, that thou never see me more in the visage. Well, madam, said he, God defend but I should forsake the world as ye have done.'

APPENDIX

COLLECTS COMPOSED FOR A MARRIAGE, 1938

ALMIGHTY God, in whom the acts of men are fulfilled at the moment of their origin: Grant that as by Thy power their ends are known already in heaven so on earth we may find them easily acceptable to Thy will: through Jesus Christ our Lord, Amen.

Almighty and everlasting God, who from Thy eternity dost always direct the operations of Thy glory: Mercifully subdue Thy beauty to our understanding and with Thy bounty illumine our distress, through the intercession of Jesus Christ our Lord, Amen.

Almighty and most merciful God, who by the glorious Incarnation and Atonement of Christ Jesus hast made men capable of eternal life: Increase among us the knowledge of the exchanges of Thy love, and from the common agony of our lives redeem us to the universal joy of Thy only City: through the fructiferous mediation of the same Jesus Christ our Lord and Saviour, Amen.

God, who by the teaching of holy doctors hast called us in all images and patterns to the unimaginable peace of goodwill: Grant that we may so study felicity with our minds that we may attain it in our lives: Who in the Triune Mystery art the perfect and only Godhead, Amen.

May the Sacred and Incarnate Intelligence excite in us the graces of belief and disbelief, of labour and humility, of clarity and devotion, of faith, hope, and love: to whom be ascribed, as is most justly due, in the unity of the Father and the Holy Ghost, all might, majesty, dominion, glory, and power, now and to the end of all the dispensations, Amen.

A BIBLIOGRAPHY

THIS is intended simply as a sketch-map for students, and only the dates of first publication are given. It is as much the work of others as of myself, and I am especially indebted to Mr. Linden Huddlestone for lending me the detailed bibliography (still to be completed) which he made on the basis of work done by Miss Joyce Coates—as she then was. I should like also to acknowledge the help and advice of the staff of the Press and of Mrs. E. W. Shideler, though I must take the responsibility for any inaccuracies.

It is impossible to classify some of C. W.'s work satisfactorily under any one heading. I have divided his critical, historical, and theological writings into three sections, but have printed them successively.

POETRY

The Silver Stair, Herbert & Daniel, 1912.
Poems of Conformity, Oxford, 1917.
Divorce, Oxford, 1920.
Windows of Night, Oxford, 1924.
Heroes and Kings, (limited edition) Sylvan Press, 1930.
Taliessin Through Logres, Oxford, 1938.
The Region of the Summer Stars, Poetry (London) Editions, 1944. (Now published with *Taliessin*, Oxford.)

Minor works include *An Urbanity*, written for the actors in the Amen House Masques (see below), and privately printed, *c.* 1927; also verse composed for the Oxford Press Music Department in the nineteen-twenties, as follows: *The Moon*, a cantata written for music taken from Purcell's operas; a translation of the 'Stabat Mater', set by George Oldroyd; and words for several songs by Handel. Some of these are still in print.

Early poems were printed in two anthologies published by the Press—*Poems of Home and Overseas*, 1921, and *A Miscellany of Poetry*, 1922; and in the *London Mercury* and the *New Witness*. Much of the verse written after 1924 (*Windows of Night*) remained unpublished; a handful of poems appeared in obscure periodicals, for which I have not the dates, such as: *Glasgow University Magazine*, *Elmfield Review*, *Monthly Paper* of St. Silas, Kentish Town, *St. Pancras People's Theatre Magazine* (Apr. 1937); others, apart from the *Taliessin* versions listed below, in *Theology* (Sept. 1941) and *Time and Tide* (Dec. 1940 and Nov. 1941). Also in house periodicals of the Oxford Press, namely: the *Lantern* (June and Sept. 1928, Sept. 1930, June 1931); the *Dominant* (June 1928); the *Periodical* (July 1939).

Some of the earlier cycle of *Taliessin* poems appeared in *New Poems*, ed. Lascelles Abercrombie, Gollancz, 1931, and in Williams's own *Heroes and Kings* and *Three Plays*. Poems from the final cycle, in some cases differing from the versions published in book form, appeared in *Christendom* (Mar. 1938), *Theology* (Dec. 1939), the *Dublin Review* (Jan. 1941), the *Wind and the Rain* (Spring 1942), and *Poetry, London* (1943).

DRAMA

Two Masques, privately printed by Henderson & Spalding: *Of The Manuscript*, 1927; *Of Perusal*, 1929. (The third, 1930, was not performed or printed.)

A Myth of Shakespeare, Oxford, 1929. (*A Myth of Bacon*, 1932, was never published, and the manuscript was lost.)

Three Plays, Oxford, 1931.

Thomas Cranmer of Canterbury, Oxford, 1936. (Acting Edition of the same year, printed for the Friends of Canterbury Cathedral, H. J. Goulden.)

Judgement at Chelmsford, Oxford, 1939.

The House of the Octopus, Edinburgh House Press, 1945.

Seed of Adam and other plays, Oxford, 1948. (A version of the title play appeared in *Christendom*, Sept. 1937.)

FICTION

War in Heaven, Gollancz, 1930.

Many Dimensions, Gollancz, 1931. (See also under *Periodicals*.)

The Place of the Lion, Gollancz, 1931.

The Greater Trumps, Gollancz, 1932.

Shadows of Ecstasy, Gollancz, 1933. (This was drafted in the late nineteen-twenties, with the title of 'The Black Bastard'.)

Descent into Hell, Faber, 1937.

All Hallows' Eve, Faber, 1945. (Faber now publishes all the novels.)

CRITICISM

Poetry at Present, Clarendon Press, 1930.

The English Poetic Mind, Clarendon Press, 1932. (An extract from this was reprinted in *Shakespeare Criticism 1919–35*, World's Classics, together with an essay on *Henry V* written for that book.)

Reason and Beauty in the Poetic Mind, Clarendon Press, 1933.

The Figure of Beatrice, Faber, 1943. (See also a pamphlet on Dante, under *Theology*.)

Arthurian Torso, Oxford, 1948. (The unfinished 'Figure of Arthur', with a commentary on the *Taliessin* poems by C. S. Lewis. Williams had planned a 'Figure of Power', about Wordsworth, and had drafted some pages of it.)

THEOLOGY

Passages in *Christian Symbolism* by Michal Williams, Talbot & Co., 1919.

He Came Down from Heaven, Heinemann, 1938.

The Descent of the Dove, Longmans, 1939. (This and the above are now published by Faber.)

The Way of Exchange (pamphlet, see p. 147 of this book), James Clarke, 1941.

Religion and Love in Dante (pamphlet), Dacre Press, 1941.

The Forgiveness of Sins, Geoffrey Bles, 1942. (Now included with *He Came Down*, Faber.)

Essay contributed to the symposium *What the Cross Means to Me*, ed. J. Brierley, James Clarke, 1943. (See p. 131 of this book.)

BIOGRAPHY AND HISTORY

Bacon, Arthur Barker, 1933.

'Lord Macaulay' in *Six Short Biographies*, ed. Goffin, Oxford, 1933. (See p. 6 of this book.)

James I, Barker, 1934.
Rochester, Barker, 1935.
Queen Elizabeth, Duckworth, 1936.
Stories of Great Names, Oxford, 1937. (Short biographical studies. Two editions issued, with slightly different contents.)
Henry VII, Barker, 1937.
'Queen Victoria' in *More Short Biographies*, ed. Goffin, Oxford, 1938.
Witchcraft, Faber, 1941.
Flecker of Dean Close, Canterbury Press, 1946.

EDITORIAL WORK

Poems of Home and Overseas, selected, with V. H. Collins, Clarendon Press, 1921.
A Note on possible endings to *Edwin Drood*, in the World's Classics, Oxford, 1924.
Notes to *A Book of Longer Modern Verse*, ed. Parker, Clarendon Press, 1926.
A Book of Victorian Narrative Verse, selected with an introduction, Clarendon Press, 1927. (See p. 1 of this book.)
Regency Verse, Clarendon Press, 1928. (Chosen and introduced by H. S. Milford. On the reverse of the title-page appear these words: 'the selection is at least equally the work of the editor's two friends and collaborators, Mr. Frederick Page and Mr. Charles Williams . . .', and I was given to understand by C. W. that he had in fact drafted the Preface—as the style implies.)
The Poems of Gerard Manley Hopkins, Oxford, 1930. (Second edition, with an appendix of additional poems and a critical introduction.)
A Short Life of Shakespeare, Clarendon Press, 1933. (Abridged by C. W. from Sir Edmund Chambers's book.)
The Ring and the Book, Oxford, 1934. (Retold by C. W., with brief introd.)
Landor's Imaginary Conversations, Oxford, 1934. (Selected by T. Earle Welby, with an introduction by C. W. See p. 15 of this book.)
The New Book of English Verse, Gollancz, 1935. (Edited with a long introduction by C. W.)
The Story of the Aeneid, Oxford, 1936. (The story retold by C. W., with an introduction.)
The Passion of Christ, Oxford, 1939. (A selection of passages illustrative of the Passion.)
The English Poems of John Milton, Oxford, 1940. (Introduction to the World's Classics edition. See p. 26 of this book.)
The Present Age, &c., by Søren Kierkegaard, Oxford, 1940. (Short introduction by C. W.)
The New Christian Year, Oxford, 1941. (Another religious prose anthology.)
The Letters of Evelyn Underhill, Longmans, 1943. (Edited with a long introduction.)
The Duchess of Malfi, by John Webster, Sylvan Press, 1945. (Introductions by George Rylands and C. W.)
Solway Ford, by Wilfrid Gibson, Faber, 1945. (Selected by C. W.)

PROSE IN PERIODICALS

Two articles in the *Contemporary Review*:
'The Hero in English Verse', Dec. 1920.
'The Commonwealth in English Verse', Aug. 1923.

Two articles in the *Dominant* (O.U.P.):
'The One-eared Man', Dec. 1927.
'The History of Critical Music', Apr. 1928—supplement.
An unsigned article on H. M. Peacock ('Personalities of the Press') in the *Lantern* (O.U.P.), Jan. 1939.
'Autocriticism' (on his *Reason and Beauty*) in the *Week-end Review*, Nov. 1933, with a caricature by 'Coia'.
In the *London Mercury*:
'Et in Sempiternum Pereant': short story about a character from *Many Dimensions*, Dec. 1935.
'The New Milton', July 1937. (See p. 19 of this book.)
In *G. K.'s Weekly*: six 'Letters to Peter', 5 Mar.–23 July 1936.
'Notes on Religious Drama' in the *Chelmsford Diocesan Chronicle*, May 1937.
'Religious Drama' in *Good Speech* (Quarterly Review of the Speech Fellowship), Apr. 1938. (See p. 55 of this book.)
'On Byron and Byronism' (extracts from Sorbonne lecture) in the *Bulletin* of the British Institute of Paris, Apr. 1938. (The *Bulletin* is only to be found in Paris, as far as I can ascertain.)
'Mr. Tillyard on Milton', a review in the *Criterion*, July 1938.
Two articles in *Theology* (reprinted in this book):
'Sensuality and Substance', May 1939.
'Natural Goodness', Oct. 1941.
Also several reviews: 1940–2.
Two reviews in *Life and Letters Today*, on books by Dylan Thomas and Edith Sitwell, Nov. 1939 and May 1940.
Six articles in the *Dublin Review* (five are here reprinted):
'The Image of the City in English Verse', July 1940.
'Blake and Wordsworth', Apr. 1941.
'The Redeemed City', Oct. 1941.
'The Index of the Body', July 1942.
'A Dialogue on Mr. Eliot's Poem', Apr. 1943.
'Malory and the Grail Legend', Apr. 1944.
Also a number of reviews: 1940–3.
'The Church Looks Forward', *St. Martin's Review*, July 1940. (See p. 154 of this book.)
'The Recovery of Spiritual Initiative', *Christendom*, Dec. 1940.
'Charles Williams on Taliessin through Logres', *Poetry Review*, Apr. 1941. (See p. 179 of this book.)
Also a letter defending his comparison of Hopkins with Milton, July/Aug. 1939—the only piece of correspondence I list here.
'The War for Compassion', the *Sword*, May 1941.
Two reviews in the *Spectator*, on books by Edward Hutton and Denis Saurat, 20 Nov. 1942 and 18 Aug. 1944.
Two reviews in the *New English Weekly*, on books by J. C. Powys and Owen Barfield, 10 Sept. 1942 and 10 May 1945.
Five reviews in *Britain Today*, 1942–5, including one on Binyon's *Paradiso*, Mar. 1944.

Many reviews and articles in *Time and Tide*, easily traced in its excellent index, from 1937 (one review and a letter only) to May 1945.

I have mentioned in my Introduction that Williams reviewed detective stories for the *Daily News* and its successor the *News Chronicle*, but I do not know exactly when these contributions began and ended. In the thirties he occasionally reviewed for the *Sunday Times*.

www.ingramcontent.com/pod-product-compliance
Lightning Source LLC
Chambersburg PA
CBHW060314100426
42812CB00003B/774
* 9 7 8 1 9 4 7 8 2 6 3 6 6 *

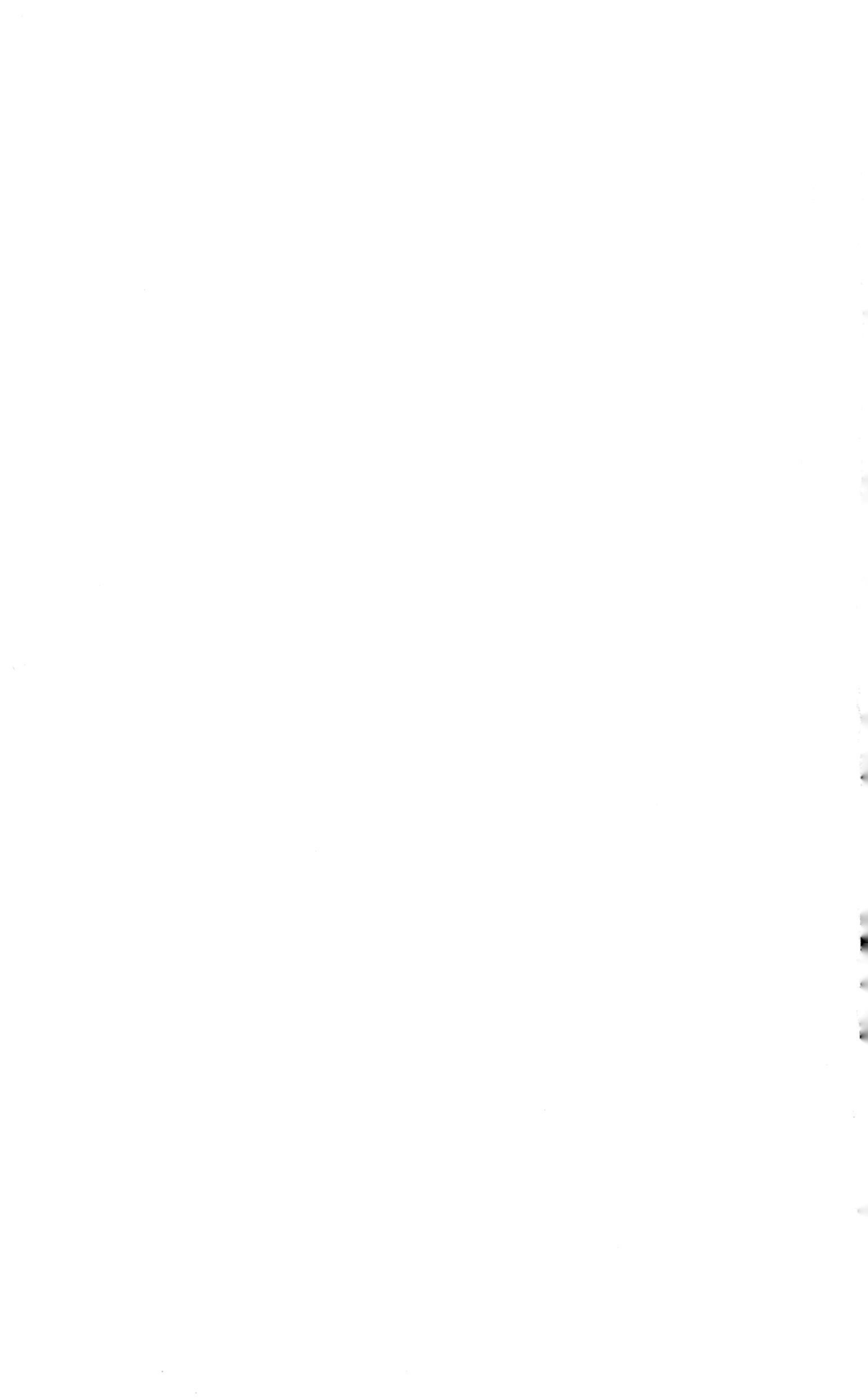